ADVANCE PRAISE

"In *Polyvagal Theory and the Developing Child*, Marilyn Sanders and George Thompson apply the principles of Polyvagal Theory to explore the disruptions to connection the children and families they serve experience on the journey from conception through adolescence and the impact of those traumatic moments. Drawing on wisdom from years of practice, they present a framework grounded in neurobiology and brought alive in clinical stories that weaves the essential ingredients of safety and connection into clinical interactions. With this beautifully written exploration of the science of safety, Drs. Sanders and Thompson offer a guide to engaging the vagal pathways embedded in our biology and creating the social connections that are the foundation of well-being."

—**Deb Dana**, LCSW, author of *The Polyvagal Theory in Therapy: Engaging the Rhythm of Regulation* and *Polyvagal Exercises for Safety and Connection: 50 Client-Centered Practices*

"Marilyn Sanders and George Thompson skillfully employ Polyvagal Theory to elucidate the biological underpinnings of emotion regulation in attachment relationships, showing how vagal tone supports social connections essential for a feeling of safety needed to cope with childhood adversity. The authors buttress their conceptual framework with scholarly research and clinical examples. Most importantly, they infuse their writing and practice with the key ingredient for healing that transcends the remarkable vagus nerve's contribution: a compassionate spirit."

—**Jon G. Allen**, Ph.D., Clinical Professor, Menninger Department of Psychiatry and Behavioral Sciences, Baylor College of Medicine, Voluntary Faculty; author of *Trusting in Psychotherapy*, American Psychiatric Association Publishing

"In their brilliant text, Sanders and Thompson deliver an inspiring call to action. After carefully explaining how the polyvagal system works, they make a convincing argument for educating others (especially those caring for infants, children, and families) with the goal of establishing a trauma and polyvagal-informed society. This book could and should be required reading for teachers, physicians, psychotherapists, and any other professional caregivers interested in the development of resilience as an optimal outcome."

—**Deborah L. Korn**, Psy.D., Faculty, Trauma Research Foundation and EMDR Institute, coauthor, *Every Memory Deserves Respect*

Polyvagal Theory and the Developing Child

A NORTON PROFESSIONAL BOOK

Polyvagal Theory and the Developing Child

SYSTEMS OF CARE FOR STRENGTHENING KIDS, FAMILIES, AND COMMUNITIES

MARILYN R. SANDERS AND
GEORGE S. THOMPSON

FOREWORD BY STEPHEN W. PORGES

W. W. NORTON & COMPANY
Independent Publishers Since 1923

Note to Readers: Standards of clinical practice and protocol change over time, and no technique or recommendation is guaranteed to be safe or effective in all circumstances. This volume is intended as a general information resource for professionals practicing in the field of psychotherapy and mental health; it is not a substitute for appropriate training, peer review, and/or clinical supervision. Neither the publisher nor the author(s) can guarantee the complete accuracy, efficacy, or appropriateness of any particular recommendation in every respect. As of press time, the URLs displayed in this book link or refer to existing sites. The publisher and author are not responsible for any content that appears on third-party websites.

Certified by Polyvagal Institute as accurately representing the principles described in Polyvagal Theory.

Copyright © 2022 by Marilyn R. Sanders and George S. Thompson
Foreword copyright © 2022 by Stephen W. Porges

All rights reserved
Printed in the United States of America
First Edition

For information about permission to reproduce selections from this book, write to Permissions, W. W. Norton & Company, Inc., 500 Fifth Avenue, New York, NY 10110

For information about special discounts for bulk purchases, please contact W. W. Norton Special Sales at specialsales@wwnorton.com or 800-233-4830

Manufacturing by Sheridan Books
Production manager: Katelyn MacKenzie

ISBN: 978-0-393-71428-9

W. W. Norton & Company, Inc., 500 Fifth Avenue, New York, N.Y. 10110
www.wwnorton.com

W. W. Norton & Company Ltd., 15 Carlisle Street, London W1D 3BS

1 2 3 4 5 6 7 8 9 0

MARILYN SANDERS

*To my husband, Peter Adomeit, who has supported me
with love every step of the way . . .
And to our children, Matthew, Ian, and River,
the best teachers a parent could have.*

GEORGE THOMPSON

*To Dr. AnnMarie Glodich, my constant partner
in learning to love deeply and well,
And to our children, Seth and Tara Jampa, whose joy
and appreciation warm the hearts of all they touch.*

CONTENTS

FOREWORD BY STEPHEN W. PORGES *IX*

ACKNOWLEDGMENTS *XV*

OUR INTRODUCTION TO THE POLYVAGAL THEORY *XXI*

SECTION I **BUILDING A HEALTHY BRAIN FOR THE FUTURE**

CHAPTER 1 PREGNANCY, THE INTRAUTERINE ENVIRONMENT, AND BIRTH: NURTURING A BRAIN UNDER CONSTRUCTION *3*

CHAPTER 2 SAFE, CALM, AND SECURE: PARENTAL ENVIRONMENT AS THE SECOND WOMB *23*

CHAPTER 3 PREPARING YOUNG CHILDREN TO LIVE IN THEIR FAMILIES AND THEIR LARGER WORLD *47*

SECTION II **DISRUPTIONS OF SOCIAL CONNECTEDNESS AND REPAIR**

CHAPTER 4 CHALLENGING DISRUPTIONS IN CHILDHOOD: TRAUMATIC SEPARATIONS THAT IMPACT CHILDHOOD EXPERIENCE *67*

CHAPTER 5 CHRONIC DISRUPTIONS OF CONNECTEDNESS FROM A LIFESPAN PERSPECTIVE *93*

SECTION III — HOW PROFESSIONALS STRENGTHEN THE SAFETY CIRCUIT IN CHILDHOOD CAREGIVING

CHAPTER 6 TAKE YOUR OWN PULSE: SELF-REGULATE TO CO-REGULATE CHILDREN, FAMILIES, AND COLLEAGUES   *115*

CHAPTER 7 SUPPORTING AN EMERGING HUMANITY: POLYVAGAL THEORY FOR PHYSICIANS, THERAPISTS, TEACHERS, AND OTHER PROVIDERS   *151*

CHAPTER 8 THE POLYVAGAL-INFORMED ORGANIZATION: BUILDING A SAFE ENVIRONMENT TO NURTURE OPTIMAL HUMAN FUNCTIONING   *187*

SECTION IV — EMBODYING POLYVAGAL THEORY IN LIFE AND IN THE WORLD

CHAPTER 9 SOCIAL CONNECTEDNESS IN THE TIME OF COVID-19   *223*

CHAPTER 10 SAFE TO DO WHAT? THE VITALIZING POWER OF THE SOCIAL ENGAGEMENT SYSTEM   *245*

APPENDIX   *271*

REFERENCES   *273*

INDEX   *291*

FOREWORD

BY STEPHEN W. PORGES

On a personal level, I am pleased to write this foreword. The authors independently took an interest in the potential of embedding Polyvagal Theory in the clinical care of children. Drs. Sanders and Thompson were passionate and insightful contributors to the volume I co-edited with Deb Dana entitled *Clinical Applications of the Polyvagal Theory: The Emergence of Polyvagal-Informed Therapies*. The goal of the edited volume was to stimulate clinicians to expand their treatment models and strategies by utilizing features and insights of the Polyvagal Theory. The goal was not to concretize theory, but to adapt the theory to the challenges that providers continuously face in the clinic. Consistent with this goal, in their book, *Polyvagal Theory and the Developing Child: Systems of Care for Strengthening Kids, Families, and Communities*, Drs. Sanders and Thompson have creatively elaborated on how Polyvagal Informed therapies and health strategies can be implemented in caring for the developing child.

From my perspective, Drs. Sanders and Thompson are an important part of the expanding "Polyvagal family." They actively and effectively live the role of a "super co-regulator" as they manage patients and their patients' support teams and in their clinical interactions, they understand and respect the power of safety in enabling access to their patients' nervous systems. As physicians, Drs. Sanders and Thompson have a uniquely sophisticated biobehavioral perspective of diagnosis and treatment, which is articulately expressed in this volume.

Although both physicians work in different clinical disciplines focusing on different phases of development, their work shares common features. As emphasized in this volume, they both attempt to optimize treatment outcomes by attempting to recruit their patients' nervous systems as collaborators on a shared journey of healing. They acknowledge that outcomes are compromised when the child's nervous system reacts defensively. In Polyvagal terms, their work is about removing cues of threat and providing sufficient cues of safety to ensure that their patients experience a neuroception of safety. It is through this process that their patients can move along a positive maturational trajectory optimizing both mental and physical health.

As the authors emphasize throughout their book, cues of safety shift the autonomic nervous system into a state that supports health-related homeostatic processes and optimizes the social engagement processes necessary to ensure co-regulation and the establishment of trusting relationships with family, friends, and other relevant people. From a Polyvagal perspective, the authors provide insights to reach these important goals by emphasizing three core principles related to the theory: maturation, social engagement, and neuroception.

Dr. Sanders's work with high-risk preterm neonates illustrates the impact of maturation on the neonate's capacity to regulate state and vulnerability to cues of threat. From a Polyvagal perspective, the degree of prematurity influences the neural resources available to calm, self-soothe, and to spontaneously socially engage. Survival for the newborn is about recruiting a suck-swallow-breath circuit. Without this circuit efficiently functioning, the infant will not thrive. Polyvagal Theory identifies the neural mechanisms underlying the suck-swallow-breath circuit as the same neural pathways that underly the Social Engagement System. Both behavioral manifestations require the neural regulation of pathways known as special visceral efferent, which regulate the striated muscles of the face and head. The brainstem area controlling these pathways is integrated with the vagal regulation of the heart and bronchi via a ventral vagal pathway. In general, the ventral vagal pathways in a preterm newborn are not sufficiently myelinated to function as an effective "vagal brake" to efficiently down-regulate autonomic defense reactions. In the absence of an effective vagal brake, cues of threat will trigger a destabilization of autonomic state by recruiting a metabolically costly sympathetic response observed in tachycardia or a potentially lethal shutdown response via dorsal vagal pathways.

Ventral vagal pathways start to myelinate at about 30 weeks' gestational age. As the fetus approaches term, the regulation of ventral vagal pathways become functionally integrated in an area in the brainstem that regulates the striated muscles of the face and head. This integrated system coordinates the regulation of the heart and bronchi with the processes of sucking, swallowing, breathing, and vocalization. At birth, this circuit is critical for survival since it enables ingestion and coordinates sucking with breathing. Beyond these ingestive responsibilities, the circuit evolves into the Social Engagement System. This powerful social communication system enables the infant and caregivers to engage in the reciprocal communication that leads to the establishment of secure social bonds and trusting relationships. Since this system is not sufficiently mature to function in most preterm infants, the naturally forming reciprocal bond between parent/

caregiver and infant is often delayed or compromised. Without the neural circuit promoting facial expressivity and vocal intonation, the parent/caregiver may feel that their love and concern is not reciprocated; they may express feelings that they love their child, but their child does not love them. This same Social Engagement System provides the portal for a Polyvagal Informed physician to calm their client's physiological state, which will simultaneously optimize their client's accessibility to treatment.

If a preterm's nervous system detects life threat, then the autonomic nervous system may shift states and move into a dorsal vagal state in which the heart rate slows (i.e., bradycardia) and breathing may either slow or stop (i.e., apnea). Physiologically, this state would not provide sufficient oxygen to the brain, which if prolonged could result in brain damage or death. Fortunately, the autonomic state (i.e., heart rate and breathing) of these vulnerable infants is continuously monitored and when these shifts occur medical staff is immediately alerted to intervene.

In the neonatal intensive care unit, monitoring the vital signs of heart rate, breathing, and blood oxygenation take the highest priority and function as cues of threat, not only to the preterm infant, but also to the clinical staff. The detection of these cues of threat requires immediate intervention to insure optimal outcome. However, chronic exposure to these life-threatening cues can disrupt the autonomic state of medical staff and potentially lead to 'burnout' and stress-related health disorders. Similar chronic disruptions occur in the psychiatric clinics when it is difficult to co-regulate dysregulated children.

A compromised Social Engagement System is often a core feature of the children that Dr. Thompson sees in his clinic. Similarly, when a child is dysregulated and neurophysiologically appears to be in a chronic state of threat, the child's nervous system will not support an active and reciprocal Social Engagement System capable of cuing the parent that the child loves them. This is observed in flat facial affect and lack of prosodic vocal intonation. In addition, a similar blunting of the Social Engagement System occurs in the workplace during chronic stressful demands that lead to colleagues not being co-regulated by each other and misreading facial cues as cues of lack connection or concern.

Dr. Thompson's work focuses on accessing the Social Engagement System of his clients through a deep understanding of neuroception. His work emphasizes that the trajectory of outcome changes when the autonomic nervous system is retuned to calm and to co-regulate via ventral vagal pathways. This retuning in autonomic state regulation occurs when the cues of safety are expressed in the dyadic exchange with the patient. An ability to listen to and to witness a patient with facial cues of accessibility and vocal cues of warmth is critical to being a successful clinician. Dr. Thompson's work acknowledges that co-regulation is an antecedent for self-regulation. Thus, an ability to calm and to soothe a patient through voice, face, and gesture of the clinician acknowledges the power of the Social Engagement System in triggering a neuroception of safety in the patient. This ability to calm and to shift the patient from defense to accessibility should be the foundational requirement of all healthcare providers.

In the world of medicine, generally physicians are dedicated to improving outcomes by focusing on the function of specific organs. This "end organ" orientation has led medicine on a journey of tests and evaluations looking for molecules or structural anomalies. This journey has led physicians towards strategies that they believe will "fix" and alleviate suffering. Unfortunately, it has overestimated the role medical interventions (e.g., pharmaceutical, surgery) and underestimated the collaborative role of the patient in the journey of healing. It has assumed that the physician and not the patient was the active healer. It is refreshing to see how Drs. Sanders and Thompson have integrated principles of Polyvagal Theory into their medical practices. By emphasizing the importance of social engagement strategies as portals of physiological regulation, their treatments functionally invite their patients and families to be active partners in a shared journey of physical and mental healing. Their successes reflect an understanding that the neural circuits involved in social behavior overlap with the neural circuits that support health, growth, and restoration.

Although Polyvagal Theory was proposed approximately 25 years ago, the clinical problems discussed in *Polyvagal Theory and the Developing Child: Systems of Care for Strengthening Kids, Families, and Communities* have been a focus of my research since the early 1970s. As I read this book, I reflected on the five decades of my research, which crossed the clinical domains of Drs. Sanders and Thompson, and felt a sense of gratitude as I have had the opportunity to witness the translation of my research into clinical practice. I feel fortunate that Polyvagal Theory has contributed to the authors' passionate journey to improve the clinical outcomes of the developing child and look forward to their future contributions.

ACKNOWLEDGMENTS

From Marilyn and George:

In 2012, the personal and professional journey that led to this book began with a request from Marilyn's friend and colleague, Jeffrey Magnavita. Jeffrey handed Marilyn a copy of Stephen Porges's *The Polyvagal Theory: Neurophysiologic Foundations of Emotion, Attachment, Communication, and Self-regulation* with a request that she review it. Jeffrey's request set in motion a series of fortunate events leading to the book you read today.

Shortly after the publication of the review, Marilyn met Stephen Porges at a conference. They met several more times over the next few years. Steve offered her the opportunity to write a chapter for a book underway that he was co-editing with Deb Dana. Thus began a friendship replete with warmth, humor, curiosity, joint inquiry, and mutual respect.

George also learned of Steve Porges's Polyvagal Theory in 2012, when he began training with Dan Hughes, creator of Dyadic Developmental Psychotherapy (DDP). He soon applied PVT to his work with traumatized children as well as in teaching medical students. When George met Steve at a conference, Steve invited

George to write a chapter on PVT and doctor-patient communication in the book to which Marilyn was contributing. Deb Dana in turn introduced Marilyn and George.

Through a series of conversations, we discovered that the work of a neonatologist/pediatrician and a child psychiatrist bore more resemblances than differences. When Marilyn sought a co-author for this book, she turned to George. The writing of this book reflects our joint passion for our work with children and their families. Our passion is embedded both in our commitment to "do no more harm" and to use the principles of Polyvagal Theory to develop unique partnerships with the infants, children, and families we serve.

The publication of our book by W. W. Norton reflects a professional dream we both share. Many thanks to editor Deborah Malmud and project editor Mariah Eppes. You shepherded this book from its early proposal and acceptance through to its finished manuscript and production with grace, a steady hand, and support as needed.

From Marilyn:

I am grateful for George's excellence as a psychiatrist, his patience, his warmth, and his sense of humor. We share a commitment to writing a book that both introduces Polyvagal Theory to child-serving professionals and gives practical applications and advice to those who want to incorporate Polyvagal Theory into their lives and work.

There are many others in my life who contributed to our success individually and together—a series of microcultures whose wisdom and experience are indelibly etched into my mind and reflected in my work.

Many thanks to my mental health microculture including Jeffrey Magnavita, Anne Shapiro, Lisa Namerow, Mary Himelstein,

John Santopietro, and Lori Calabrese. Your wisdom and guidance kept me and my family on a path of exploration, inquiry, and enjoyment of our abundances. And to Ann Halsell Appelbaum, who passed away in 2015, thank you for introducing me to John Bowlby in the 1970s. It made an enduring mark on my life and career.

None of this would be possible without the microculture of my dear friends whose daily camaraderie, laughter, and willingness to share joys enrich my life, especially during this difficult time of COVID-19. To Marge Julian, Karen O'Brien, Stephanie McGuire, and Barb Theurkauf, my hat is off to you and everything you do to make daily life and the world around us a better place. And to Isabella Knox, you are the best "best friend forever" a woman, mother, and doctor could ever have. Thirty-six years of friendship, and we are still moving forward.

My deepest gratitude to my workplace, Connecticut Children's Medical Center. The Connecticut Children's NICU remains the home of my experience with vulnerable babies, their families, and a world-class staff of physician colleagues, advanced practitioners, nurses, developmental and lactation specialists, social workers, and other staff. Many thanks to my two supervisors, Jim Moore and Vic Herson. Both men gave me the flexibility to write this book during a busy clinical career and wholly supported the concept and importance of improving the outcomes and experiences of babies and their families through integrating trauma-informed care and The Polyvagal Theory.

And of course, not least, my undying devotion to my family of origin and my chosen adult family. In 1921, my grandmother set sail from Poland with her family to a better life in America. My grandparents were the predictable constant in life from early childhood into adulthood. My mother gave me the gift of her expectations that I would accomplish anything I set my mind to, including becoming a physician. She fostered my love of books and music and was a steady presence in my children's lives, though she lived far away. From my father, I learned how a sense of humor will get you a long way when things are tough and the value of a strong work ethic that stays with me today. I am blessed with four siblings; twin sisters, Paula and Shelly, and brothers, Marvin and Michael. We are consistently there for each other and are steadfast companions to each other.

Finally, my chosen family of adulthood. Thirty-six years ago, I met my husband, Peter Adomeit. Life changed forever as our first family together included his 3 adolescent and young adult children, Kristin, Hans, and Paul. I am grateful to them for their ready acceptance of me as a stepmom and for introducing me to parenting. In 1990, Peter and I had our first child, Matthew, followed by Ian in 1994, and River in 1996. They are all now adults with careers of their own. Two are professional musicians, and one is an engineer. They are all kind, considerate, and compassionate. They fill my life with joy and belief that the best is yet to come.

From George:

Without Marilyn's invitation to participate in this project, I would not be writing these words now. Marilyn's medical competence, understanding of Polyvagal Theory, concern for patients and their families, and good-heartedness make her the ideal physician, teacher, and colleague. I am blessed by others' love, support, wisdom, and expertise as well.

I am grateful to my wife, AnnMarie Glodich, and our children, Seth and Tara Jampa, for believing in me and this project, and for their encouragement to keep going through the rough patches. They excitedly read book drafts a number of times and were patient as writing cut into family time.

My mother, Patty Streater, has been a shining example of tireless perseverance in doing whatever it takes to help children in need over the past 50 years. She and her husband Allen provided useful feedback as we talked through selected chapters.

My father, George Thompson, Sr., taught me that it is possible to create a sacred space in one's professional office and to see the face of God in each person we meet.

On my parents' bookshelves I found many treasures, but *Dibs in Search of Self* by Virginia Axline shaped my life purpose: to awaken people to the power and grace and interconnectedness that arises from wholeheartedly embracing our humanity.

I value the faithful companionship of my siblings John and Teal, along with that of my extended family, Kathy, Tim, Tam, and Ted.

I am forever grateful to Steve Porges and Deb Dana who welcomed me into the polyvagal family and have patiently supported my efforts to understand and apply Polyvagal Theory. I hope that I can do their unlimited generosity justice by passing their gifts along to others.

I don't know what I would do without the support of the DDP community. Dan Hughes has been a mentor, supervisor, organizational consultant, and trusted ally. Grey McKellar, another true friend, helped me integrate principles of PVT and DDP at KidsTLC and other places. Kim Golding and Edwina Grant also provided vital guidance regarding safety and connection in organizations. Jon Baylin brought clarity and good humor to all our DDP work. I am also grateful to the board of the DDP Institute and the DDP practitioners, consultants, and trainers working around the world.

I truly appreciate the leadership of KidsTLC, Inc., who supported our audacious goal of creating a polyvagal-informed organization. I have deep affection for Mark Siegmund and Brandon

Mock, comrades in a *daring band of misfits* setting out to change the world. Great thanks as well go to our other teammates: Roy Rotz, Renee Azzouz, Cindy Whitney, and Kelly English. KidsTLC teachers, Sherrie Dupree, and Kylie Larson, provided important consultation by sharing how they applied Polyvagal Theory in the classroom. Lastly, my love goes out to the early adopters of DDP and PVT, Jan Moore, Mitchell Cloud, and Mary Stuck Eibes, who have accompanied me on this journey with warmth and enthusiasm.

I would like to thank Nikkia Young, who provided invaluable insight into racial equity issues. I knew she would help make the book better, and, fortuitously, the work with her made me a better person as well. In addition, I am grateful to Nancy Michael for her work on the neurobiology of implicit bias, racism, and transgenerational trauma, which informed several sections of the book. Caryn Mirriam-Goldberg occupies a special place in my heart for her coaching in how to tell the stories that want to be told. To paraphrase Khalil Gibran, she has helped my writing become "love made visible."

I have learned a great deal from the families and children with whom I have had the honor to work. I am indebted to Rebecca and Jermey for instructing me in what works when creating safe and secure bonds after life has been terrifying.

Finally, I am indebted to Harry Palmer and Avra Honey-Smith for the love and support they have shown me over the past 20+ years. Any growth in my ability to be courageous, compassionate, and curious comes from their guidance in learning and teaching the Avatar Course tools, along with the clear-eyed care of my cherished Avatar teammates.

OUR INTRODUCTION TO THE POLYVAGAL THEORY

We are both physicians with decades of experience caring for babies, children, adolescents, and families in extreme circumstances. Marilyn Sanders is a pediatrician and neonatologist, working with sick or premature babies in a newborn intensive care unit. Her patients are born unexpectedly too soon, before they are physically ready to face the world. Her team must provide a nurturing environment that allows babies' bodies and brains to mature and their families to embrace their parenting role despite the interruption of their expectations of a healthy pregnancy, delivery, and baby.

George Thompson is a child psychiatrist who leads a residential facility for children who have suffered abuse, neglect, and disrupted relationships early in life. Though his patients are older, they are equally unprepared to face the world and often use anger, manipulation, and control to survive. His team must also provide a safe and nurturing environment where his patients can learn to trust the parents who are raising them now.

At its heart, the Polyvagal Theory (PVT) describes how the brain's unconscious sense of our safety or danger impacts our emotions and behaviors. As do all other mammals, human infants and children require the presence of an adult caregiver to survive. From the earliest moments after birth, healthy babies and their mothers seek each other out and send each other signals of safety and security.

When we learned about Stephen Porges' Polyvagal Theory,[*] we recognized it as a powerful organizing principle, a new way of understanding relationships, a way that validated what we had observed and sometimes challenged what we previously assumed or were taught. Safe relationships wire children's brains to engage with and attach to their adult caregivers, as well as, over time, learn to trust and thrive. These children can respond appropriately to cues of safety or danger. Their sense of security in relationships scaffolds them as they take on challenges and buffers them when they are stressed. They are both adaptable when encountering predictable stressors and resilient in their ability to reestablish their equilibrium after more significant changes.

When children don't have safe relationships, or emotional, medical, or physical traumas punctuate their lives, their ability to love, trust, and thrive is damaged. Children who have multiple and sustained disruptions of their safe relationships may have physical, behavioral, or mental health concerns that follow them into adulthood, affecting the longevity or quality of their lives.

Humans are unconsciously and continuously monitoring for friendly or dangerous environments. This automatic process runs in the background of our consciousness. The Polyvagal Theory

---

[*] Stephen W. Porges is the creator of Polyvagal Theory. Dr. Porges first outlined his theory in his Presidential Address at the annual meeting of the Society for Psychophysiological Research in 1994. His address was then published in the society's journal, *Psychophysiology* (Porges, 1995). Dr. Porges has continued to elaborate and expand the theory in articles, books, and lectures. Since its introduction, Polyvagal Theory has been referenced in thousands of peer-reviewed research articles and has been incorporated into the clinical work of thousands of therapists around the world.

describes three behavioral responses that are sequentially activated as an unconscious alarm system registers internal or environmental changes associated with danger or a life-threatening challenge. When we are among friends, we relax and prepare to engage in work or play with others. When a dangerous environment is detected, such as a dark street at night, we go on the defensive, preparing to fight or flee. If we are trapped and the danger is overwhelming, life threatening, and inescapable, we may shut down and collapse—becoming emotionally numb, dissociating, or even fainting. In each of these states, our attention, interpretation, and reactions may differ significantly.

Porges named this unconscious processing of sensory information both in the environment and in our bodies *neuroception* to distinguish it from *perception*. Neuroception originates in unconscious awareness. Perception involves the gray matter or thinking parts of our brains.

Polyvagal Theory is a foundational infrastructure built upon mammalian evolutionary biology that provides the "Why?" for the goals and behaviors in the attachment relationship. The take-home message of Polyvagal Theory is crystal clear: the brain's sense of safety, danger, or life threat is the organizing principle for mammalian behavior. The evolutionary expectation of physical and emotional proximity to a sensitive and caring adult is hardwired into the newborn and young infant brain. Social engagement with the caregiver over time leads to social connectedness, a biological imperative for survival. Porges defines social connectedness as "the ability to mutually (synchronously and reciprocally) regulate physiologic and behavioral state" (Porges, 2019).

The Polyvagal Theory impressed upon us a transformative lesson: it is crucial for adult caregivers to be aware of their children's neuroceptions, as an infant or child may act quite differently depending on the cues of safety, danger, or life threat their unconscious nervous system broadcasts to them. We transitioned from questioning what was wrong with a child who was reacting or disruptive, and our motto became *it's not what's wrong with them; it's what happened to them that caused their current state.* When we address only infants' and children's behaviors without understanding their neuroceptions, we may choose approaches that are suboptimal or at worst harmful. Only through awareness and understanding of their neuroceptive state, as defined by Porges, will we as medical caregivers truly know what actions to take at what time.

The Polyvagal Theory also taught us that healthcare providers can play a critical role in the neuroception of our patients and their families. For example, the doctors and nurses may prepare to transition a sick baby from the ventilator to a less invasive form of respiratory support. His mother may be very worried because the last time the tube came out of his throat, the team quickly needed to replace it. The neonatologist, recognizing the mother's sense of danger, remains calm and reassuring as the staff do their work. She looks the mother directly in the eyes and uses a soft voice to assure the mother that everything is going to be fine. The physician's face is relaxed, and she smiles. While the neonatologist appreciates the mother's worry and sense of danger, she uses her own calm and therapeutic presence to help the mother move toward a sense of safety, security, and confidence in the healthcare team.

Other settings care for older children with social-emotional struggles who become dysregulated. This child's neuroception of danger and life threat becomes contagious. While the staff members are trained extensively in de-escalation and management, their own fears and sense of danger may easily be triggered as they cooperate to assist the child. If the medical provider or team leader broadcasts a sense of calm and self-regulation that will co-regulate the staff, the entire team will be more effective in helping the child to regain their own sense of safety and security.

As medical providers, the Polyvagal Theory taught us that a sense of safety is not simply a nice experience. It is necessary for healthy physical and emotional growth, development, and healing to occur. We now have a way to understand our patients, their families, our staff, and our own work in ways that we hadn't before.

Section I (Chapters 1 through 3) addresses early childhood social-emotional development and the importance of attachment and caregiver-child dyadic regulation as the building blocks for later social relationships. Here, we describe optimal infant and early childhood relationships and the underlying neuroanatomy, neurobiology, and neurophysiology that support the developing child. Our perspective is influenced by the evolutionary biology from which Polyvagal Theory derives.

Section II (Chapters 4 and 5) discusses disruptions of social connectedness in childhood and the implications for later life. We include environments that physically separate the caregiver and young infant, for instance, the immigration crisis or parental imprisonment. We also explore environments where the caregiver and the infant or child may be in physical proximity but lacking emotional reciprocity. For example, primary caregivers who are challenged by substance misuse or serious social-emotional difficulties may be located together with their children but are not emotionally available. Included are discussions of why disruptions happen, as well as the visual, metabolic, physiologic, or behavioral clues that alert us. Finally, we elaborate upon both short- and long-term health consequences for the individual child and family as well as for their communities.

Section III (Chapters 6 through 8) focuses on the prevention and repair of relationship disruptions that place children and their families at risk for poor health and social-emotional well-being. We include a Polyvagal Theory perspective on self-regulation for the professional caregivers of children and families that assists them in co-regulating others. We highlight examples of excellence in relationship-based care for families that demystify the autonomic nervous system–driven behaviors and foster social connectedness. We address building polyvagal-informed organizations to broadcast that patients, families, and staff are in good hands.

Section IV (Chapters 9 and 10) applies Polyvagal Theory to larger issues of life. As we wrote this book, the COVID-19 pandemic emerged and intensified. Suddenly, the presence of others spelled danger, and social connectedness was threatened by *social distancing* and *sheltering in place*. On a daily basis with family, friends, community, and professional worlds, we had to find new ways of feeling emotional proximity and resonance. Our worlds were upended as we yearned for safety and security through proxies of presence. Chapter 9 considers the COVID-19 pandemic from the viewpoint of Polyvagal Theory.

As disturbing as the COVID-19 pandemic was, as we were writing, another cataclysm rocked the United States and beyond, when footage of police killings of Black Americans went viral and gave birth to wide-spread protests and an intense social reckoning. We were horrified by these killings, which focused our collective attention on anti-Black violence and racism. In response, we contemplated together the dramatic cultural shifts we were watching, and we both did our own soul searching and examined the implicit biases lodged deep within our own limbic systems. We realized we needed to include sections in this book describing the polyvagal neurobiology of threat and harm caused by racism.

In our final chapter, we address the emergent properties of a global community built upon Polyvagal Theory. Just as we struggle to emerge from the COVID-19 pandemic, we hold similar hope for eventually transcending what can only be considered a pandemic of oppression, both explicit and nonconscious. Using embodied Polyvagal Theory as one tool to end oppressive behaviors will take longer than ending a viral pandemic, but to survive as a species, we must make progress on this front. We can put practices and understandings into action that help us heal from the deep wounds of childhood trauma, systemic racism, and all else that divides and harms us.

We write this book as clinicians who care for babies, children, adolescents, and their families and as parents of our own adolescent and young adult children. Learning Polyvagal Theory often evoked our memories of things that went well in our lives and things that didn't. As you read this book, we invite you to reflect upon how Polyvagal Theory applies to your own clinical or educational practice with children and families. Consider your roles for others' children, your own children, and other family members. Reflect upon your own childhood with the template provided to you by nature and prior generations' experiences. In addition, we invite you to pay attention to your own autonomic state as you read. Notice how you feel about words, concepts, and scenarios. Do they make you feel a little nervous, does your mind wander, or do you suddenly relax and let out a long breath? Consider possible neurobiological meanings of your reactions. Allow Polyvagal Theory to further inform what you know and do.

Aided by an understanding of the neurobiology of safety and cooperation, we can build a safer, kinder, and better resourced world framed by principles of compassionate justice, equity, and thoughtful investment in children and their families.

Marilyn Sanders and George Thompson
Winter 2020

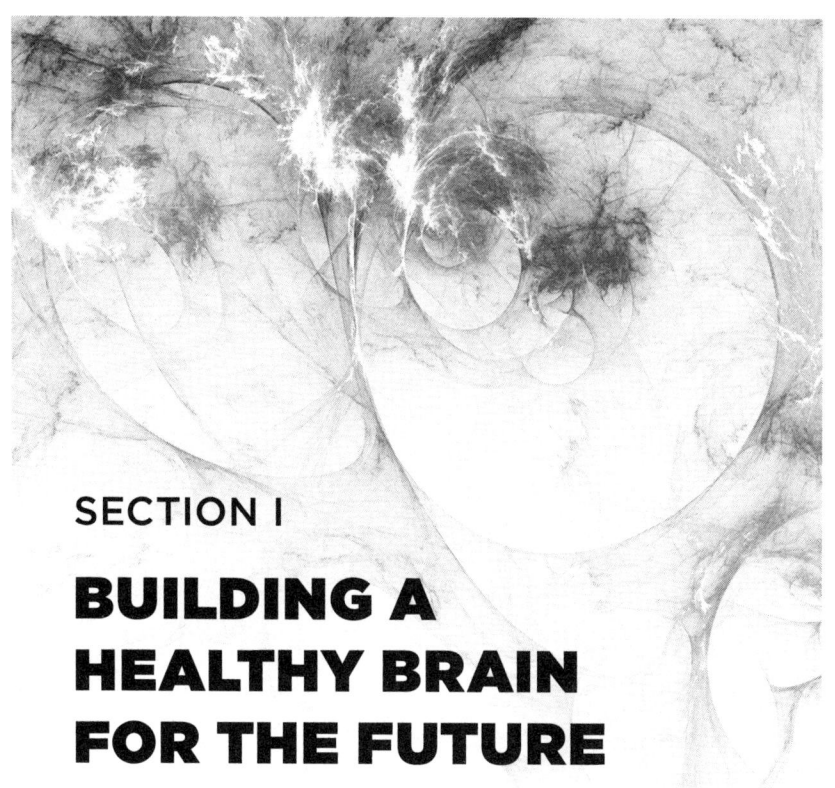

SECTION I

BUILDING A HEALTHY BRAIN FOR THE FUTURE

CHAPTER 1

Pregnancy, the Intrauterine Environment, and Birth: Nurturing a Brain Under Construction

We were born at the mercy of someone else's care. We grew up and survived into adulthood because we received care from others.
—THUPTEN JINPA, 2015

Mammals, including human infants, experience a prolonged period of dependency upon adult caregivers to meet our needs. As babies, our biological expectation is that our caregivers are sensitive and attuned. In proximity to caring adults, we are open-faced, calm, and engaged increasingly in a dance that communicates our pleasure in our caregivers. Without the physical and emotional proximity of a responsive caregiver, we are distressed and signal our struggle to engage others. If successful, we return to our state of calm and content. If we are repeatedly unsuccessful, we may eventually give up, withdrawing into aloneness, our lives in peril.

EVOLUTIONARY BIOLOGY LAYS THE GROUNDWORK

The seeds of the human infant's sense of peril were sown in the evolutionary biology of the autonomic nervous system (ANS). At the most basic level, our brain's sense of safety, danger, or life threat is the organizing principle of our emotions and behaviors. We understand at an unconscious level that our connections to others keep us safe, and without them, we are in danger. When we are in danger, our sympathetic nervous system prepares us to fight or flee. If the danger is so overwhelming we feel trapped, as if we may indeed perish, we feel buried alive and experience terror.

Porges (2011) names the unconscious barometer range from safety to life threat *neuroception* to distinguish it from perception that derives from the conscious or thinking portions of the brain. Neuroception is the brain's rapid and constant assessment of safety or threat. Our neuroception derives from the limbic system, one of the most primitive brain structures. The limbic system includes the amygdala (the central alarm, responsible for attentional, emotional, and social processing); the hippocampus (enabling learning and storing memories); the hypothalamus (directing endocrine processes and including pathways to other central and peripheral nervous system components); and the thalamus (serving as a thoroughfare for sensory information).

THE EVOLUTIONARILY DETERMINED HIERARCHY OF BEHAVIORS

The limbic alarm system broadcasts when we feel *safe*, in *danger*, or in a *life-threatening* situation. An evolutionarily determined hierarchy of behaviors is associated with these three neuroceptive states (see Figure 1.1). As mammals, our first response to danger is to look for safety through social engagement with our caregivers. If

The Evolutionary Timeline

parasympathetic	sympathetic nervous system	parasympathetic
dorsal vagus		ventral vagus
life-threat	danger	safety
immobilization	mobilization	social engagement

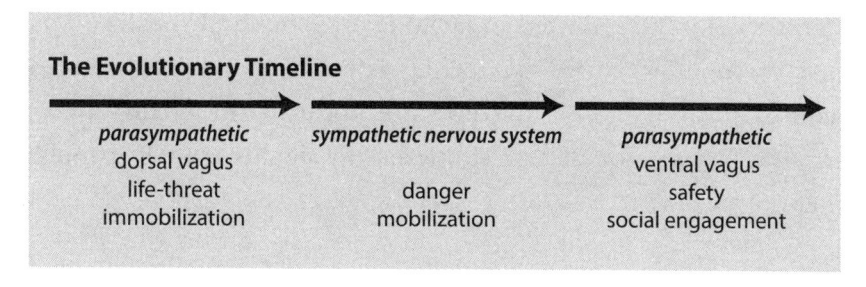

FIGURE 1.1

The evolutionarily-determined hierarchy of behaviors. From THE POLYVAGAL THEORY IN THERAPY: ENGAGING THE RHYTHM OF REGULATION by Deb Dana. Copyright © 2018 by Deb Dana. Used by permission of W. W. Norton & Company, Inc.

this strategy fails, we either fight back or flee to escape the lurking predator. Finally, and only if our social engagement system and ability to fight or flee fail, we seek safety in immobilizing, disappearing, and hoping the predator will look for other prey.

The behaviors associated with these states reflect the autonomic nervous system's (ANS) parasympathetic and sympathetic components. The well-modulated parasympathetic (PNS) and sympathetic systems (SNS) work together, both in the central nervous system and in the periphery to regulate our bodily functions. Neither is good nor bad; we need both components to survive and thrive. The PNS works through the many branches of the 10th cranial nerve, *vagus*, or *wandering nerve*. Porges coined the term *Polyvagal Theory* to describe the roles of the vagus nerve with its two components, the primitive or dorsal vagus and the smart or ventral vagus. Each component has a distinct origination in the brainstem.

The fibers of the vagus bring critical sensory information back to the brain where neuroception then evaluates the incoming information and relays the felt sense of safety, danger, or life threat. The co-location of the vagal nerve body with the nerve bodies of the muscles of the face, eye, and mouth creates the *face-heart connection*. The face-heart connection causes the heart's neural regulation to be reflected in facial expressions and vocalizations. For example, when we are feeling safe and secure, the muscles controlling our mouth and eyes are upturned in an inviting or *approach* expression. These subtle bodily signals are felt through neuroception.

SAFETY IS REFLECTED IN THE VENTRAL VAGAL SOCIAL ENGAGEMENT SYSTEM

The mammalian social engagement system is mediated by the more recently evolved ventral vagus and its branches (see Figure 1.1). When the ventral vagus is operative, mammals find safety in the presence of and connection to others. We feel the protection of caring others, and our sympathetic reactivity quiets. We become calm and are free to enjoy continuing social engagements that over time lead to social connectedness and attachments. When socially connected, we "mutually (synchronously and reciprocally) regulate each other's physiological and behavioral state" (Porges, 2019). As Thupten Jinpa (2015, p. 3) noted above, we survive to adulthood (and beyond) because our ANS finds safety in the warm smile, soft touch, and comfort in the presence of others.

Vagal tone can be measured by either respiratory sinus arrhythmia (RSA) or heart rate variability (HRV). For more detail, please see Chapter 2. Both methods assess the neural input to the heart by quantifying the variability from one heartbeat to the next. Quantification of the distance between two heartbeats yields information about the flexibility of the central nervous system to respond to stress. When a person is neurologically damaged and said to be brain dead, there is no variability between the heartbeats because the communication between the brain and the heart is absent. Thus, although the person may have a beating heart, he is legally dead.

When there is good variability in the heart rate, the central nervous system is able to respond flexibly to stresses or challenges to the system. When necessary, for example, the heart rate can increase, yielding a higher cardiac output and more energy available to overcome stresses. When there is diminished or poor variability in the heart rate, the brain has little reserve and cannot successfully meet significant stresses.

When mammals breathe, the heart rate increases during inspiration and decreases during expiration. Respiratory sinus arrhythmia (RSA) (Porges, 2011) measures the "phasic increases and decreases" (p. 68) in ventral or smart vagal output to the heart. The higher the amplitude of the increases, the greater the flexibility of the system to respond to stresses or challenges

THREAT OR DANGER REQUIRES SYMPATHETIC MOBILIZATION

As evolution proceeded, increased species complexity required alternative strategies for responses to danger (see Figure 1.1). The sympathetic nervous system (SNS) and hypothalamic-pituitary-adrenal axis (HPA) came online. As in a home security system, the blaring alarm of the limbic system led to an escalation of emotional responses and behaviors, known as *fight-or-flight*. The SNS mediated through hormonal and neurotransmitter pathways uses epinephrine or adrenaline and cortisol, the stress hormone, to facilitate mobilization and movement. Sympathetic responses may be recognized as anger, hostility, panic, or more subtly, hypervigilance or intrusiveness. Irritation or heightened anxiety may turn to panic or rage as the ANS seeks the reset alarm button and attempts to escape the felt danger (Delahooke, 2019).

WHEN LIFE THREAT IS FELT, FREEZE IN PLACE

The primitive dorsal vagus arises from the part of the brainstem responsible for our vegetative systems and innervates bodily organs below the diaphragm, including the stomach, intestines, and bladder. If the limbic system is the home security alarm (Delahooke, 2019), the dorsal vagus is the basement where the utility functions fuel the infrastructure of the body to keep the lights, heat, and water going. Without the metabolic energy provided by digestion and water balance provided by the kidneys and bladder, there would be no energy to fuel higher processes.

Dorsal vagal responses are seen in reptiles, the earliest vertebrates to come on land. When the reptile senses life threat, it immobilizes, hoping to camouflage into its environment to avoid being seen. Clinically, this may be recognized as emotional shutdown, vasovagal syncope (fainting), and in extreme situations, clinical dissociation (see Figure 1.1).

THE AUTONOMIC NERVOUS SYSTEM IN FETAL AND INTRAUTERINE LIFE

Early in the pregnancy, the maternal-fetal environment indelibly links the mother and her developing fetus. A mother's experience of her own life, the circumstances surrounding conception, and her felt sense of safety, danger, or life threat are all played out in the response of her autonomic nervous system with its potential impact upon the developing fetal ANS.

These maternal and fetal bidirectional influences include a vast array of neuronal, hormonal, and immune responses that can move the interdependent systems away from safety, health, and well-being toward challenge. Throughout pregnancy, the fetal brain is actively developing the neural structures and communication pathways that are the modifiable template upon which early experience acts. Both central and peripheral nervous system structure and function are vulnerable to changes in the environment that may have downstream effects. At any moment in time, an intricate dance is playing out in the central nervous system where the neurobiologic choreography is masterminded within the limbic system's alarm broadcasting system.

BRICKS AND MORTAR OF THE FETAL CENTRAL NERVOUS SYSTEM

Nerve cells or neurons and other brain cells come together in networks that repeatedly activate each other and increase each other's efficiency (Hebb, 1949). These brain cells form recognizable structures (e.g., the cortex and the limbic system), and they constantly exchange information using energy supplied by electrical and hormonal influences. As a neuron is acting, it is being acted upon by multiple forces.

By 9 weeks after conception, the dorsal vagal nerve body appears in the fetal brainstem, making it the first and most primitive of the autonomic response systems to come online. Between 16–20 weeks' gestation, fetal movements begin, and the SNS is available to respond to intrauterine stresses. *Quickening* (appropriately named) occurs when pregnant women recognize the first subtle signs of fetal movement. Finally, after 23 weeks' gestation, ventral vagal neurons begin to myelinate, greatly increasing after 30 weeks' gestation (Porges & Furman, 2011). This prepares the newborn to participate in social engagement behaviors including vocalization, facial gesturing, sucking, and the long-awaited smile.

THE RICH FETAL SENSORY ENVIRONMENT

In the sensory-rich intrauterine environment, the fetus receives continuous feedback from its own environment as well as the external environments, the utero-placental unit, and the larger world of the mother's experience. In the third trimester ($\geq$ 24 weeks'), skin sensory receptors project to the brain, and the fetus, if born early, can discriminate pleasant vs. unpleasant touch (Olausson et al., 2002). Finally, the eighth cranial or auditory nerve forms, and the fetus develops a selective preference for sounds such as the mother's heartbeat and voice (Weinstein, 2016).

These sensory capacities lay the groundwork for attachment behaviors after birth. For example, fetuses have a preference for a nursery rhyme sung by their own mother, rather than another person (DeCasper, Lecanuet, Busnel, Granier-Deferre, & Maugeais, 1994). According to Marlier, Schaal, and Soussignan (1998), newborns are more likely to turn toward the smell of their own mother's amniotic fluid, rather than another woman's. Newborns will also prefer the scent of foods their own mother ate during gestation (Schaal, 1998).

THE NEURAL REGULATION OF THE FETAL HEART

Early in the first trimester, the fetal heart starts beating (Kirby, 2007) and is sensitized by neurotransmitters originating in the PNS (e.g., acetylcholine) and the SNS (e.g., epinephrine). As gestation proceeds, obstetric healthcare providers monitor fetal well-being using both the biophysical profile and fetal heart rate tracings, both reflections of integrity of the fetal ANS. For the at-risk or laboring pregnant woman, fetal heart rate and heart rate variability are invaluable indicators of well-being (Robinson, 2008).

In an optimal zone with a healthy mother and fetus with good heart rate variability, the fetal autonomic nervous system broadcasts an intrinsic sense of safety and well-being. Through the lens of Polyvagal Theory, the healthy fetus with a stable heart rate and good heart rate variability is *autonomically* safe, resilient, and able to adapt to evolving challenges in the maternal-fetal environment. When the fetus' well-being is challenged, the fetus is sympathetically activated, and the fetal heart rate increases. When severe and potentially lethal fetal bradycardia intervenes that fails to recover after typical resetting interventions, there is a dire need to deliver the fetus immediately. Now the overwhelmed fetal autonomic nervous system reverts to dorsal vagal influence to protect the fetus by minimizing metabolic demands through shutting down activities that are not vital to immediate survival, such as digestion.

The biophysical profile used after 24 weeks' gestation combines fetal heart rate tracing and five ultrasound measures to gauge fetal well-being (Manning, Morrison, Harman, Lange, & Menticoglou, 1987). The fetal heart rate, fetal breathing, diaphragmatic motion, movements, and muscle tone are reflections of the integrity of the fetal ANS. Good heart rate variability forecasts a fetus able to manage a constantly changing maternal environment. It is a fetal reflection of autonomic nervous system resilience.

HORMONAL REGULATION AND THE INTRAUTERINE ENVIRONMENT

The major hormonal regulators and effectors of early experience, both prenatally and after birth, are the hypothalamic-pituitary-adrenal system (the HPA axis) and the oxytocin/vasopressin systems. The hypothalamus, located in the limbic system, senses disruption or metabolic stress and produces corticotropin-releasing hormone (CRH) that signals the anterior pituitary to produce and secrete adrenocorticotropic hormone (ACTH) (see Figure 1.2). ACTH travels to the adrenal gland, where it stimulates the production of cortisol. While too much cortisol may overstimulate an already taxed limbic system, leading to anger, irritability,

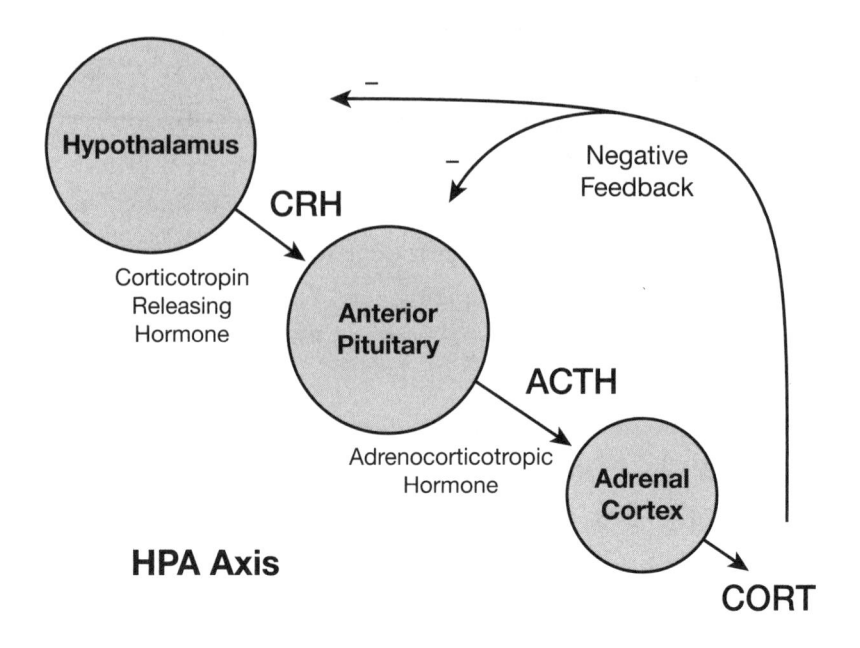

FIGURE 1.2

Basic Hypothalamic–Pituitary–Adrenal Axis.
Used with permission under the Creative Commons Attribution-Share Alike 3.0
https://commons.wikimedia.org/wiki/File:HPA_Axis_Diagram_(Brian_M_Sweis_2012).png

or even rage episodes, too little cortisol at a time of metabolic stress signals life-threatening danger to the challenged system.

When stable, the pregnant mother's circulation and placenta protect the fetus against excess cortisol surges. Levels of CRH found in the maternal circulation approach those seen only at times of induced stress. Typically, peripheral production of cortisol suppresses CRH in a negative feedback loop. During pregnancy, cortisol stimulates maternal CRH production. Cortisol may cross the placenta to the fetus but 11β-Hydroxysteroid dehydrogenase type-2, an enzyme in the placenta, deactivates cortisol to its inactive form, cortisone. This enzyme is active through much of pregnancy, protecting the fetus from cortisol overload, but decreases dramatically near term, allowing transfer of maternal cortisol. Maternal cortisol stimulates the production and release of surfactant. Surfactant plays a key role in lung maturation for the developing fetus and in preparation of the fetus for entering the air-breathing world (Sandman, Davis, Buss, & Glynn, 2011).

The hormonal oxytocin and vasopressin pathways also develop during the fetal period. Both are protein molecules that are linked to safety-seeking behaviors. Evolutionarily, vasopressin developed first and plays a critical physiologic role in metabolic adaptation to a stressful environment. Vasopressin may promote both sympathetic activation and blending in or immobilization behaviors akin to the extremes of the dorsal vagal system. Oxytocin, colloquially known as the *love hormone*, developed later and promotes social engagement, affiliation behaviors, and pair bonding (Carter, 2017).

Both hormones are synthesized and stored deep in the central nervous system in the pituitary gland close to the hypothalamus. The fetal oxytocin pathway is extraordinarily sensitive to the maternal-fetal environment and may be linked to intergenerational transmission of early maternal life stress (Toepfer et al., 2017). The implications are vast as we begin to understand that we are all the sum total of our earlier generations' experiences.

TRANSITION TO THE EXPECTED ENVIRONMENT

The fetus, now infant, is delivered and begins breathing. The umbilical cord is cut, severing the dependence upon the placenta, and continuing the transition from the previous fetal pattern of circulation that bypasses the lungs to the newborn circulation. As the newborn continues to breathe with a robust cry, blood that returns to the heart from the body goes to the lung for oxygenation and returns to the left side of the heart to be pumped to the brain and vital organs. The healthy newborn is placed on the mother's chest where the dyad begins the work of choreographing the dance of attunement and social engagement. As the dyad continues its work of social engagement, leading to social connectedness and safety, the system becomes iterative and self-reinforcing.

During the first hour after birth, the mother's body and breasts replace the placenta and uterus as infant regulators. The evolutionarily determined ecological niche for the healthy newborn is skin-to-skin with the mother where the mother satiates the senses of her newborn. Her skin provides cutaneous sensory input and temperature regulation; her breasts provide breast milk, satisfying sensations of taste and smell and nutrition; her soft voice and prosody stimulate the auditory system. The mother's oxytocin levels surge as the infant is skin-to-skin. The mother's own autonomic nervous system and sense of safety convey protection. The infant's autonomic nervous system resonates with the mother's broadcast of safety as they both calm and regulate after the necessary sympathetic activation accompanying labor and delivery (Phillips, 2013).

According to Phillips (2013), the healthy newborn on their mother's skin searches for their mother's breast and nipple in a well-documented sequence of nine stages over the first hour, beginning with the birth cry. The newborn continues to crawl toward the mother's breast as they make a series of short pushes moving toward the mother's nipple. Finally, the newborn familiarizes themself with the nipple and sucks at the breast (Widström et al., 1990).

Keeping newborns and their mothers skin-to-skin after birth is associated with both short- and long-term benefits. Mothers who have their babies skin-to-skin demonstrate increased confidence handling their babies in the birth hospitalization, and they breastfeed longer. Their infants have better self-regulation at 1 year old than babies who were separated at birth from their mothers (Bystrova et al., 2009).

Over the next several days, as mother and newborn become familiar with each other, the newborn's capacity for social engagement increases. In a well-regulated dyad, the mother's milk supply increases to meet the newborn's needs for both hydration and nutrition. Using information from all their senses, the mother and her newborn co-regulate each other, and social engagement increases. Over time, as social engagement flourishes, social connectedness emerges. With time, social connectedness of the mother and her newborn leads to attachment relationships, the keystone for promoting health and well-being over a lifetime.

DISRUPTIONS OF THE EXPECTED ENVIRONMENT

The best babies are the ones things don't happen to.
—NEONATOLOGIST, 2018

In most pregnancies, connectedness builds as both the pregnant woman and her fetus develop biologically embedded expectations of the intrauterine maternal-fetal dyadic interactions. The mother becomes acquainted with the fetus, develops a mental model, knows the patterns of movement, and begins feeling connected. At least by quickening (the maternal perception of fetal movement), typically occurring at 16–20 weeks of gestation, the mother begins bonding to her fetus (Ammaniti & Gallese, 2014).

The fetus, who becomes a baby, depends upon the mother for all forms of shelter and nurturance as social engagement comes online in the moments following delivery. Typically, a mother and her new baby need only each other. However, some babies, either through challenges in the labor and delivery, transitions from the intra-to-extrauterine environment, early problems in organ development, or premature birth, require additional support. For these mother-baby dyads, the biological expectations of the physical and emotional proximity of a sensitive and attuned caregiver with whom the delicate choreography of engagement and contingent responsiveness builds fails. The expected transition of biologically determined ecological niche from womb to maternal breast is disrupted. For some, the disruption will be as brief as a few hours. For others, the process is interrupted for days, weeks, or months.

The healthy newborn reacts to any separation from the mother with a sense of danger and is sympathetically activated with crying, increased heart rate, and agitation. The attuned and sensitive mother, recognizing the newborn's cries of danger and aloneness, instinctively consoles, calms, and comforts until the infant returns to safety. If, however, mother broadcasts her own sense of danger or life threat due to her medical condition; challenges of pregnancy, labor, or delivery: or history of early adversity, the infant's cries may go unheeded. Over time the infant eventually ceases crying and may shut down in dorsal vagal despair.

Parents who are separated unexpectedly from their babies have often experienced prior stresses in the conception and pregnancy such as infertility, preterm labor, or hospitalizations due to maternal health complications or preexisting medical conditions. For hospitalized babies, neuroceptions of danger lurk as they experience separation from their parents, multiple caregivers, and unpredictability in the environment with lights, sounds, unpleasant touch, or pain (Sanders & Hall, 2018).

Many babies are born as early as 6 months' gestation (23–24 weeks'), when the immature architecture of their brains and nervous system function place them at risk for short- and long-term developmental challenges. Preterm infants are often born during critical phases of brain development that are potentially altered by exposure to environments, such as the newborn intensive care unit, that challenge the limits of autonomic nervous system adaptability. For other parent-infant dyads, the alterations of the intrauterine environment, such as intrauterine opiate exposure, may set the stage for potential disruptions.

THE PRETERM INFANT

The preterm infant is not an inadequate fullterm organism, but a well-equipped, competently adapted organism appropriately functioning at his/her stage and in a particular environment. Suddenly, the infant is in a vastly different environment, the passage to which has irreversibly triggered subsystem functioning in an environment only poorly matched to the infant's expectations.
—HEIDELISE ALS, 1982

In a well-working parent-infant system, the parent and infant delight in each other as they volley and parry in their evolving and increasingly satisfying interactions. However, there are many challenges for the preterm infant and their caregivers as the evolutionary expectations of both parties are violated. Pioneering developmental psychologist Heidelise Als (1982) recognized the vulnerabilities and strengths of the preterm infant. While Porges was beginning his early work in heart rate variability in the newborn intensive care unit (NICU), Als framed the synactive theory to assist clinicians and parents to understand the neurodevelopment of the preterm infant. From birth onward, infants look for their caregivers, and, with increasing alertness and interactive capacity as they mature, they connect with the caregiver who affectionately rewards them for their social engagement with interaction. In synactive theory, like Polyvagal Theory, the role of the autonomic nervous system is central to and a key determinant of other bodily systems. In synactive theory, the autonomic nervous system is positioned at the center of four cones of integrated bodily systems including the motor system, state-organization, and attention/interaction. At all times, these interacting subsystems are embedded in an external environment that is mismatched to the preterm infant's needs.

For example, skin sensitivity begins early in gestation, initially around the mouth and face, and spreads sequentially to the hands, genitals, and soles of the feet. The fetus is receiving continuous cutaneous feedback from the amniotic fluid and the boundaries of the womb. This is reflected in the size of the sensory cortex serving these earliest innervated skin regions. In otherwise typical deliveries, the newborn comes directly from the rich sensory environment of the womb to the mother's chest. Yet, even though the evolutionary significance of these innervation patterns is clear, the preterm infant most often goes from the amniotic fluid and womb to an open warmer, where they are stabilized by the healthcare team and then placed in an incubator for transport to the NICU. In the NICU, they spend significant time in an incubator. Ideally, their time out of the incubator includes skin-to-skin (kangaroo) care from their parents. During kangaroo care, the infant is placed directly upon the parents' skin, typically the chest, for autonomic regulation, warmth, and nutrition. Skin-to-skin care is referred to as kangaroo care as the infant is akin to the kangaroo baby Joey who crawls to the mother's pouch for the same. Hours before, they were nourished and regulated by the maternal circulation and immediate womb environment. Now, the NICU environment and technology address the baby's needs for temperature control, respiratory support, nutrition, and autonomic regulation.

Application of synactive theory to the modern NICU led Als to develop the Newborn Individualized Developmental Care and

Assessment Program (NIDCAP). NIDCAP is a framework for caregiving in the modern NICU based upon the synactive theory that recognizes the challenges of addressing the biologically embedded needs for caregiving and social engagement while acknowledging the necessity of technological support. In the modern NICU, survival of babies previously thought nonviable is now routine, but survival comes at a cost, and short- and long-term morbidities remain a substantial concern.

In NICUs adopting NIDCAP, caregiving is relationship-based, recognizing the primacy of the parent-infant dyad as the natural ecological niche for the infant. NIDCAP is a "professional alliance that supports the parents' engrossment with their child and the child's neurobiologically-based expectations for nurturance from the family" (Als & Gilkerson, 1997, p. 178). Recognizing the infant's behavior as their language, NIDCAP invites family and professional caregivers to make ongoing assessments of what the baby is saying with their behavior; where are their strengths; what are their vulnerabilities; and what support do they need from the caring adults around them?

The NIDCAP behavioral assessment tool documents stress and self-regulatory behaviors in the autonomic, motor, state-organization, and interactive/attentional subsystems. These autonomic states mirror Polyvagal Theory's ventral vagal safety/self-regulation, sympathetic activation, and dorsal vagal immobilization/stress. The preterm infant who is resting comfortably in skin-to-skin on mother's chest with stable respirations and good color is co-regulated in ventral vagal safety. As the infant is moved from mother's chest to the incubator, they are sympathetically activated and may become tachycardic with increased nonpurposeful motor activity. If they need all their resources to manage the separation from their mother, they may ultimately become exhausted and collapse into dorsal vagal immobilization. Polyvagal Theory recognizes the neuroception of safety/danger or life threat. Individualized developmental care is a template for caregiving that relates the recognizable behaviors to the underlying autonomic neuroceptive state (Als, 1982).

Neonatologists and other newborn healthcare providers also increasingly recognize and affirm the parents' relationship as the primary caregiving relationship for infants in hospital-based care. The conceptual transformation of the newborn intensive care unit (NICU) into a newborn intensive parenting unit (NIPU) embeds "reconnection of the family and baby as a first priority" (Hall et al., 2017, p. 1261). The NIPU model also expects full partnership of family and staff to work collaboratively toward healing the baby's medical concerns and the fundamental disruptions of connectedness that occur when the mother and her infant are separated after birth (Hall et al., 2017). Validating these disruptions of connectedness as trauma lays the groundwork for integration of polyvagal-informed care in the NIPU that honors the relationship of babies and their families (Sanders & Hall, 2018; Sanders, 2018).

THE OPIATE-EXPOSED NEWBORN

Mothers who have experienced opioid misuse or dependence often had chronic disruptions of their early childhood social connectedness. In the absence of ventral vagal safety, survival-seeking, maladaptive coping strategies are implemented. Seen through the lens of neuroception, opioid dependence reflects an autonomic nervous system in chronic sympathetic activation or dorsal vagal immobilization. The ventral vagal pleasure ordinarily experienced in social engagement and connectedness is absent, and the pleasure-seeking rewards of dopamine surges associated with opioid use are substituted.

Opioid prescriptions provided to pregnant women doubled from 2005–2009 (Gomez-Pomar & Finnegan, 2018). Sixty-eight percent of infants whose mothers took chronic opioids experience neonatal abstinence syndrome (NAS), the constellation of physical and behavioral symptoms reflecting the withdrawal from intrauterine opioid exposure (Gomez-Pomar & Finnegan, 2018). Exposed infants are often irritable with excessive crying, sleep disturbances, poor feeding behaviors, and vomiting or diarrhea. The most severely affected newborns may have seizures.

Finnegan and colleagues (1975) reported the Finnegan Neonatal Abstinence Scoring System. The Finnegan score assisted healthcare providers to determine which opiate-exposed infants needed treatment with morphine. Infants were often treated with morphine to stabilize them with a slow weaning. Once started on morphine, the infant was typically maintained on morphine. Hospitalization was often prolonged for several weeks. During the hospitalization, the infant was routinely awakened on a schedule for assessment and dosing with morphine. The primary caregivers for the infant were generally hospital staff. Mother and family care was often intermittent and brief. Classic treatment of mother-infant dyads affected by opiate-use substituted morphine for the mother's innate co-regulatory capabilities.

Grossman and colleagues (2017) described Eat, Sleep, Console as an intervention that promotes the mother or primary caregiver as the medicine for the baby, strongly encouraging ongoing parental or family presence with the newborn. With scaffolding provided by experienced healthcare providers, family members provide complete care for the baby. Morphine doses are used intermittently only if the baby cannot eat, sleep, or be consoled with nonpharmacologic interventions and supports. The primacy of the parent-infant relationship is prioritized. Staff are in the background, and the parent is the expert on the baby. Grossman reported outcomes for mother-baby dyads treated using the Eat, Sleep, Console intervention. Hospitalization days and morphine doses dramatically decreased compared to historical cohorts. Breastfeeding rates at discharge increased significantly (Grossman et al., 2017).

When hospitals use the Eat, Sleep, Console intervention, the staff support the opioid-misusing parents as security-engendering caregivers. As the opioid-misusing mother's neuroception recognizes respect and support, her dysregulated ANS calms. As she begins to experience a ventral vagal sense of safety and security, her newborn's ANS responds in kind. The mother's sense of self-efficacy increases and results in higher sensitivity and attunement to her newborn, whose ANS is often sympathetically activated by the effects of withdrawal from intrauterine opioids.

In Chapter 2, we discuss the first year after birth and how the parental environment becomes the second womb regulating the newborn and young infant, promoting safety, security, connectedness, and over time, secure attachment.

CHAPTER 2

Safe, Calm, and Secure: Parental Environment as the Second Womb

The intrauterine womb provides regulation of nutrition, hydration, temperature, and moderation of stress for the fetus. From the moment of birth through early childhood, the parental caregiving environment is the second womb taking over these regulatory activities to promote early health and well-being. Evolution prepared mammals to transition these regulatory functions from the intrauterine to extrauterine environment as the capacities for social engagement came online.

SECURE ATTACHMENT: THE COIN OF THE REALM

In his seminal series, *Attachment and Loss*, first published in 1969, Bowlby painstakingly detailed the evolving attachment relationship of the mother-infant dyad. Bowlby theorized the proximity-seeking behavior of the young infant or child is an instinctive behavior that is a product of the "genetic endowment with environment" (Bowlby, 1982, p. 38) with the goal of ensuring "maximum chances of survival" that requires a "nice balance between stability and lability" (p. 46).

Bowlby (1982) embedded the mother-infant dyadic relationship within the "environment of evolutionary adaptedness" (p. 50), describing a psychological construct that includes biological and physiologic events. As Bowlby remarked, "No single feature of a species' morphology, physiology, and behavior can be understood or even discussed intelligently except in relation to that species' environment of evolutionary adaptedness" (p. 64).

Within this environment, mother and infant engage in a series of instinctive behaviors with the set goal of achieving and maintaining proximity to each other. Through these interactions, they are able to organize information about their world into predictable schemata or maps. To Bowlby (1982), these self-organizing systems include the anatomical and physiological structures as well as the control systems that organize and direct the behaviors of both members. Finally, "within the environment of adaptedness, the whole performance as rule has effects that promote the survival of the individual and/or its kin" (p. 49).

Bowlby (1982) expanded upon proximity-seeking behavior, recognizing the infant's perceived responses are internalized and shape his psyche through his internal working model, derived from his experience with his attachment figure. Costello (2013) describes the internal working model as a "kind of guidance system that tells us what to do and what to expect when we are with another person. They are scripts for social interaction" (p. 85).

Developmental neuroscientist, psychotherapist, and analyst Allan Schore (1996) suggested "The self organization of the developing brain occurs in the context of another self, another brain" (p. 60). Furthermore, this robust maturation is "experience-dependent" (Schore, 2014, p. 1). Schore cited the science of interpersonal neurobiology to describe the role of mother-infant interactions within the environment of evolutionary adaptedness either to facilitate or inhibit the emergence of the self-regulatory role of the right hemisphere. Unlike other body organ systems, only a small portion of brain development and maturation occurs in utero. The heart, lungs, and kidneys, the critical visceral organs necessary to permit survival outside the womb, are typically sufficiently mature at term birth. Dobbing (1973), however, noted an exponential increase in brain mass, volume, organization, and myelination from delivery until 18–24 months.

Anatomic as well as structural and functional neuroimaging studies support the dominance of the right hemisphere in early infancy and toddlerhood as the seat of the emotional brain, affect regulation, and the attachment relationship (Trevarthen, 1996). Porges recognized the dominance of the right brain in emotional processing and the corresponding lateralization of the ventral vagal nucleus in the nucleus ambiguus, receiving input from the right amygdala. Porges, Doussard-Roosevelt, and Maiti (1994) elaborated the right-sided responsibilities of regulating homeostasis and modulating physiological state in response to both "internal (i.e., visceral) and external (i.e., environmental) feedback potentially enabling the control of other functions to evolve on the left side of the brain" (p. 175). They noted this asymmetry is reflective of the unique evolutionary demands of mammalian species with their long period of infant dependency upon the mature caregiving adult.

Social engagement and social connectedness are preconditions to the evolution of the attachment system. Early pioneers, including Bowlby and Robertson, described and documented what they saw in both typical and atypical interactions. Bowlby's student, psychologist Mary Ainsworth, elaborated upon and expanded Bowlby's theory of proximity-seeking beyond mere physical closeness to include emotional proximity and availability. The resulting theoretical shift emphasized maternal behaviors and communication patterns within the maternal-infant dyad. To assess these behaviors and the infant's response, Ainsworth developed and validated the Strange Situation paradigm. The Strange Situation evaluates attachment patterns by examining attachment (proximity-seeking) versus exploratory behaviors with the attachment figure and a stranger. Ainsworth's (1978) original work documented three major patterns of attachment and a fourth was later added by Main and Solomon (1990). The three original attachment patterns were (1) secure: an infant who seeks closeness to the attachment figure and is readily comforted by her return; (2) avoidant: an infant who displays little need for closeness nor comfort upon her return; and (3) resistant: an infant who shows intense emotion upon separation but is not easily comforted upon her return.

The development of video technology moved the study of infant behavior from empirical observations to hypothesis-based scientific research of infant face-to-face interaction with measurable outcomes. Using video analysis, Main further identified the fourth pattern as disorganized: an infant who shows a combination of secure/avoidant/resistant strategies that form an incoherent whole. While the intent of the pattern recognition was meant to indicate protective or risk factors, not diagnostic categories, the disorganized pattern has most often been associated with the later development of psychopathology (Beeney, 2017).

BEYOND THE MOTHER-CHILD INTERACTION

The single most common factor for children who develop resilience is at least one stable and committed relationship with a supportive parent, caregiver, or other adult. These relationships provide the personalized responsiveness, scaffolding, and protection that buffer children from developmental disruption.
—CENTER ON THE DEVELOPING CHILD

According to the Pew Research Center (2015), about two-thirds (69%) of all children under 18 years old live with two parents; one quarter (26%) live with one parent, and a small number (5%) live with no parent. In the Pew Research data, parent means an adult parental figure who may be a biological or adoptive parent, or the spouse or partner of a biological or adoptive parent. A decreasing number of parents are married. Black children and those children whose parents have less education are less likely to live with two parents.

Also noted by the Pew Research Center (2015) is the decreasing numbers of children who live in traditional two-parent families in their first marriage. It is beyond the scope of this book to discuss child attachment and well-being across the many family caregiver constellations now common in this country. Although adult caregivers for children may range by demographic factors, including marital status, gender, age, sexual orientation, biological relationship to the child, level of education, economic status and others, it is the stability and quality of caregiving relationships that most affect children's development and well-being (Center on the Developing Child, n.d.). While conventional wisdom may have previously claimed the advantages of being raised by a biological parent, Raby et al. (2017) report that adoptive parents' attachment representation are more likely to have "autonomous (secure) states of mind." Three-quarters (75%) of parents who adopt internationally or domestically are classified as having secure attachments on the Adult Attachment Interview, exceeding the typical rate of 55-60% in the general population (p. 4).

Braun and Champagne (2014) reviewed the evolving literature on the specific role of paternal caregiving on the health and well-being of their offspring. They identified three potential mechanisms through which paternal caregiving influences development: (1) direct paternal care of offspring; (2) epigenetic paternal variations transmitted to offspring, and (3) the influence of paternal caregiving on maternal care. The data derives predominately from bi-parental mammalian caregiving species such as the prairie vole. In general, mothers and fathers have similar behavioral repertoires, excluding lactation and nursing. However, their interactive styles suggest more high energy and playful behaviors between fathers and their offspring, compared to mothers.

Building upon variation noted in biparental species, Verschueren (2020) points out that, "The dominant focus on mothers as attachment figures [in the research literature] is likely influenced by societal and cultural factors shaping Bowlby's early theorizing" (p. 105). Verschueren (2020) says that one way of examining the role of the father is to look for ways that it differs from the role of the mother:

> Specifically, the "safe haven" function of attachment, referring to the provision of comfort and reassurance when the child is stressed or upset, may be more prominent among mothers. In contrast, the "secure base" function of attachment, implying the provision of support and encouragement when the child explores the wider social and non-social environment, may be more typical among fathers. (p. 107)

Verschueren (2020) gives us another reason to focus on the safe haven and secure base functions. She proposes that by shifting our focus from considering the differential impact that mothers and fathers have on child development to considering the differential impact of safe haven and secure base functions, we can move beyond biological and social gender constructions and appreciate the wide diversity of today's family configurations. Although we still refer to *mother-infant* and *mother-child* relationships, the descriptions of relationships in this book are also seen between the child and the non-birth parent, as well as other people important to the child.

Porges (2015b) proposes that "Functionally, play is a neural exercise in which cues triggering neuroception alternate between danger and safety" (p. 3). He points to the game of peek-a-boo, in which the mother gives her child a mild scare by disappearing and suddenly reappearing. The "game is ended, when the mother uses a prosodic voice with warm facial expressions to calm the startled infant" (p. 4). Porges theorizes that alternatively stimulating fight-or-flight responses and then calming them with prosodic speech and a friendly face builds resilience by guiding the child to practice going back and forth between the two states and by repeatedly accessing the ventral vagal state to regulate sympathetic fight-or-flight.

Paquette (2004) summarizes research in this area: "Men seem to have a tendency to excite, surprise, and momentarily destabilize children; they also tend to encourage children to take risks, while at the same time ensuring the latter's safety and security, thus permitting children to learn to be braver in unfamiliar situations, as well as to stand up for themselves" (p. 193). So, from the attachment perspective, the father who plays peek-a-boo and similar games with a pattern of alternating fright and calming is functioning as a secure base from which the child can safely explore the external world. As Verschueren discusses, either the safe haven or the secure base role can be provided by a caregiver irrespective of their gender.

MISMATCH AND REPAIR IN MOTHER-INFANT INTERACTIONS

Building upon the observations of Brazelton and colleagues, Tronick (2007) further refined the goal of the mother-infant dyad as reciprocity. He used video microanalysis to document interaction patterns in both naturalistic and experimental settings. The experimental Still Face intervention parallels Ainsworth's Strange

Situation but is validated in infants as young as 3–4 months. In the Still Face, the mother faces her infant and interacts typically for 2 minutes. She then turns around and when she returns to the infant's view, she adopts a masklike Still Face showing no reaction. During the Still Face, a well-regulated infant becomes increasingly distressed as she tries to get her mother's attention and engagement. Finally, after another 2 minutes, the mother abruptly returns to her prior interactive style. A healthy infant noticing her mother is back will begin to interact again, smoothly moving back to their usual interactive style (Cohn, 1987). While typical mother-infant interactions were often described as mutual delight, these times of synchronous interactions alone do not define the range of dyadic behaviors. Tronick focused upon infant coping behaviors by which infants can signal their caregivers of a mismatch, opening the opportunity for repair.

Mother-infant dyadic interactions were matched for behavioral states for typical 3-, 6-, and 9-month-old infants the minority of the time: 28%, 30%, and 36% respectively (Tronick, 1989). Infants are active participants in their repair process, not passive recipients. In the repair, they engage in both self-directed regulatory behaviors (e.g., thumb sucking or looking away) and other-directed regulatory behaviors (e.g., affective displays that signal the caregiver the infant is not achieving his goal). The stability of an infant's coping behaviors is in place by 6 months.

Using split screen video microanalysis, psychologist Beatrice Beebe (2010) brought further clarity to mother-infant dyadic communication by relating maternal styles of interaction with 4-month-old infants to 12-month attachment patterns. Beebe identified mothers' behaviors with their 4-month-olds that fell into patterns predicting secure or insecure attachments. Mothers who were themselves well-regulated displayed midrange-tracking of the infant. Beebe characterized the translation of

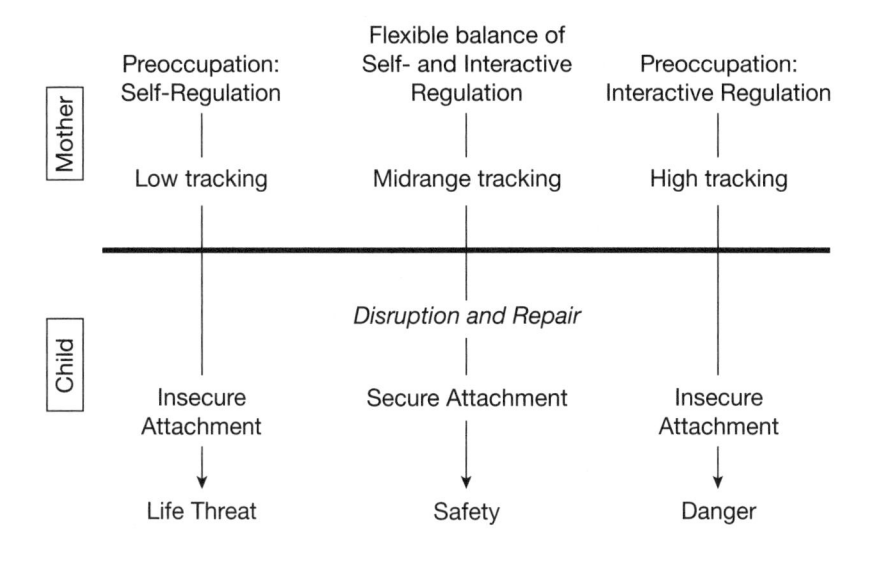

```
                    Flexible balance of
    Preoccupation:    Self- and Interactive    Preoccupation:
    Self-Regulation        Regulation         Interactive Regulation
Mother   |                  |                       |
     Low tracking     Midrange tracking       High tracking
         |                  |                       |
─────────┼──────────────────┼───────────────────────┼─────────
         |           Disruption and Repair          |
Child    |                  |                       |
      Insecure          Secure Attachment       Insecure
     Attachment                |               Attachment
         ↓                     ↓                    ↓
     Life Threat            Safety               Danger
```

FIGURE 2.1

Midrange balance model of attachment. Created with data from from Beebe, B. & Lachman, F. (2002).

the procedural expectation shared by the midrange tracking mothers as "We follow each other's direction of attention as we look and look away from the other's face" (p. 60). The internal working model of her infant might be translated as "I know your rhythms of looking at me; I feel seen by you" (p. 60). The infants of midrange-tracking mothers generally had secure attachments at 12 months. In contrast were mothers who demonstrated either low-tracking/preoccupied or high-tracking/intrusive styles. Low-tracking mothers may, themselves, sense less ability to focus on their infants. The infant's translation of his procedural expectation might be translated, "I do not know when you will look at me or for how long; I cannot count on your gaze" (p. 64). Alternatively, mothers may make intrusive head movements in a chasing pattern to which the infant may feel "I don't feel free to look away. I can't get away when I need to settle down" (p. 64) (see Figure 2.1).

SEPARATION THREATENS INFANT SURVIVAL

Through the lens of Polyvagal Theory and neuroception, prior to any separation, the infant or young child over 6 months of age grows to expect the presence of a supportive caregiver. He is an active participant in an increasingly well-developed game of the give and take of ventral vagal mutual delight promoting safety and security in both members of the couplet. When he appears to lose his mother, he senses danger, becomes sympathetically activated, and protests with cries and facial expressions of displeasure as well as frantic, chaotic movements. He has lost his ballast: the person who previously anticipated, understood, and responded to his needs with a warm smile and reassurance. If his protests go unheeded, the hope of her return fades. He despairs, becoming quiet, losing muscle tone, and withdrawing. He has exhausted his reservoir of metabolic energy in protest. Finally, when it is clear there is no way out, he minimizes the necessary metabolic energy by blending into his environment in a dorsal vagal state of despair and detachment.

Bowlby (1982) discusses the attachment relationship derived from observations of "loss of mother" (p. 4) between 6 months and 6 years of age. From these observations, Bowlby and James Robertson, a psychiatric social worker and psychoanalyst at the Tavistock Clinic in London, defined predictable phases as the infant appreciates the loss. The observed infants were either in the hospital or in an institutional setting with variable and often unpredictable access to their mothers. Infants initially protested the loss, interpreted by the observers to indicate an expectation that mother would return. Subsequent to their protest, they entered a phase of despair suggesting that they were becoming less hopeful of their mother's return. Finally, they became detached. Bowlby and Robertson emphasized that detachment may actually seem like recovery to the casual observer. The infant begins to show more interest in his environment; however, in his detachment, the infant may show little interest either in his mother or in any human contact (Bowlby, 1982). With additional observational data, Robertson and Bowlby concluded that children who have had good relationships with their mother will have robust protests when separated. Indeed, they noted that the lack of protest when separated from mother was potentially cause for concern about the prior relationship.

THE EVOLUTIONARY NEUROANATOMY OF THE MAMMALIAN BRAINSTEM

The NA vagus provides the vagal brake that mammals remove instantaneously to increase metabolic output to foster fight-or-flight behaviors. The NA vagus provides the motor pathways to shift the intonation of vocalizations (e.g., cry patterns) to express emotion and to communicate internal states in a social context.

—STEPHEN PORGES, 2011

Porges (2011) details the structure of the mammalian brainstem that includes distinct central locations for the ventral vagus complex (nucleus ambiguus, NA) and the dorsal motor complex (the dorsal motor nerve nucleus, DMNX). In reptiles, there is no anatomically distinguishable border between the DMNX and the NA. In mammals, the DMNX and NA are anatomically distinguishable. Direct neural connections between the amygdala and the NA are documented.

The more primitive, dorsal motor nucleus, or DMNX, is associated with restorative functions such as breathing, glandular secretion, and digestion. It is often called the *vegetative vagus* because of its role in supporting internal homeostasis. The later developed ventral vagal, myelinated, or *smart vagus* is associated with the heart, soft palate, pharynx, larynx, esophagus, and bronchi. The vagus is bidirectional, both receiving sensory input from bodily organs and innervating motor nuclei. The co-location of NA with the nuclei for the cranial nerves of the face, mouth, and throat linking cardiac function and the face are known in Polyvagal Theory as the *face-heart connection*. These vagal nerve branches enable behavioral responses including facial expressions, prosody, and cadence associated with emotional expression. Cardiac function is also regulated predominantly by the NA through input to the heart's pacemaker, the right sinoatrial (SA) node. The SA node controls the atrial rate and communicates with the atrioventricular (AV) node that controls the ventricular rate (Porges, 2011).

MEASURING VAGAL TONE AS A REFLECTION OF NEUROCEPTIVE STATE

The unique face-heart connection opens the door to measuring vagal influence or tone and associations with behavioral responses linked to emotional states. Since the NA regulates the SA node, the heart's primary pacemaker, vagal tone can be indexed by evaluating vagal influence to the SA node. Components of vagal tone measurement include both the heart rate and the interval between heartbeats. Vagal tone is captured in measurement of respiratory sinus arrhythmia (RSA) or heart rate variability (HRV), a naturally occurring phenomenon of changing heart rate over the inspiratory cycle. When we take a breath and expand our chests, the pressure on our paired vagal nerves diminishes, decreasing vagal influence and thus accelerating our heart rate. When we breathe out and our chest deflates, pressure on the paired vagal nerves increases, thus increasing vagal influence, and our heart rate decreases. Porges and colleagues (1994) developed and patented a methodology to extract RSA in spontaneously breathing persons. The heart rate pattern is a sinusoidal waveform with both height and time period components. The height or amplitude of the waveform is a measure of cardiac vagal tone.

Changes in RSA amplitude reflect the relative cardiac vagal tone in response to internal or environmental challenges to the autonomic nervous system. When all is well, and the infant is in ventral vagal safety, the vagus supports internal homeostasis, growth, and restoration. However, when environmental or visceral demands increase, the ANS marshals metabolic energy by withdrawing vagal tone and increasing sympathetic excitation. The mammalian myelinated vagus thus acts as a *vagal brake* that increases or decreases vagal influence to the heart as required by the sense of safety or danger. When the internal and external environments are calm and supporting approach behaviors, requiring low resting metabolic load, vagal tone is high, and the brake is on. When danger is sensed, avoidance behaviors are required, and the vagal brake is lifted to supply additional metabolic energy for mobilization (Porges, 1996).

Porges (1996) studied vagal tone in preterm infants hospitalized in a newborn intensive care unit. He measured RSA before, during, and after feeding. Both earlier born (< 30 weeks') and later born infants (> 31 weeks') had decreased RSA and increased heart rates during feeding, reflecting withdrawal of vagal tone necessary to provide metabolic energy for ingestion and digestion. The later born infants, however, showed increases in RSA to pre-feeding levels after feeds. The earlier born infants continued to show low RSA (i.e., decreased vagal tone). Porges proposed the discrepancy could be explained by the lesser degree of myelination of the NA in less mature neonates with dependence upon the unmyelinated fibers of the DMNX for vagal input to the heart. The flexibility of the NA myelinated fibers results in a finely tuned system that can respond to the need for increased metabolic energy without compromising other systems (Porges, 2011).

HORMONAL INFLUENCES DRIVE SAFETY AND THREAT BEHAVIORS

Changes in vagal tone are only one subsystem of the larger neurobiologic-neurophysiologic regulatory system. Vagal tone cannot be considered in the absence of examining the critical hormones that influence the bodily *felt state* of the mother-infant dyad. Chief among the hormonal influences are cortisol and oxytocin. The release of adrenocorticotropin releasing hormone (ACTH) from the anterior pituitary gland signals the adrenal gland to produce cortisol. Basal cortisol is vital and necessary for visceral functioning and support of the cardiovascular system. Without cortisol, we cannot maintain blood pressure and cardiac output or release and use metabolic fuels such as glucose. When humans face any type of stress, cortisol rises to meet the bodily need to overcome a challenge, whether it be facing novelty or a saber-toothed tiger. Given the relative absence of animal predators, today the largest challenge faced by humans is often social interactions. This is true for older children and adults as well as infants and young children. For infants and young children, the challenges often lie in their perceptions of whether the attachment figure is available and how the attachment figure is responding to their communication of their needs. Disruptions of the sense of safety and security that are brief and quickly repaired will lead to transient increases in cortisol. Chronic disruptions of safety and security may lead to prolonged stresses resulting in high cortisol levels. Over time, if the disruption is not repaired, the hypothalamic-pituitary-adrenal axis (HPA axis) is suppressed by feedback of high cortisol, and the infant or child may experience low cortisol associated with poor physical and social emotional well-being (Agorastos, 2019).

Oxytocin is made in the hypothalamus and stored in the posterior pituitary, from which it is secreted into the bloodstream. Oxytocin is involved in reproduction, including sexual intercourse and childbirth, mother-baby care, and formation and maintenance of social relationships. Both men and women make oxytocin and release it during sexual intercourse (Neumann, 2008). In labor and delivery, oxytocin causes uterine contraction and cervical dilation (Carter, 2017). In the breastfeeding mother, oxytocin causes milk letdown (Carter, 2017). Oxytocin is also involved in social relationships by increasing trust and decreasing hostility (Kosfeld, 2005). Like cortisol, the oxytocin system is exquisitely sensitive to our early experiences. For example, infants who experienced long-term separations or disruptions from their parents (e.g., infants raised in orphanages) have altered patterns of oxytocin secretion compared to family-reared infants (Fries, 2005). Cortisol and oxytocin are also synergistically regulated in our neurobiology—activation of cortisol when we are stressed leads to increases in oxytocin, causing us to seek out attachment figures to assist us in regulating ourselves (Onaka, 2012). The roles of transgenerational stress and aberrant cortisol and oxytocin responses are discussed in Chapters 4 and 5.

MATERNAL-INFANT CO-REGULATION SETS THE STAGE FOR LATER ATTACHMENT

Bowlby's (1982) attachment theory identified the critical role of the primary attachment figure, usually the mother, and the "set goal" of establishing proximity between a mother and her infant (p. 69). Ainsworth (1978) emphasized maternal sensitivity and communication as she described patterns of attachment that are either protective for typical development or risk factors for later social emotional challenges. Later, Tronick (1989) and Beebe (2010) called attention to the critical partner in the mother-infant dyad, the infant who is an active participant as the relationship is shaped and choreographed.

How then do the primary caregiver and infant regulate each other's physiologic and behavioral states to leverage their ini-

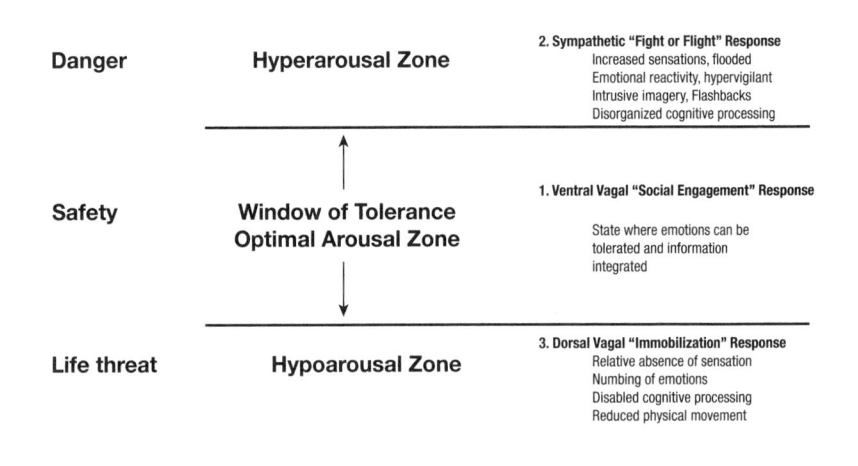

Danger	Hyperarousal Zone	**2. Sympathetic "Fight or Flight" Response** Increased sensations, flooded Emotional reactivity, hypervigilant Intrusive imagery, Flashbacks Disorganized cognitive processing
Safety	↑ Window of Tolerance Optimal Arousal Zone ↓	**1. Ventral Vagal "Social Engagement" Response** State where emotions can be tolerated and information integrated
Life threat	Hypoarousal Zone	**3. Dorsal Vagal "Immobilization" Response** Relative absence of sensation Numbing of emotions Disabled cognitive processing Reduced physical movement

FIGURE 2.2

Arousal zones, maternal tracking, and neuroceptive states.
Figure 2.2 Arousal Zones by Pat Ogden, Kenkuni Minton, Clare Pain, from TRAUMA AND THE BODY: A SENSORIMOTOR APPROACH TO PSYCHOTHERAPY by Pat Ogden, Kenkuni Minton, Clare Pain. Copyright © 2006 by Pat Ogden. Copyright © 2006 by W. W. Norton & Company, Inc. Used by permission of W.W. Norton & Company, Inc., with data from Korn, D. (2015).

tial engagement around birth into social connectedness by several months, resulting in a secure attachment by a year? Trauma therapist Deborah Korn (2015) embeds appraisals of windows of tolerance and models of attachment within a Polyvagal Theory framework (see Figure 2.2). As in a therapeutic situation, the primary caregiver and infant are in a continuous pas de deux, where each both anticipates and responds to the other's signals. Primary caregivers may include from birth mothers, fathers, adoptive parents, grandparents, foster parents or other relatives.

When primary caregivers are in an optimal arousal zone, engaged in midrange tracking of their infants, both the parent and the baby have a neuroception of safety. The autonomic nervous system, in ventral vagal engagement, has a green light to engage that can range from mutual delight to periods of disruption and repair. The parent understands the infant may need to glance away momentarily to regulate himself. The parent is open to the momentary disruption, and the parent's neuroception of safety persists until the infant returns to them. The infant has a neuroception of safety, since he understands both that he can bring himself back to his parent and that his parent will come back to him. As Beebe et al. (2010) comment, both a mother and her baby "feel seen by the other" (p. 60).

In contrast, the hyperaroused or high-tracking parent is sympathetically activated on an emotional roller coaster. The parent may begin the engagement in ventral vagal social engagement; however, when the infant glances away momentarily, the parent has difficulty with repair. The parent's intense anxiety does not allow them to see the infant, as Beebe et al. (2010, p. 64) describe, or recognize that the infant may be overly aroused. The parent's neuroception of danger does not allow the baby to have the time he needs for self-regulation, and the parent may chase the infant, using intrusive gestures, a loud voice, or other signals to get him back. The infant, who may share the parent's arousal, also has a neuroception of danger, as he has no place to hide. Wherever he goes, the parent will chase after, not allowing him the time to regulate himself. Over time, and in desperation, the infant may shut down to a dorsal vagal life threat state. There he collapses into a death-feigning pose as a maladaptive coping mechanism against the hyperarousal of his parent that he experiences.

Finally, the hypoaroused primary caregiver, who is in dorsal vagal shutdown, has little energy to bring to the dyadic interaction. The caregiver's neuroception is one of life threat, and their

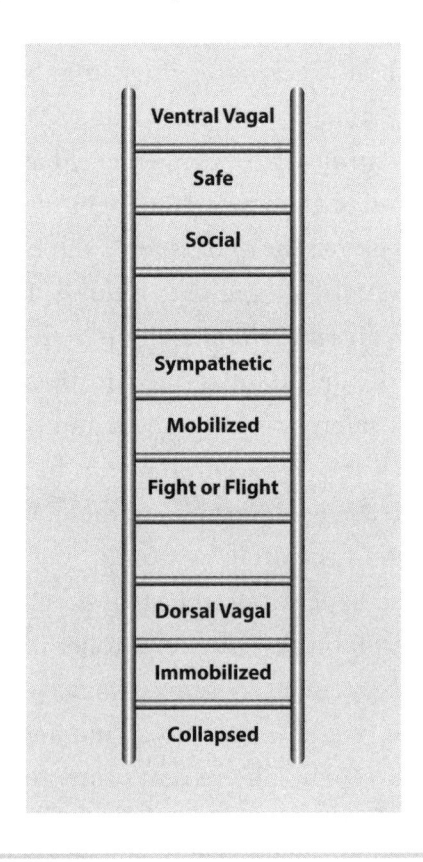

FIGURE 2.3

The automatic, autonomic ladder.
From THE POLYVAGAL THEORY IN THERAPY: ENGAGING THE RHYTHM OF REGULATION by Deb Dana. Copyright © 2018 by Deb Dana. Used by permission of W. W. Norton & Company, Inc.

focus is inward and on their own survival. They are numb and often without much emotion. Their infant may try to engage them. He may use all the tricks in his bag. He may smile and point as he looks for joint attention. When these gestures fail, he becomes sympathetically activated, sensing danger in the loss of his primary caregiver. He may begin to shriek and arch as if trying to say, "Look at me," "See me," and "Feel my presence." As he exhausts his available metabolic energy, he, too, falls into dorsal vagal shutdown to preserve what energy is left for basic vegetative functions.

PRIMARY CAREGIVERS AND BABIES ASSUME THEIR PLACES ON THE AUTONOMIC LADDER

Maintaining a ventral vagal state requires primary caregivers to regulate their vagal brakes, allowing for dynamic and corrective changes in emotions and behaviors. To do so, a caregiver needs sufficient autonomic bandwidth to have flexible responses to their baby as the baby responds (or doesn't) to their presence and engagement.

A primary caregiver in the optimal arousal zone is at the top rung of the autonomic ladder in a ventral vagal state of relaxation (see Figure 2.3). A caregiver at the top of the ladder will typically connect with their birthing partner and others, seeking support for the transitions associated with parenting. They will have flexibility around the getting-to-know-you period and accept that they will learn their baby's patterns and needs over time. A birth mother accepts the changes her body is undergoing with ease. A primary caregiver, whoever that might be, greets the baby with an open face, gentle smile, and soft voice. When primary caregivers have a difficult day or night, they draw upon their strengths to get through to an easier time. If primary caregivers are to remain at the top of the ladder, they will be supported through these many transitions and disruptions by family and friends who themselves are well-anchored at the top of the ladder.

We assume our position on the ladder based upon the net impact of a large series of interactions and engagements, beginning in our own fetal period transitioning through early infancy and toddlerhood, into childhood, and onward. No one is always at the top of the autonomic ladder. Our place on the autonomic ladder is specific to an individual interaction and the person or other mammal with whom we are engaging. If we have experienced Winnicott's (1960) "good enough maternal care" (p. 594) (or have had good enough therapy), we transition more easily to the top of the ladder as we assume our parenting roles. Even for those, however, who have had their own positive early experiences, circumstances around the pregnancy, labor and delivery, or birth may disrupt our autonomic nervous systems, requiring a reset.

Even in relatively uneventful fertility histories, pregnancies, labors and deliveries, and births, women undergo neurobiologic and physiologic transitions to parenting akin to the transition the newborn undergoes from the fetal/aquatic to the air breathing/land environment. From conception onward, women's bodies are in constant change as the hormones, necessary to promote implantation and survival of the embryo and prevent uterine contractility, surge. At the very least, there is discomfort. For some women, hormone-associated changes present challenges to daily living and activities. Finally, the birth itself is bathed in additional hormones as the uterus responds to increases in oxytocin-stimulating uterine contractility.

As the labor proceeded toward delivery, a 35-year-old physician and first-time mother who was in the final stages of delivering her first-born son commented:

> I was lying on my back with my feet in stirrups and experienced this extraordinary sensation of how my life was going to change. In just a few minutes, I will be a parent. Life will never again be the same.

Some mothers with complicated pregnancies or labors or primary caregivers whose early histories are complex may be sympathetically activated and be part-way down the ladder (see Figure 2.3). These primary caregivers are often hyperaroused and hypervigilant. When there is unpredictability or uncertainty, they experience symptoms associated with surges of adrenaline/epinephrine or cortisol. Their hearts race; they may breathe quickly; they experience many unusual sensations such as tingling; they may say their skin is crawling. The trigger for their autonomic experience may be contemporaneous (e.g., they may feel their baby is not responding to them), or early experience may have left them with deeply embedded and encoded signals that challenge their neuroception of safety and security in relationships. These experiences are not consciously processed in the forebrain. They derive from limbic-level signalling that is experienced by caregivers as a sense of dis-ease or danger, as if a predator they cannot see lurks in the midst. These caregivers may be perceived as extremely diligent and attentive parents. As a consequence, the baby may seem overwhelmed, irritable, or inconsolable because his attempts to get some space for resetting his autonomic nervous system are often seen as danger signals by a caregiver who needs to keep him close.

Sympathetically activated parents will benefit from their own caregivers who emphasize the inconsistency and unpredictability of the early, post birth, getting-to-know-you time. There is no roadmap to safety and security. An agile autonomic system, fueled by a series of positive relationships and experiences, will find the way. A rigid and less flexible autonomic nervous system will be in a feedback heightening of prior experience. The disruption of this feedback loop may be an opportunity for incremental repairs that build a parent's confidence in their caregiving and restructure their autonomic nervous system responses.

In contrast to babies who are in ventral vagal states who depend upon their parent's return, or those who are sympathetically activated who fear their loss, the baby in a dorsal vagal state knows his caregiver is gone. He cannot see, hear, or feel his caregiver and is in a state of isolation that may be life threatening. Because he is shut down, he rarely cries or demands attention. Ironically, these babies may be seen as good or easy babies.

Primary caregivers who are at the bottom of the autonomic ladder experience life threat and may feel buried alive (see Figure 2.3). They are isolated and cannot either reach out or accept comfort from others. Their world is increasingly small. They see no sustaining hope that their experience can change. Far from cortisol surges, their cortisol responsiveness may be burned out. They are in dorsal vagal shutdown, akin to the reptile who blends into the environment to avoid notice when a predator is at striking distance. Obviously, caregivers in a dorsal vagal state will not be able to parent as they would prefer.

Hughes and Baylin (2012) coined the term *blocked care* to describe how "stress can suppress a well-meaning parent's capacity to sustain loving feelings and empathy toward his or her child" (p. 6). They identified 5 core parenting functions, each with its separate brain system, including circuits that enable a parent to be safe and open with their child; to attune to their child's emotions and experiences; to enjoy and make sense of their parenting; and to manage their own emotions and the parent-child relationship itself, including its repair.

A unique feature of their model is that 4 of the 5 systems are reciprocally reinforced by complementary systems and functions in the child. For example, under typical circumstances, as the parent enjoys his child, the child feels pleasure too. In return, the child's pleasure strengthens the parent's enjoyment circuit, in a mutually reinforcing cycle. When a child's response is not typical, like when they have experienced early trauma or if they have autism, the child may not feel pleasure in response to the parent's enjoyment and this reinforcement breaks down. The absence of joyful positive reinforcement from the child eventually winds these systems down. As Baylin and Hughes (2016) say:

> The concept of blocked care refers to a scenario in which too much stress suppresses the higher brain functions needed for caregiving, engendering a self-defensive stance toward a child. In blocked care, the parent's nurturing capacities are suppressed, temporarily out of commission. Caregiving is supported by the social engagement system, not the defense system; defensive states of mind inhibit the caring process. When a parent gets stuck in a defensive state of mind, this puts the parent–child relationship in jeopardy because, in effect, there is no caring mind "in the room." (p. 77)

Hughes and Baylin (2012) say that the caregiver in blocked care needs their own social engagements that scaffold and assure them they are safely connected. Their state of shutdown will be relieved only when they have experienced sufficient care, concern, and rapport themselves. If the blocked care is persistent, they may need intensive interventions and supports to move back up the autonomic ladder.

Children who are chronically in a dorsal vagal state will need substantial support as well. Parents need to notice even small micro-moments of responsiveness of the baby to reinforce their own sense of efficacy. Additionally, the baby will need to have a village of other warm caregivers to provide surround-sound experiences of caring and warmth. Helpful professional caregivers will focus upon what happened and is happening to the parent's mind and body, not what is wrong with them.

Noticeable in the language of Polyvagal Theory is an absence of *Diagnostic and Statistical Manual (DSM)* or *Diagnostic and Procedural Coding (ICD)* labelling. The value of naming and language lies in assisting the parent to recognize their neuroceptive states, the emotions they generate, and the behaviors that result. Likewise, as the parent recognizes their own neuroceptive states, so too will they recognize iterations of those states in their baby.

CHAPTER 3

Preparing Young Children to Live in Their Families and Their Larger World

In order to develop normally, a child requires progressively more complex joint activity with one or more adults who have an irrational emotional relationship with the child. Somebody's got to be crazy about that kid. That's number one. First, last, and always.

—URIE BRONFENBRENNER, 1991

The presence of a supportive caregiver mediates the young child's ability to manage short-term or even moderate stresses building resilience and confidence. Over time, this explicit social connectedness, reinforced by the caregiver's physical presence, becomes embedded connectedness and secure attachment. Once securely attached, the child can venture out into the world, have novel experiences, and take risk. Too big a challenge is dangerous, but too little challenge is neglect. Providing access to developmentally appropriate challenges with available supports nurtures young children and supports their growing independence.

How then, do we as parents, families, and professional caregivers provide the right balance between safety and risk to support infants, toddlers, and young children to begin to venture out into the larger world? Secure attachments are critical to the foundation for play and exploration. However, as necessary as secure attachments are, they are not sufficient. Infants and young children need to build skills and experience success and just enough stress to achieve their expanding goals. The implicit goal of the very young infant is proximity to the adult caregiver. As the infant acquires motor skills and becomes curious, his goal shifts to achieving mastery. While once he needed only his parent's soft smile as a reward for attention to him, now the infant seeks a prize. The prize may be acquiring the toy that is just out of reach or the excited feedback of a parent as he lets go of the couch for the first time and takes a step.

THE INFANT EXPLORES THE WORLD

Whatever the reward, the infant will experience some stress as she dares to reach beyond her boundaries to reach the toy. As she lifts the vagal brake, decreasing vagal tone, she becomes sympathetically activated. With sympathetic activation, she experiences an epinephrine surge that increases both her heart rate and the amount of blood pumped by her heart. With increased output from the heart, she has more oxygen to her vital organs and metabolic energy to support her musculoskeletal system as she strives to meet her goal—acquiring the toy. Cortisol too may increase, leading to release of glucose to fuel her efforts. As she reaches the toy and picks it up, all smiles, she looks to her parent. Her parent appreciates the significance of the victory and in facial expression and vocalization gives her the grand prize, the hearty approval for her perseverance, efforts, and skill. "Look at you! You are such a good girl!" the parent says while beaming approval. Basking in her parent's ventral vagal approval and joyful in her own acquisition of a new skill, the infant's short-term epinephrine and cortisol surges wane, and heart rate and cardiac output return to baseline. The system returns to an equilibrium and vagal tone returns to baseline.

Consider, however, another scenario, the infant spies the toy several feet away and adopts a set goal of acquiring the toy. The vagal brake is released; she is sympathetically activated; she redoubles her effort as she becomes upset. Sympathetic activation increases; epinephrine and cortisol surge, the now frustrated infant begins crying and ceases her efforts to reach the toy. As her parent recognizes her frustration, the parent begins speaking to the infant in a reassuring tone. "It's okay. I'm here, and I'll help you," the parent says. As her parent senses she is becoming more activated and upset, the parent crosses the room to retrieve the toy and pick up the infant who is wailing in frustration. The infant soon begins to quiet and buries her head in the parent's shoulder as the parent's calm co-regulates her. Feeling safe and secure in her parent's arms, she returns to a quiet, alert state over a few minutes. Here, the parent's scaffolding and support of her during her distress assist her in tolerating mild stress.

In a third scenario, unable to reach the toy, the infant becomes increasingly distressed. The parent ignores her, turns away, and appears preoccupied. The infant cries louder and louder and reaches out to her parent, who continues to ignore her. Finally, in an angry voice, the parent says, "If you think I am going to come over and rescue you, you better think again." With this, parent turns their back on the infant, eventually getting up and leaving the room. The infant continues to cry for several minutes; gradually her cries become whimpers; and finally she collapses on the floor, staring blankly across the room. She was not scaffolded by her parent. She is now left to experience her despair alone in dorsal vagal shutdown. Over time, such experiences become intolerable or toxic stresses for the infant. If persistent and compounded, they result in suboptimal outcomes in health and well-being unless the young child experiences and attaches to another supportive caregiver who provides the necessary scaffolding.

MOTIVATING YOUNG CHILDREN TO SEEK NOVELTY

As infants gain mobility and curiosity, their experience leads them to *seek or approach* novel objects and situations or to *avoid* them. Again, the infant's sense of her safety internally and in her environment versus the danger or threat posed guides her responses and behaviors. Over time, infants and young children need to develop both approach and avoidance behaviors. At the extremes, either hypervigilance due to perceived threat or excessive risk-taking may result in undesirable short- or long-term outcomes. The modifying presence of a caring and supportive adult caregiver protects the child both against excessive caution or excessive risk-taking (Center on the Developing Child, n.d.).

For the young child, the anticipation of a reward leads to a dopamine surge signalling a pleasurable experience is coming. The child is at the top of the autonomic ladder as she seeks her goal. The message to the deep parts of her brain—the amygdala or seat of emotion and the hippocampus, the center of memory and learning—are reassuring. The goal or reward is in clear sight. If her caregiver cheers her on, supporting her effort, she gets additional pleasure from her caregiver's tone and facial expression. The face-heart connection brings her neurobiology back into equilibrium as the sensory input from her read of her parent's face and voice both calm her heart. When she achieves the goal, acquires the toy, or lets go of the couch to take a step, the experience-dependent portions of her brain reinforce the memory of pleasure and satisfaction. The next time, it is easier because the novelty of the task is diminished (Berridge, 2013).

Motivators for young children may either be intrinsic, internally driven, or extrinsic, deriving from the environment. Young children are curious and novelty-seeking when supported. They will work hard, both short- and long-term to please an adult, especially an attachment figure. While small positive reinforcers such as candy are promoted to encourage activities as disparate as toilet training and behavior control, the rewards are often short term rather than associated with any meaningful change (Deci, 1999).

Sometimes young children are motivated by a need to avoid an experience. A previous experience with novelty-seeking may have led to an undesirable outcome, a punishment, or an unexpected, harsh response from a parent or other caregiver. For this infant, the amygdala is already on high alert as the hippocampus encoded the prior experience as undesirable or even dangerous. Now the young child begins to tumble down the autonomic ladder as she becomes sympathetically activated with cortisol and epinephrine surging. If an adult catches her as she tumbles, bringing ventral vagal safety and connectedness with a soothing voice and kind face, a repair of the disruption takes place. The adult eases her back up to the top of the ladder. Young children who face ongoing chaos and threat may tumble to the bottom of the ladder where they sit alone. Chapter 4 addresses the short- and long-term impact of disruptions due to toxic stress when children sit chronically at the bottom of the ladder.

SOCIALIZATION FOR SAFETY AND DANGER

When caregivers support children to venture out, engage in novel experiences, and take reasonable risks, they prepare them to navigate safely in the world. Caregivers can steer curious youngsters away from unhealthy risks, such as reaching for something too hot or sharp, with subtle hints, such as a glance or simple request, that can escalate up to fearful or angry rebukes. A child may be startled by Grandma yelling, "No don't!" to keep the child from grabbing a knife, and with one shout the child knows: knives are dangerous. Nancy Michael (2020a) explains that nonverbal communication is the language of the threat detection system. Caregivers' nonverbal declarations, their cheers of approval or cries of fear, socialize children to what enhances or threatens their well-being.

Michael (2020a) goes on to say this nonverbal communication gets encoded in the child's brain, whether a stepdad gives his son a loving look, indicating things are okay, or he shoots his son a worried look, signaling an approaching hazard. Michael reminds us that we won't truly understand learning until we comprehend its neurobiology. Michael points to Hebb, who explored learning in his 1949 book, *The Organization of Behavior: A Neuropsychological Theory*. Hebb said, "When an axon of cell A is near enough to excite a cell B and repeatedly or persistently takes part in firing it, some growth process or metabolic change takes place in one or both cells such that A's efficiency, as one of the cells firing B, is increased" (p. 62). Neurons that repeatedly activate each other increase each other's ability to communicate efficiently.

Following Hebb, Shatz (1992) coined the poetic phrase neurons "that fire together wire together" (p. 64) to capture the increased efficiency from coincident neuronal communication. As neurons fire, they send signals across synaptic gaps to other neurons downstream, which fire in turn. Experience causes neurons to fire, and the more an experience is repeated, the easier it is for neurons to trigger downstream responses. This strengthening of communication across gaps between neurons is called long-term potentiation. Shatz identified that, while a basic architecture of neurons may be in place when mammals are born, those neurons must fire to make the further, smaller adjustments needed for these circuits to work as designed. Shatz says, "within limits, the maturing nervous system can be modified and fine-tuned by experience itself, thereby providing a certain degree of adaptability" (p. 67). This is the neurobiological process of learning. When we repeat or practice something, it becomes easier to do. When a lesson is well-learned, nerve signals travel easily along the circuits of the lesson.

EARLY ASSESSMENTS OF DANGER LEAD TO DEVELOPMENT OF IMPLICIT BIASES

Even very young children look toward their parents to gives cues of which situations are safe and which interactions may represent potential dangers. Young children watch their parents faces, prosody, and body language to signal *safe to seek* or *watch out and avoid* experiences in a form of social learning recognized by Michael (2020a). Although caregivers don't usually realize they are changing their children's brains, their looks of approval and disapproval, via long-term potentiation, are consolidated in the neural architecture of the amygdala (e.g., LeDoux, 2007). As we have seen, the amygdala is the part of the brain that mediates what Porges (2011) calls neuroception: a fast nonverbal assessment of safety or danger.

Michael (2020a) says that neurocepted messages, in addition to protecting us from actual danger, also serve as a mechanism to transmit and encode implicit biases that don't fit with our conscious values. For example, if a white* mother's face flashes

---

* Norton Professional Books currently follows AP's style guide on the capitalization of *white*, *Black*, and other racial and ethnic identifiers. Here is a link that explains the rationale of this style choice (from July 20, 2021). https://apnews.com/article/archive-race-and-ethnicity-9105661462

fear as her daughter approaches a Black family, the daughter's amygdala neurocepts threat. Because neuroception occurs outside awareness, neither mother nor daughter may consciously perceive that a warning was communicated. But, Michael maintains, the lesson that Black people are dangerous gets wired into the white child's amygdala just as it was wired into her mother's. Through this nonconscious socialization, inappropriate fears and the injurious behaviors they precipitate persist in communities for ages despite being inaccurate and harmful. Méndez-Bértolo and colleagues (2016) presented adults with images of various facial expressions and demonstrated that their amydalas responded to fearful faces in about 70 milliseconds. Neither happy nor neutral faces resulted in similar fast processing in the visual cortex. Interestingly, very fast processing occurred only when subjects viewed blurry photos of faces, literally when they were faced with ambiguity. Méndez-Bértolo and colleagues (2016) hypothesize that, in order to survive, humans needed to respond rapidly to minimal cues of danger from our fellow humans. Within milliseconds, our amygdalas react without the need for thought or a clear image. Michael (2020b) concludes that responding quickly to threat is crucial, and speed is more important than accuracy. But this protective response sets the stage for acting out implicit bias.

In this section, we have explored the unconscious and neurobiological processes informing how caregivers teach children what is safe, who is safe, and who can be trusted. As we will discuss in more detail in Chapter 6, we will not be able to stop the harm caused by acting out implicit bias unless we understand how nonconscious mechanisms perpetuate it. Quite simply, we can't and won't change something we don't see. Once we do understand neuroception and can identify it, we will recognize the importance of managing the serious repercussions of implicit bias. After that, we will want to learn more about healthy development of a well-functioning autonomic system. That desire to learn about healthy development motivates our pivot from the serious issues we have been discussing to the lighter but still consequential topic of the neurobiological purpose of childhood play.

TO PLAY IS TO LEARN ABOUT THE SELF AND THE WORLD

To paraphrase Stephen Porges (2015b), play is a neural exercise. Affective neuroscientist Jaak Panksepp (1994) identified seven primary mammalian emotional systems. Panksepp's positively valenced primary emotional systems are SEEK/Expectancy, CARE/Nurturing, PLAY/Social joy and LUST. The negatively valenced primary emotions are RAGE/Anger, FEAR/Anxiety, and PANIC/Sadness. These primary emotional systems are observed in juvenile rats whose neocortex (frontal lobes/most recently derived part of the brain) is absent. To Panksepp (2003), these systems derive subcortically and need not be learned. Indeed, the evolutionary purpose of social play may be to facilitate the maturation of higher brain areas, including the neocortex. By promoting the development of behavioral inhibition and self-regulation, PLAY may be decreasing the likelihood of impulsive or risk-taking activities.

Consider for a moment the prior scenario of the infant reaching for a toy without success. What if the parent's response is to be playful? Perhaps they take the toy in hand and begin a game of peek-a-boo. Peek-a-boo is often the first game of reciprocity enjoyed by the parent and the infant. As the infant exhibits some distress when he is unable to acquire the toy, the parent may then take the toy and hide it behind their hands as they bend down and momentarily disappear. Where have they gone, and will they reappear? After a few moments, the parent takes their hands away, says peek-a-boo in a gentle and lilting voice and displays the toy. At first the infant may seem slightly anxious and a bit confused. The parent and toy he feared he lost are sighted. When the parent is assured the infant is regaining her equilibrium, the parent again hides with the toy. This time, when parent and toy return, they are greeted by a big smile. After several more repetitions, both parent and infant are laughing as the infant realizes the playful nature of the game. He now anticipates the return of the parent and toy. His expectations are met, and he reflects his sense of safety with squealing and giggling. With each repetition, the parent moves slightly closer to the baby, bringing the toy into reach. Finally, the baby grabs the toy and responds with joy as his parent now lavishes praise on him: "Aren't you a good boy? You did it!"

Tracing the autonomic nervous system response, the infant who was trying to get the toy was sympathetically activated. His set goal of achieving the toy was interrupted. His hypothalamic pituitary adrenal axis was activated, and he generates a cortisol surge. As he becomes more activated, his parent acts quickly to change the game. Now, the parent uses themselves as a reward, and the toy follows. Initially, the infant is confused and remains somewhat activated. However, on repetition, his expectation is met, the parent's presence and smile become the reward, and dopamine surges as the infant's pleasure increases. As dopamine increases, his amygdala reads the changing external environment as pleasurable, and he experiences ventral vagal joy. As the game continues through cycles of peek-a-boo, his vagal brake lifts slightly as he generates energy to meet his excitement. The cycle continues as repetition, with the reward of parent's presence and the toy in sight. The infant gradually understands autonomically that this is a game—there is no risk of loss—and he responds appropriately and joyfully.

This parent and infant are engaging in *serve and return* or *back and forth* interactions that build a sense of mastery, competence, and tolerance of stress. The Center for the Developing Child (n.d.) lists five explicit steps in serve and return interactions that build healthy brain architecture.

1. Notice the serve and share the child's focus of attention
2. Return the serve by supporting and encouraging
3. Give it a name
4. Take turns and wait
5. Practice endings and beginnings

There are frequent opportunities for building, sustaining, and reinforcing serve and return interactions. As a social worker sees the mother share joint attention with her infant, he may offer supportive feedback to the mother: "Look how she looks where you look." As the infant returns the serve to the mother, the social worker with a gentle smile may say, "Look how you throw the ball back to Mommy. You are playing a game!" By sharing his delight in the infant's part in the game and the mother's responsiveness, the social worker reinforces the dyad's function and the sense of mastery for both members. For many mothers and their children, such reinforcement is a pleasant recognition of their dyadic success. For others, who have struggled to share attention and play the game, the recognition of their nascent skills is life changing. The attentive social worker recognizes and seizes these moments and knows there is no positive connection too small to merit comment and reinforcement.

The recognition of joint attention is particularly important when working with parent-infant dyads whose development may be challenging. For example, if the infant is premature and remains hospitalized, parents may not experience the sensory and emotional feedback cues that prompt healthier infants to connect in noticeable ways. The first time her infant glances at her may be a momentous landmark for a parent. A nurse's recognition reinforces both the occurrence of the glance as well as the emotional importance to the parent.

What are the important lessons of this simple game? The infant learns she can manage mild stress. The infant learns that she has agency—she is a competent person, can set a goal, and can achieve it. She develops a working model of self that she is validated as her mother responds to her with joy. She learns to trust another person. The mother develops a sense of increasing competency as a parent. She knows the needs of her baby and meets them.

A PARADIGM SHIFT IN PROMOTING HEALTHY DEVELOPMENT

Prior to the 1990s, the accepted developmental pathway for healthy development was a one child/one parent/one trajectory model. Beginning with the publication of Shonkoff's and Phillips' *From Neurons to Neighborhoods* (2000), child health professionals increasingly recognized additional promotive or protective factors along with risk factors that impact the development of individual children and populations of children. This new paradigm recognized the critical importance of "nature dancing with nurture over time" (Shonkoff et al, 2012, p. e235) and led to the development of the eco-bio-developmental (EBD) model. The eco-bio-developmental model recognizes both the biology or genetic predispositions and the ecology or social and physical environments that impact the health and development of individual children (Shonkoff et al., 2012).

We now recognize the biology of a child is affected both by physiologic disruptions and adaptations she has made as well as changes in the genetic code passed through generations. The changes do not affect the DNA itself but affect how genes express themselves. The expression of genes is altered by changes in proteins that either facilitate or inhibit behaviors. Such changes in the genetic code are called epigenetic changes because they alter how genes express themselves rather than the DNA itself. We will have more to say about epigenetics in Chapters 4 and 5.

Each child will also be affected by the social and physical environment(s) in which she lives. She will also impact those environments in both large and small ways. The cumulative dynamic system representing the multilayered interactive components is reflected in her health and development. For child-serving professionals across physical and mental health, education, child welfare, and policy, the intersection of these components represents the rapidly evolving basic science of pediatrics. Building upon the invaluable observations of Bowlby, Roberston, Ainsworth, and others, we can now layer functional MRI, molecular studies, and additional basic science data explaining the critical need for sustaining relationships to manage stress and thrive.

Since 2012, the Committees of the American Academy of Pediatrics have published 16 policy guidelines and 21 clinical reports that emphasize the importance of developing resilience in typical development, care of special populations, working with family challenges, and exposure to environmental and other toxic stresses (www.aap.org, n.d.). If the child-caregiver dyadic relationship is the foundation of childhood health and well-being, the development of *resilience* is the optimal outcome.

MASTERING ORDINARY DISRUPTIONS BUILDS THE PLATFORM FOR RESILIENCE

Curiosity and novelty-seeking are stressful for the young infant. As she reaches out to expand her world, she will need additional energy for both the emotional and physical components of play. Ideally, stress is meted out in small packets that are manageable for the young child. When stress increases, the presence of the buffering support of an adult caregiver mitigates the impact of stress. A stress-free infancy is both impossible and undesirable. According to Parker and colleagues (2006), "People with the capacity to maintain healthy emotional functioning in the aftermath of stressful experiences are said to be resilient or stress-resistant" (p. 3000).

There are always disruptions of the equilibrium of the larger environment and the dyadic interactions. In early infancy, disruptions can be as brief as a look in another direction. As the infant grows and matures, she hones her skills to reestablish equilibrium under the watchful eye of a caregiver. As motor activity and capability increase, the newly found movement brings its own stresses.

A former preterm infant is seen in a neurodevelopmental follow-up clinic. As she is being examined on a floor mat, she tumbles over. The examining physician rushes to rescue her as her mother remarks, "It's okay. Sometimes I actually let her tumble over so she knows she can get up." The physician responded with cues of danger, sweeping down to rescue the child. This mother responded with cues of safety to her infant, conveying both her availability and her confidence in the increasing mastery of her daughter. The infant who tumbles over, rolls on her stomach and resumes the seated position now has the wired-in expectation that she can do this. Being competent even in the smallest ways (i.e., small to us but big to the infant) now has the neural expectation that she can right herself.

The *righting reflex* is a neurologic reflex that is initiated by the vestibular (balance) system when the body is not in the usual upright position. Components of the reflex are seen shortly after birth in healthy infants. By 6–7 weeks, the infant will turn her neck back toward the body when she is tipped to the side. The development of this reflex is, however, dependent upon the presence of a supportive care provider. The righting reflex in mammals is impacted by maternal separation. Newborn rats who were separated from their mothers for 6 hours daily showed changes in the righting reflex in the first 2 weeks after birth (Mesquita et al., 2007).

The disruptions get longer and more sustained. A new sibling may come into the house who receives attention once paid to the child. The child may begin to spend time with trusted others, such as a grandparent, while parents work or refuel their own relationship. As the infant becomes a toddler and becomes mobile, she may run after a ball, briefly losing sight of the parents. If early life was full of serve and return interactions with the availability of attentive and sensitive caregivers, the toddler both tolerates these brief absences of the parents and in the course of seeking novelty and play extends the disruptions herself.

THE SCIENCE OF RESILIENCE

The Center on the Developing Child, the Center for the Study of Social Policy, the American Academy of Pediatrics, and the American Psychological Association all identify the ongoing presence of an attentive and supportive caregiver as the keystone to promoting healthy development. The caregiver scaffolds the infant and child whose response to stress is buffered. As a strategy to monitor, understand, and investigate the impact of stress upon young children, the Center on the Developing Child (n.d.) proposed a stress taxonomy with three distinct stress responses:

1. **POSITIVE:** "a normal and essential part of healthy development characterized by brief increases in heart rate and hormone levels." When experienced in the presence of a supportive relationship, the stress can be growth-promoting.

2. **TOLERABLE:** "exposure to non-normative experiences that present a greater magnitude of adversity or threat." The presence of a buffering relationship greatly reduces the likelihood of significant long-term consequences.
3. **TOXIC:** "strong, frequent or prolonged activation of the body's stress response systems in the absence of the buffering protection of a strong, supportive adult relationship" (Center on the Developing Child. n.d.).

One child's manageable positive stress may be another child's tolerable but negative or even toxic stress. The child's prior experiences and supports will make the difference. No one is born resilient. We are all vulnerable in utero and in early life. If we are fortunate enough to have the presence of "good enough" (Winnicott, 1960, p. 594) supportive caregivers, graduated stresses, and a safe environment, we are likely resilient at times of stress. As trauma therapist Deb Dana remarks, "Good enough is better than perfect parenting" (personal communication, 2019).

If parents fall on either side of good enough parenting to either hypervigilance or dismissive reactions, there is little room for learning to manage the everyday challenges such as skinning a knee, tumbling down the last few steps, or being called a name. Being secure that a bandage strip and a hug prepares a child to get back in the game lays the groundwork to meet the continuum of challenges that lie ahead.

Considering the ordinary or everyday stresses facing young children, resilience might be considered, according to Panter-Brick (2013, p. 333), "a process to harness resources to sustain well-being." Masten (2018) presents a transdisciplinary framework of "life course health development" that is grounded in "developmental systems theory" (p. 2). Developmental systems theory views each child as an individual in a framework emerging from "myriad interactions across system levels, at multiple levels of function from the molecular to the macro-level systems of culture, society, and ecology" (2018, p. 2). Furthermore, there is redundancy in these interconnected, adaptive systems as relationships with others in young children's homes and communities may be brought to bear if primary caregiving relationships are challenging.

Key resilience factors salient for young children documented in the literature by Masten (2018, p. 6) include: (1) caring family, sensitive caregiving; (2) close relationships, emotional security, belonging; (3) skilled parenting; (4) agency, motivation to adapt; (5) problem-solving skills, planning, executive function skills; (6) self-regulation skills, emotion regulation; (7) self-efficacy, positive view of self or identity; (8) hope, faith, optimism; (9) routines and rituals; (10) engagement in a well-functioning school; and (11) connection with well-functioning communities.

Examples of stress inoculation from both animal and early childhood research support the value of graduated exposure to ordinary stress in the presence of sensitive caregivers to build adaptability and resilience. Monkeys who had brief (1 hr) weekly separations from their mothers had increased emotional and psychosocial indications of resilience at 9 months of age compared to non-inoculated monkeys. At 2 and a half years of age, the stress-inoculated monkeys were more curious and had more exploratory behaviors (Lyons & Parker, 2007; Parker & Maestripieri, 2011).

Responses of children and their parents to childhood vaccinations, a medically indicated and ordinary stressor, are predictive of adaptive responses and cognitive outcomes. Child and caregiver coping responses were sequentially studied at 12-month vaccination and preschool vaccinations. A subset of children also had preschool psychological assessments. Infant responses to 12-month vaccinations predicted preschool responses. The researchers concluded that "caregiver behaviors during vaccinations are not only critical to both child pain coping responses and outcomes in the short- and long-term but also show relationships to broader child cognitive abilities as well" (Campbell, Pillai Riddell, Cribbie, Garfield, & Greenfield, 2018).

The only constant throughout evolution was the presence of other humans. It is in the context of the presence of other humans that we grow, develop, and thrive. We are wired to read each other, so that we can see the world's threats and the world's beauty through each other's eyes. Secure attachment and attunement and shared narrative communicate to the child that she is safe, she is seen, and she is part of the story. With these messages, she can learn how to take initiative and create, as well as to ask for help and to cooperate.

However, for an enlarging population of young children, early relationships and environments are mismatched to the stresses they experience. These mismatches occur across all socioeconomic, racial or ethnic, and educational levels of caregiver attainment. Now, both child and caregiver stresses increase and the caregiver-child relationship is threatened. In Chapters 4 and 5, we will explore the impact of significant stress and early adversity upon the health and well-being of the child-caregiver dyad in the short-term and across the lifespan.

SECTION II

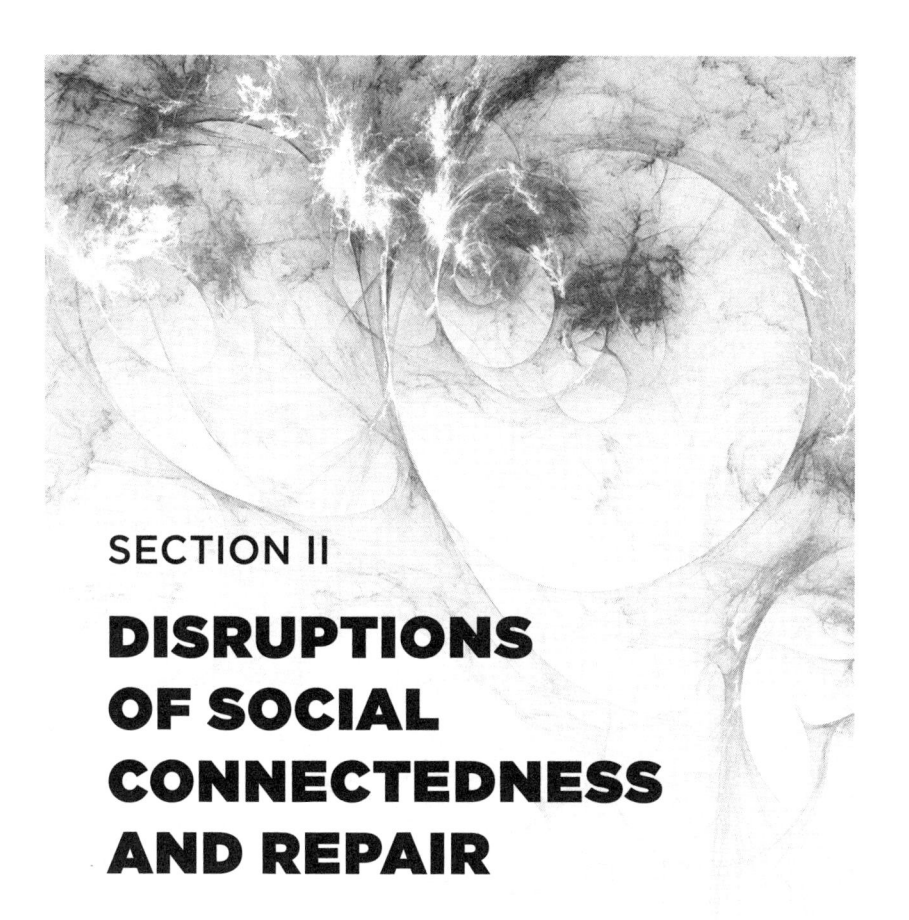

DISRUPTIONS OF SOCIAL CONNECTEDNESS AND REPAIR

CHAPTER 4

Challenging Disruptions in Childhood: Traumatic Separations That Impact Childhood Experience

Trauma is a chronic disruption of connectedness.
—STEPHEN PORGES, 2014

During early infancy and young childhood, parents and their babies are ideally in close physical and emotional proximity. The social ecology of the environment includes a network of family and community support, allowing the dyad to establish secure attachments with only mild stress and brief disruptions of connectedness. Physical resources are adequate—there is minimal or no concern about housing, nutrition, and clean water. The parent-infant dyad has enough money to buffer against interruptions of support or emotional or physical needs. Parents and infants get adequate sleep and have internal resources and external environments to support them when stresses are exacerbated. As infants become toddlers and young children, interruptions of parental proximity increase.

In 2016, more than half (54%) of children under 6 years old lived in a household where both parents worked (Bureau of Labor

Statistics, 2016). Family members or others become caregivers. Children may go into daycare locations, either home-based or center-based. Parents hope other caregivers have the right combination of safety and exploration, compassion and caring, adequate staffing, and curiosity about our children. We work hard to be secure bases for our children as they begin to explore the world. We also want their other caregivers and teachers to do so.

Sadly, for a significant proportion of young children both nationally and internationally, the stresses of infancy and early childhood range from moderate to severe, or from tolerable to toxic. For these children, the neuroception of danger and life threat looms. Some children respond to stress with sympathetic activation, anxiety, anger, or impulsivity. Others, struggling against toxic stresses without buffering support, may present with apathy, depression, or even apparent dissociation.

ACCESS TO MEDICAL CARE DOES NOT FULLY EXPLAIN HEALTH OUTCOMES

Despite our enormous global health care budget, the United States lags behind other industrialized countries in critical health outcomes including life expectancy and infant mortality (United Health Foundation, 2017). The public health community increasingly identifies factors, in addition to access to quality medical care, that are associated with variability in health outcomes. For example, even within racial or ethnic groups, persons who are better educated typically have better health than those who have less than a high school or high school education (Braveman & Gottlieb, 2018). The World Health Organization identifies social determinants of health as "the conditions in which people are born, grow, live, work and age" and the "fundamental drivers of these conditions" (World Health Organization, 2008). New England Journal of Medicine Catalyst (2017) details social determinants including: income level, educational opportunities, occupation, employment status and workplace safety, gender inequity, racial segregation, food insecurity and inaccessibility of nutritional food choices, access to housing and utility services, early childhood experiences, social support and community inclusivity, crime rates and exposure to violent behaviors, availability of transportation, neighborhood conditions and physical environments, access to safe drinking water, clean air and toxin-free environments, and recreational and leisure opportunities.

Braveman and Gottleib (2018) consider the pathways through which the social determinants influence health. As an example, the authors discuss the impact of educational attainment. They hypothesize educational attainment may affect health knowledge, literacy, coping and problem solving; where persons work exposing them to different working conditions, environmental exposures, and incomes; as well as their social standing, social networks, and belief systems (2018, p. 26). Braveman and Gottleib also describe protective factors such as social support, self-esteem, and self-efficacy that may mitigate the impact of social determinants.

Research on the impact of social determinants is challenging as they are the basic conditions in which infants, children, adolescents, and adults live—they do not allow randomization and their impact upon any individual person or family is variable. Social determinants can contribute exponentially to caravans of risk passageways, discussed later in this chapter, if factors align disadvantageously. When people face issues or obstacles with a single social determinant, it can be challenging. When they must contend with complications and difficulties in multiple social determinants, the combination may produce toxic stress. Consider the predicament, for example, of a child and family who are experiencing poor access to quality education, and also live in an urban environment with contaminated drinking water, community violence, food and energy insecurity, and a lack of social supports. When the number of difficulties reaches a tipping point, family functioning will suffer, no matter how capable or resilient they might be under more typical circumstances.

TOXIC STRESSES OF CHILDHOOD ARE TRAUMATIC

Originally, trauma described breaches of bodily integrity, that is, physical wounds or injuries. A more holistic understanding of the implications and impact of childhood trauma led to more expansive definitions. The National Child Traumatic Stress Network (2021) defines a traumatic event as a "frightening, dangerous, or violent event that poses a threat to a child's life or bodily integrity. Witnessing a traumatic event that threatens life or physical security of a loved one can also be traumatic. This is particularly important for young children as their sense of safety depends on the perceived safety of their attachment figures."

The traumas of today's children and adolescents are often the "chronic disruptions of connectedness" described by Porges (2014). Such trauma exposures are violations of our mammalian survival strategy of social connectedness with adult caregivers. They are disruptions without repairs, disruptions that stimulate sympathetic activation or isolate the developing child from the caregivers whose evolutionary biological imperative is to protect and shield them from danger, ensuring their safety, security, and connectedness.

TRAUMATIC LOSSES ARE THE MOST COMMON TRAUMATIC EXPOSURES OF CHILDREN

The National Childhood Traumatic Stress Network (NCTSN) database describes the epidemiology of childhood trauma and identifies evidence-based approaches to working with children who experience trauma. The NCTSN database of over 10,000 children in trauma treatment (Pynoos et al., 2014) details the type(s) of trauma exposure and mean duration(s) of trauma. The four most common types of childhood trauma exposures are traumatic loss, bereavement, or separation; domestic violence; impaired caregiver; and emotional abuse. Mean durations of these trauma exposures are typically 4 to 6 years. Children in the NCTSN dataset experienced an average of four types of trauma. With each additional trauma type, the odds of adolescent risk-taking (e.g., substance use, criminal activity) or internalizing behaviors (e.g., attachment problems, self-harm, suicidality) increased.

Pynoos et al. (2014), reported the types of trauma exposure shift as infants and children mature. The youngest children (birth to 5 years old) are most frequently exposed to impaired caregivers, neglect, domestic violence, and emotional abuse. School-aged children (6–12 years old) experience war, terrorism, or political violence; school violence; natural disasters; and sexual abuse. Finally, adolescence (13–18 years) was more typically the age of onset in physical assaults and extreme interpersonal violence.

Psychological maltreatment (emotional abuse and emotional neglect), called *unseen wounds* by Spinazolla and colleagues (2014), is a common childhood trauma. Psychological maltreatment results when either a series of caregiving episodes or a single severe episode conveys to the child he is unloved, unworthy, or worth only what he can do for another (often the very caregiver who is supposed to protect him). Chamberland, Fallon, Black, & Trocme (2011) reported 36% of all maltreated children experienced emotional abuse, and 52% of all maltreated children experienced emotional neglect.

Children who experience psychological maltreatment have a working model of self in relationships that they are unworthy of the other's love or care. Imagine children who repeatedly hear they are stupid, lazy, good for nothing, or to blame for the difficult circumstances surrounding them. They do not know what it feels like to be at the top of the autonomic ladder in safety and security. Their neuroceptions are of danger or life threat. They are hypervigilant, scanning the environment constantly waiting for the other shoe to drop. They are easily triggered. Even hearing a caregiver's voice in the distance may bring them to full attention and on guard. Early in life, they respond with sympathetic activation. Their amygdalas signal the central and peripheral nervous systems to come to life. The neurotransmitter epinephrine, made in the adrenal medulla, is released into the bloodstream. Heart rate and blood pressure increase. If able, they may run away and seek cover. Over time, their hypothalamus produces CRF; the pituitary makes ACTH, and the adrenal cortex responds by making cortisol (see Figure 1.2).

The child who has a secure attachment experiences comfort and caring that interrupt this feedback loop. In contrast, the child who has trauma due to chronic disruption of social connectedness experiences surges of epinephrine and cortisol long after the trauma exposure. These surges result in chronic irritability or anxiety that may lead to additional traumatic exposures when an inattentive, dysregulated caregiver with their own sympathetic activation struggles to attend to their irritable, anxious, or preoccupied child. At times, the caregiver, at the peak of their activation, may strike the child or resort to mind-altering substances, both of which increase their disconnectedness from their child.

With repeated exposures to severe psychological maltreatment, sympathetic activation may wane and the child may tumble to the bottom of the autonomic ladder in dorsal vagal despair. They may appear lifeless, unresponsive, or out of touch. They have exhausted their reserves and are depleted of cortisol. Their heart rate and blood pressure are low. They cannot mobilize. They cannot fight. They can only hope to be invisible.

The National Child Traumatic Stress Network (2004) notes, "The child's perception, rather than the cause of death, plays the key role in determining the development of symptoms following the death of a significant person. Not every child develops traumatic grief after a death that happened in a particularly dramatic or threatening manner. On the other hand, some children may experience what most of us would consider an expected and normal death of another person as a traumatic event" (p. 4).

CHILDREN ARE DIFFERENTIALLY EXPOSED TO RISK FACTOR CARAVAN PASSAGEWAYS

The social and physical ecology of the traumatized child's larger environment exposes him to *caravans of risk* described by the National Childhood Traumatic Stress Network (Steinberg et al., 2014, p. S52). The caravans of risk passageway build upon the conservation of resources (COR) theory that describes personal, social, and material resources that co-develop and travel together to optimize developmental trajectories (Hobfoll, Stevens, & Zalta et al., 2015). Layne (2014) proposed using the term *risk factor caravan passageway* to describe the "often disadvantaged, resource poor and danger-laden socioeconomic conditions that foster the co-occurrence of multiple risk factors that accumulate and constellate across development" (p. S3). Travelling together as if in a caravan, these risk factors often become additive or even exponential in their impact over time.

Consider, for example, the risk factor caravan passageway that develops for Julia, a white infant who was born to a mother who was incarcerated for substance misuse. Julia's mother never saw her after the delivery. Julia stayed in the hospital for 14 days while she was treated for neonatal abstinence syndrome (NAS) and was placed in medical foster care after discharge. During her 4 months in medical foster care, her irritability subsided as she received loving and compassionate care from her foster family. In the meantime, child welfare services identified a maternal aunt who lived in another city. The aunt raised her own children and was eager to care for Julia. With little to no transition, Julia was placed with her aunt. In her new family, Julia's irritability and sleep problems returned. However, with her aunt, who was an attuned caregiver, Julia gradually began to sense safety and security again, and her irritability and crying subsided. For the next four years, Julia was cared for by her loving aunt and extended family. Child welfare services were pursuing termination of parental rights so her aunt could adopt her. Shortly before the court date, Julia's aunt was killed by a hit-and-run driver in a parking lot just after she placed Julia in her car seat and closed the door. The police ensured that child welfare services were notified, and Julia was placed in emergency foster care. Julia, who was now well-attached to her aunt/mommy, again moved into the foster care system while another pre-adoptive home was identified. By 4 years of age, Julia had experienced multiple traumatic separations.

STRESS ALLOSTASIS CAUSES WEAR AND TEAR ON BRAIN AND BODY SYSTEMS

Stress allostasis describes the repetitive wear and tear of multiple and additive toxic exposures without repair. McEwen (2005) defined allostasis as the "adaptive processes that maintain homeostasis through the production of mediators such as adrenaline, cortisol, and other chemical messengers" (p. 315) or "the superordinate system by which stability is achieved through change" (p. 316). Szabo (2012) described Hans Selye's general adaptation syndrome in three stages of stress exemplifying the response of the sympathetic nervous system: (1) alarm with release of epinephrine and glucocorticoids leading to restoration of homeostasis; (2) defense and adaptation or the classic fight-or-flight paradigm; and (3) exhaustion after persistent stress without adaptive response. Students of Polyvagal Theory can easily recognize the states of sympathetic activation and dorsal vagal collapse. Missing, however, is the core contribution of ventral vagal states, the initial mammalian attempt to leverage social engagement to remain safe and secure, rather than to tumble into danger or life threat states.

JULIA'S STORY OF STRESS ALLOSTASIS

Julia's life began in sympathetic activation as the effects of withdrawal from maternal opiate misuse resulted in her irritability and sleep problems. As her irritability receded, she became safe and secure in a ventral vagal state with her medical foster care parents, leveraging her social engagement system. Unfortunately, just as she was settling in with her foster care family, she was separated from them abruptly. The delicate sense of safety and security she had developed was interrupted as she was placed with her aunt. Again, danger loomed to Julia's immature nervous system, and her sympathetic activation returned. Fortunately, her aunt, an experienced mother, was prepared to socially engage her, and over time the dyad became socially connected. Julia attached to her aunt/mommy, sought her out at times of stress, and was moving into a larger world of playdates, friends, and outings. As her world was continuing to open up with new experiences, each of which represented micro-challenges or stresses with good scaffolding, her aunt/mommy was killed. What will Julia's future be? Her early prenatal intrauterine exposures, separations, and losses were the foundation of a risk caravan passageway. Will she instead experience a *resource caravan passageway* in another home with sensitive and attuned caregivers who will recognize her traumatic loss and support her in her bereavement and grief? Or will Julia's risk factor caravan passageway continue as she moves from foster home to foster home?

McEwen (2010) introduced the term *allostatic load* to refer to the "wear and tear on the body and brain resulting from chronic overactivity or inactivity of physiological systems that are normally involved in adaptation to environmental change" (p. 194). Julia's early life included considerable sympathetic activation, but over time she was scaffolded by the loving and attentive care of her medical foster care family and her maternal aunt. Julia's early allostatic load was buffered by her social engagement, connectedness, and attachment with her aunt/mommy. When her aunt/mommy was killed, Julia faced the most significant traumatic loss and separation of her life. If the social service system finds another caregiver who will support and scaffold her as she recovers, her allostatic load, while considerable, may ease over time. If not, she may become either chronically sympathetically activated with challenging behaviors or she may sink into inactivity with depression and withdrawal. Hopefully, there are multiple potential times for reset. The earlier she finds safety and social connectedness, the less the wear and tear on her system.

In the Bucharest Early Intervention Project, Zeanah et al. (2009) shed light on the impact of early separation upon infants, toddlers, and young children. In the 1960s and 1970s, Romania had overwhelming population growth resulting in abandonment of 170,000 children who were cared for in large orphanages. Conditions in the orphanages and the poor health and well-being of the children later came to light. Zeanah et al. hypothesized children who were raised in high-quality foster care would have better outcomes than those who remained in orphanage settings.

The children in the orphanages were randomly assigned either to high-quality foster care placements or continued orphanage placement. Children who were placed in foster care before 2 years of age were less likely to have any psychiatric morbidity, more likely to be securely attached, and less likely to have disorganized attachments than children in institutional care (Smyke, Zeanah, Fox, Nelson, & Guthrie, 2010; Zeanah et al., 2009). Longer term implications included dose-related telomere shortening, which is a reflection of premature aging seen in institutionalized children in middle childhood (Drury et al., 2012).

A common thread in childhood traumatic exposures, both explicit and unseen wounds, is the loss of physical or emotional proximity of the parent. Such traumatic exposures are more common than frank physical or emotional abuse, whose poor long-term outcomes are well documented. Whether it is due to traumatic losses and bereavements, forced separations, school or community violence, substance misuse, or war or genocide, social connectedness is disrupted repeatedly, often chronically. Even when the parent maintains a physical presence, they may be emotionally unavailable due to competing priorities (e.g., accessing safe housing, adequate nutrition, daycare, etc.). Even when a parent is physically and emotionally present, there is often the lingering fear of unpredictable violence that threatens even the best relationships.

TRAUMATIC LOSSES OR BEREAVEMENTS: FORCED BORDER SEPARATIONS AND UNACCOMPANIED MINORS

Despite centuries of contributions by immigrants to the United States, immigration policy and potential benefits for immigrants and their children are diminishing. Khullar and Chokshi (2019) detailed specific actions that limit immigration and increase the risk of deportation. In 1996, President Clinton introduced a 5-year waiting period for eligibility for Medicaid and Children's Health Insurance Plan (CHIP). In 2010, President Obama introduced a 5-year waiting period for eligibility for the Affordable Care Act (ACA) marketplace. At the same time, he introduced Deferred Action for Parents of Americans (DAPA), an executive action that provided 3-year renewable work permits and exemption from deportation for some undocumented adults with children who are citizens or lawful permanent residents. In 2012, Obama announced the Deferred Action for Childhood Arrivals (DACA) program, an executive memorandum that offered immigrants who came to the United States as children a renewable 2-year period of deferred action from deportation and eligibility for a work permit. In 2017, shortly after he was sworn in, President Trump began a series of executive actions and rescissions of DAPA and DACA. These actions were part of a zero-tolerance policy that continues to narrow the possibilities for persons to immigrate to the U.S. Hundreds of thousands of children, adolescents, and young adults are also at risk for separation from parents and deportation with or without their families.

In 2013, one in four children (~18 million) in the United States lived in an immigrant household with at least one noncitizen parent (Council on Community Pediatrics, 2013). In 2018, after implementation of Trump's zero-tolerance policy, ~2400 children under 12 years old were detained in federal custody at so-called "tender age" facilities. According to Elizabeth Frankel, associate director of the Young Center for Children's Rights, quoted in the *New York Times* (Dickerson, 2018), "The young kids think that their parents have abandoned them, or that something very bad has happened to them. They're in crisis. They're just crying uncontrollably. We've seen young kids having panic attacks, they can't sleep, they're wetting the bed. They regress developmentally, where they may have been verbal but now they can no longer talk."

In addition to the forcible separations, unaccompanied minors, largely fleeing their violence-ridden home countries, are detained. Between October 2017 and September 2018, more than 50,000 unaccompanied minors were detained at the borders (U.S. Customs and Border Protection, 2018). In 2018, on average, these unaccompanied children were held for more than 2 months before release to local sponsors (Office of Refugee Resettlement, U.S. Department of Health and Human Services, 2018).

Forced separation of children from their parents is a fundamental human rights concern. Forced separation violates the biological imperative of social connectedness. Forced separation also places children at high risk of physical and emotional maltreatment and neglect, sexual abuse, and death, as documented by reports of maltreatment and death in detention facilities (Pompa, 2019).

TRAUMATIC LOSSES OR BEREAVEMENTS: PARENTAL INCARCERATION

In many respects, when a parent is incarcerated, the entire family serves the sentence.
—ELIZABETH BARNETT, 2018

Parental incarceration is both an antecedent to a risk factor caravan passageway and a result of cumulative risk. On any day, more than 2.7 million children under 18 years of age have a parent who is currently incarcerated (Reilly, 2013). The Sentencing Project (Schirmer, Nellis & Mauer, 2009) reported that 10 million children between 1991 and 2007 experienced parental incarceration.

There are dramatic differences in the risk of having an incarcerated parent by ethnic or racial background. In 2007, one in 15 African American children; 1 in 42 Hispanic children, and 1 in 111 white children had an incarcerated parent (p. 7).

The epidemiology of parental incarceration has changed dramatically. Men represent the vast majority (92%) of persons in prison. Yet the population of women in prison increased 587% between 1980 and 2011, or from ~15,000 to ~111,000 women. When women in local jails are included, there are ~ 200,000 incarcerated women (Mauer, 2013). Across the country, there are more than 120,000 incarcerated mothers and 1.1 million incarcerated fathers who have minor children (0–17 years old) (Glaze & Maruschak, 2010). In 2010, 93% of persons in federal prisons and 47% of persons in state prisons were convicted of nonviolent crimes. The most common reasons for imprisonment were drug, immigration, property, and public order offenses (Carson & Sabol, 2012). Almost two-thirds (62%) of all women in state prisons are imprisoned for nonviolent offenses (Kajstura, 2019).

Short- and long-term risks for children associated with parental incarceration include: (1) migraines, asthma, and subsequent poor adult physical health; (2) anxiety, post-traumatic stress disorder, attention deficit disorder, substance misuse, and subsequent poor adult mental health; and (3) homelessness, delinquent behaviors, school problems, economic hardship, and increased adverse childhood experiences (ACEs) (Morsy & Rothstein, 2016; Murray, Farrington, & Sekol, 2012). The daily life of children of incarcerated parents is captured by a qualitative analysis of adolescents (13–18 years old) who had an incarcerated parent. Participants poignantly discussed the abrupt disruptions of their home lives, unpredictable visitations with no physical contact, the despair of broken promises for parental involvement, and the stigma of parental incarceration resulting in isolation.

As one young man, Omar, then 15 years old, described, "they made sure I couldn't touch her or give her a kiss on the cheek. I could talk to her but couldn't touch her" (Nosek, Stillman, & Whelan, 2019, p. 6).

Understanding the richness of sensory experience that ideally begins at the birth mother's chest, skin-to-skin, after delivery, the cumulative impact and longing for kind touch burst from Omar's description. All he wanted was to kiss her cheek, to have some physical contact with the mother who bore him and raised him. Depending upon who the substitute caregivers are for Omar and others, this lack of physical contact can reach the level of sensory deprivation. If the only touch is harsh or unloving, it is easy to imagine how quickly this is incorporated as lack of trust, being unloved, and unworthiness.

TRAUMATIC LOSSES OR BEREAVEMENTS: MENTAL HEALTH CONCERNS THAT IMPACT EMOTIONAL PROXIMITY

Over 5 million U.S. children currently live with a parent with serious mental illness (Sherman & Hooker, 2018). For these children, parental mental illness may travel with low socioeconomic status, poor social support, and homelessness in a risk factor caravan passageway. The Center on the Developing Child (n.d.) highlights the impact of moderate to severe maternal depression on serve and return interactions, the platform for developing brain architecture and connectivity that facilitates or inhibits typical development. Additional critical factors are the chronicity of mental health concerns and the timing of impaired caregiving (Center on the Developing Child, 2009).

Estimates of serious parental mental health problems are highest when the index population is either children who are being treated for their own mental health disorders or populations that have multiple psychosocial risk factors, for example, women who receive social support services. Among children receiving inpatient psychiatric services, one in two (48%) parents also had a diagnosable mental health disorder. Over 60% of children whose parents have depression develop a mental illness during childhood or adolescence. Substance misuse disorder was also reported in one in five (20%) of these parents. In contrast, in the general population, one in 20 (4.5%) parents are affected by substance misuse (Mattejat & Remschmidt, 2008).

Postpartum depression can affect both mothers and fathers. One in four (23.8%) mothers and one in 10 (10.4%) fathers experience postpartum depression. Rates for both mothers and fathers are highest during the 3–6 month postpartum period (Paulson & Bazemore, 2010). In a birth cohort with an overrepresentation of mothers with depression followed over 10 years, the depressed mothers had higher evening cortisol and sIgA levels. sIgA is an inflammatory marker associated with chronic stress. Depressed mothers were more negative, hostile, and intrusive. Children of depressed mothers had higher evening sIgA levels, more psychiatric disorders, and more externalizing and internalizing symptoms (Ulmer-Yaniv, Djalovski, Priel, Zagoory-Sharon, & Feldman, 2018).

In addition to neurobiologic correlates, there are significant neurophysiologic indices of infants' psychological functioning that may be disrupted by parental mental illness. Most research reports outcomes of birth mother and infant dyads. There is little research on the relationships between non-birthing partners, including fathers, and infant outcomes. The paucity of such data highlights the need to better study all the adult caregiver infant interactions.

The immaturity of the parasympathetic system due to lack of

myelination of the vagus makes the newborn and young infant particularly vulnerable to the effects of parental depression. The peak of parental perinatal depression is 3–6 months postpartum (Mattejat & Remschmidt, 2008), and the greatest increase in myelination of vagal fibers is the third trimester to 9 months postpartum (Pereya, Zhang, Schmidt, & Becker, 1992), overlapping the 3–6 month peak of postpartum depression. This convergence may be yet another allostatic load in the caravans of risk passageway. Mothers with postpartum depression may find particular challenges in the diminished responsiveness of young infants due to their developmentally-regulated myelination of the vagus nerve. Infants of depressed birth mothers were more likely to show lower baseline RSA, a reflection of decreased vagal tone and diminished autonomic flexibility. They also did not show the typical robust increase in vagal myelination noted in 3–6 month old infants (Field, 2008).

Studies of the effects of parental depression on the HPA axis, the immune system, and RSA suggest that the impact of parental depression on children is pervasive. Furthermore, alterations of neurobiologic and neurophysiologic processes potentiate vulnerability and potentially lead to intermediate- and long-term poor social-emotional and cognitive outcomes.

Alterations in the body's stress system, the HPA axis, are potentially linked to depression and intergenerational transmission of vulnerability to depression. Alteration in both morning cortisol and the cortisol awakening response (CAR) are noted in persons with current and past depressive episodes. In urban parent–preschool-aged child dyads studied over 3 years, there was a strong parent-child adrenocortical attunement of morning cortisol for parents with and without a history of depression. For parents with depression and their children, higher adrenocortical attunement predicted increased parent hostility, impaired child social functioning, and increased child depressive symptoms (Merwin, Barrios, Smith, Lemay, & Dougherty, 2018).

The experience of living with a seriously mental ill parent brings a host of concerns for the young child, school-aged child, or adolescent. As psychiatrist Alan Cooklin (2006) comments, "Children with a parent with mental illness often fall through the cracks and are seen as nobody's responsibility. Nothing is explained to them, and they often receive no help at all . . . These children need to be seen and heard."

Yamamoto and Keogh (2018) identified four themes in their systematic review of qualitative studies of children's experiences of living with a parent with mental illness: children's understanding of mental illness, their relationship with their parents, their coping strategies, and their social connections. For the young or school-aged child, there are often basic questions about their parent's behavior and a lack of access to knowledge about their parent's illness. Lacking an understanding of their parent's mental health concerns, children will often simply describe what they see. Children may also describe feeling disrespected by the medical staff. Many children also expressed fear of a parent's hospitalization with both the loss of proximity as well as the potential disruption of kin care or foster care. Children experienced sadness and isolation and a sense of responsibility for their parent. They often poignantly described both their concern for their parent as well as the burden of needing to take on significant additional responsibility. To protect their parent, children tried to hide their own negative emotions.

Coping strategies were quite variable. Both playing games and sports as well as talking to someone were described as good ways of refueling. Younger children with less understanding were likely to leave the room or play with stuffed animals. Making social connections was challenging due to stigma associated with mental illness or concern that friends would gossip. Nonetheless, children valued friendships and looked for people to trust, irrespective of whether they wished to share information about their parents (Gladstone, Boydell, Seeman, & McKeever, 2011; Murphy, Peters, Wilkes, & Jackson 2018; Yamamoto & Keogh, 2018).

IMPAIRED CAREGIVING: SUBSTANCE MISUSE

A body does not inject drugs in a social vacuum: it may become subject to the physical intervention of the law, the coercive force of medicine, the reductive classification of psychiatry, the intervening categorization of public health, the disapproving gaze of moral reasoning, the restrictions of spatial planning. . . . It may suddenly find itself a "risky" body; a "dirty" or "polluted" or "criminal" body.

—PETA MALINS, 2004

Caravans of risk passageways are often exemplified by the experiences of children whose parents are engaging in substance misuse. These children are often concurrently affected by poverty, poor social support, low educational levels, community violence, single parenting, and complicating mental health concerns. Often they are currently involved or have a history of involvement with child welfare systems. Lipari and Van Horn (2017) reported that approximately 1 in 8 U.S. children 17 years old or younger (8.7 million) live with a parent who had a substance use disorder (SUD) in the previous year. Included in the survey are alcohol, marijuana, cocaine, heroin, hallucinogens, inhalants, and nonmedical uses of psychotherapeutic drugs. Most of these children, 7.5 million, had a parent with an alcohol use disorder. Another 2.1 million children aged 17 years or younger lived with a parent who misused illicit drugs. Young children (< 5 years old) who were in critical stages of establishing reciprocity and brain development were as likely to live with a parent who had a SUD as older chil-

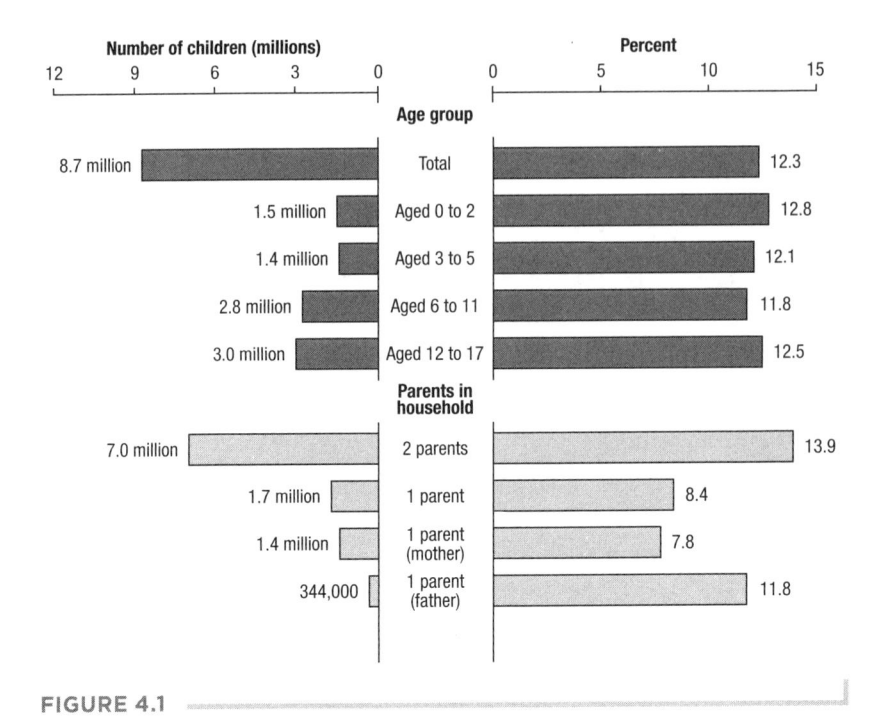

Number of children (millions)	Age group	Percent
8.7 million	Total	12.3
1.5 million	Aged 0 to 2	12.8
1.4 million	Aged 3 to 5	12.1
2.8 million	Aged 6 to 11	11.8
3.0 million	Aged 12 to 17	12.5
	Parents in household	
7.0 million	2 parents	13.9
1.7 million	1 parent	8.4
1.4 million	1 parent (mother)	7.8
344,000	1 parent (father)	11.8

FIGURE 4.1

Number and percentage of children aged 17 or younger living with at least one parent with a past year substance use disorder, by age group and household composition: Annual average, 2009 to 2014.
Source: SAMHSA, Center for Behavioral Health Statistics and Quality, National Surveys on Drug Use and Health (NSDUHs), 2009 to 2014.

dren. Only a minority, 7.6% of the parents with SUD, received any SUD treatment in the previous year (see Figure 4.1).

SUBSTANCE MISUSE IN PREGNANCY AFFECTS THE DEVELOPING BRAIN

The impact of parental substance use is potentially dramatic for any child. However, pregnancy and perinatal substance use carry particular implications given the potential effects of alcohol and illicit drugs on the developing brain. Frequent polypharmacy challenges researchers and care providers to understand the effects of exposures on fetal development. A brief summary of the effects of perinatal use of alcohol and illicit drugs follows.

Since the central nervous system remains vulnerable to environmental and teratogenic effects throughout gestation, there is no safe amount of alcohol in pregnancy. Early alcohol use (first trimester) is associated with brain, facial, cardiac, and limb abnormalities. Babies exposed to alcohol are often born underweight and with small heads, reflecting their small brain size. Over time, children exposed in utero to alcohol have cognitive and behavioral challenges. Early intervention can mitigate the negative consequences of alcohol exposure on later development (Williams, Smith, & the Committee on Substance Abuse, 2015).

Prenatal substance use has documented short- and long-term effects on the newborn and child. Nicotine, alcohol, and cocaine have documented effects on fetal growth, withdrawal, and behaviors in newborns and on cognition in children. Though opiates account for withdrawal and behavioral changes in newborns, the impact of opiates on long-term development is less clear. Outcomes of prenatal exposure to marijuana and methamphetamines are less consistent (Behnke, Smith, & the Committee on Substance Abuse, & Committee on Fetus and Newborn, 2013). These associations are often muddied by polysubstance use, contradictory data, and areas of rapidly evolving information. For example, Short and colleagues (2019) found a potential association between maternal opioid use and gastroschisis, a severe congenital anomaly in which the fetus' intestines are outside the abdominal wall. Epidemiologic data showed that the prevalence of gastroschisis, an uncommon anomaly, was 1.6 times higher in U.S. counties with high opioid prescription rates. Prevalence was highest in mothers who were < 20 years old. There is a long-known association between young maternal age and gastroschisis. Short et al. report this potential association with opioids is difficult to interpret in light of multiple confounders including the known association of gastroschisis with young maternal age.

The summary effects of maternal substance use on children and families demonstrate multilevel disruptions of caregiving relationships. In particular, the explosion of opioid use in the U.S. in the past 20 years resulted in a dramatic increase in babies hospitalized for neonatal abstinence syndrome (NAS), the result of the infant brain withdrawing from prenatal/perinatal exposure to opiates. Between 2008 and 2012, one-third of reproductive-aged women filled an opioid prescription (Ailes et al., 2015). A recent large epidemiologic study showed that 28% of all pregnant women were prescribed at least one opioid pain reliever during pregnancy (Patrick et al., 2015). In 2014, a baby was born every 15 minutes who was diagnosed with NAS due to opioids (Honein et al., 2019). Babies who have NAS will stay in the hospital; may have clinical symptomatology due to sympathetic activation associated with absence of opioids; and may not experience skin-to-skin time, maternal caregiving, extended family presence, and breastfeeding typical of non-opioid-exposed babies. Hospital providers now collaborate with families to use the Eat, Sleep, Console methodology to care for opiate-exposed newborns. Eat, Sleep, Console leverages nonpharmacologic interventions including continuous maternal presence, quiet rooms, skin-to-skin care, swaddling, facilitation of sleep, and good nutrition, rather than opiates to treat the infant. However, the complexity of life for many mothers experiencing opioid use disorder may interrupt both their physical and emotional proximity to the baby (Grossman et al., 2017; Jansson et al., 2007).

Examining maternal substance use through a biopsychosocial lens enables providers and mothers to understand factors that influence parenting styles. Key complexities include the altered reward and motivation systems that may impact maternal caregiving among substance-using mothers. For example, decreased breastfeeding rates among substance-using mothers will impact oxytocin surges during breastfeeding that are critical to affiliative and social bonding behaviors. Oxytocin also potentially modulates drug-seeking and relapse behaviors (Cataldo, Azhari, Coppola, Bornstein, & Esposito, 2019; Williams & Johns, 2014). On functional MRI (fMRI), substance-using and non-substance-using mothers who were 1–3 months postdelivery responded differently to infant faces as well as auditory stimuli. Non-substance-using mothers had higher activation than substance-using mothers in areas related to visual and auditory processing as well as areas related to emotional processing, memory, and empathy (Landi et al., 2011).

The longer term effects of living with a parent with SUD span physical health, social emotional well-being, education, and life course trajectories. For example, one in four (25%) infants and toddlers (< 2 years old) whose parents misuse substances do not receive recommended healthcare maintenance visits (Callaghan, Crimmins, & Schweitzer, 2011). Children of parents who misuse alcohol or illicit substances are three to four times more likely to be physically or emotionally neglected or abused or sexually abused (McGlade, Ware, & Crawford, 2009).

Children are at high risk for educational problems that may relate either to cognitive or behavioral effects of prenatal exposure or the impact of other factors in the caravans of risk passageway. They have high absenteeism as well as impaired attention and behavior problems that place them at risk for disciplinary actions (Torvik et al., 2011). Children who have a parent with SUD including alcoholism have a significantly increased risk of developing a SUD compared to the general population (Sørensen et al., 2011; Yule, Wilens, Martelon, Rosenthal, & Biederman, 2013).

This chapter introduced concepts of toxic stress in childhood and allostasis, the cumulative wear and tear, on the mind and body from repeated exposures to severe stress without the buffering of a supportive adult. While the world may recognize natural disasters, wars, interpersonal violence, and mass murder as examples of traumatic exposures, the most common traumas faced by our children on a daily basis are traumatic separations due to the lack of either physical or emotional proximity to the adult caregiver. For children entangled in caravans of risk passageways, the impact of additional stresses becomes exponential. The child's life journey exposes him to more exposures with few available resources to mitigate risk.

There is, however, reason for optimism if we can leverage our social engagement and connectedness to individually and collectively extend ourselves to provide episodes and moments of safety and security even at times of disaster. Consider the individual and collective responses of families and strangers to the September 11, 2001 terrorist attacks. While there were many examples of individual heroism, the collective response of the Newfoundland town of Gander exemplifies the power of social engagement. Within minutes of closing U.S. airspace, 38 planes with 6500 passengers landed in this isolated town of 10,000. DeFede (2003) described the local response: "For the better part of a week, nearly every man, woman, and child in Gander and the surrounding smaller towns . . . stopped what they were doing so they could help. They placed lives on hold for a group of strangers and asked for nothing in return" (p. 7). With little notice, the town's population reached out with wide open faces, smiles, touch, and other cues of safety to absorb the traumatized passengers into their town and homes. The Gander townspeople anchored the passengers with their ventral vagal energy and provided a safe haven so desperately needed until the airspace reopened. As testimony to the enduring impact of the social engagement and connectedness developed over this brief time together, friendships initiated during the tragedy persist almost 20 years later.

In Chapter 5, we will examine the impact of early toxic stress on adult health and life course from both an individual and population health perspective. We will also consider the life long impact of individual, institutional, and societal structural stigma and systemic racism. Included will be discussion of genetic and epigenetic influences that may modify risk.

CHAPTER 5

Chronic Disruptions of Connectedness from a Lifespan Perspective

The Child is father of the Man
—WILLIAM WORDSWORTH, 1802

FETAL PROGRAMMING AND THE DEVELOPMENTAL ORIGINS OF HEALTH AND DISEASE (DOHAD)

The developmental origins of health and disease hypothesis (DOHaD), described by D. J. P. Barker (2007), proposed that nutrition and the fetal environment factor heavily in the risks of premature mortality and chronic diseases of adulthood. Prior to Barker's revolutionary hypothesis, the medical community attributed only adult lifestyle issues, including cigarette smoking, obesity, and high-fat diets, to the risk of developing coronary artery disease.

Supported by epidemiologic studies of United Kingdom populations linking lower birth weight to cardiovascular disease, Barker (2007) theorized that chronic fetal malnutrition and low ponderal index ([birth weight (gm) × 100] /[birth length $(cm)^3$]) resulted in fetal programming of organs, permanently changing bodily structure, function, and metabolism, predisposing to adverse health outcomes. The biological underpinning of DOHaD relates to critical periods of development for an organ system when the organ system (e.g., cardiovascular system) is plastic and sensitive to the environment, after which it becomes a fixed functional capacity. Barker developed the *thrifty phenotype hypothesis*, attributing the increased risk of adult non-insulin-dependent diabetes to poor fetal and infant growth. When calories are not readily available to the fetus in utero, fetal metabolism adjusts to caloric deprivation. For example, when fetuses are malnourished, they develop fewer pancreatic insulin-producing (beta) cells. Insulin is required to transport glucose into cells and maintain normal blood glucose levels. While this is an adaptive strategy in utero, once calories are plentiful after birth, it becomes maladaptive. These formerly malnourished fetuses grow rapidly in infancy and childhood, produce less insulin due to decreased beta cells, and develop insulin resistance. Zanetti and colleagues (2018) demonstrated that low birthweight, a proxy for fetal malnutrition and poor fetal growth, is independently associated with the risk of developing non-insulin-dependent diabetes.

Barker and colleagues (1989) showed regions of England and Wales with the highest low birth weight rates/neonatal mortality also had the highest rates of cardiovascular disease. Subsequent associations between low birth weight and chronic diseases included hypertension and mental health concerns (Schmidt, Burack, & Van , 2016; Skogen & Øverland, 2012). Global epidemiologic studies confirmed the world-wide associations between low birth weight and chronic diseases (Simmons, 2009).

EPIGENETICS AND GENETIC SUSCEPTIBILITIES

The gene is the hardware of the computer; epigenetics is the software. Genes load the gun; epigenetics pulls the trigger.
—BARRY LESTER, 2016

The complete sequencing of the human genome yielded 99% of the human DNA. There is little variability in 99.9% of the DNA between any two individuals. It is in the 0.1% variation that our individual features and certain disease states lie (National Human Genome Research Institute, n.d.). Many genetic syndromes and chronic diseases diagnosed in childhood are attributed to single gene mutations. The classic single gene mutation is sickle cell disease, which is caused by an alteration in the DNA which causes an abnormal hemoglobin protein chain (Bunn, 1997). Current genetic testing widely available in the United States can look down to the single gene level and diagnose many heretofore unknown conditions. However, we still lack a complete understanding of the variability between two individuals with the same condition.

The evolving field of epigenetics offers promise to better understand how the genotype—your genetic template—becomes your phenotype—the person you experience and the world sees. The term *epigenetics* was coined by Waddington as cited in Deans and Maggert (2015, p. 888). Waddington described epigenetics as the "the branch of biology which studies the causal interactions between genes and their products which bring the phenotype into being." Lester and colleagues (2016) further defined epigenetics as "processes and mechanisms that physically lie on top of the DNA that affect the activity of the DNA but do not change the DNA itself" (p. 29). Outside forces precipitating epigenetic changes may include nutrition; infectious pathogens, medications, or teratogens; alterations of stress management; and as yet unknown forces that affect the HPA pathway and cortisol production. These forces regulate the genes' production of proteins, changing our phenotype, that is, our appearance and behaviors, without changing our underlying genetic template.

The best studied epigenetic change sequence resulting in altered mammalian behavior is the impact of postnatal maternal handling of rats on their behaviors (Champagne, 2013). There is natural variation in maternal nurturing patterns, manifested in maternal licking and grooming (LG) levels. There are low LG (LLG) and high LG (HLG) rat mothers. Male rat pups who are handled by LLG mothers have fewer receptors to bind cortisol in the brain and a slower recovery of cortisol levels after stress than rat pups nurtured by HLG rat mothers. Finally, if male pups born to LLG mothers are raised by HLG mothers, their behaviors look like offspring of HLG mothers (Meaney et al., 2000; Meaney & Szyf, 2005). The behavior of the males of LLG mothers is associated with an epigenetic change of the gene that controls cortisol binding at the cell surface. Liu and colleagues (1997) concluded that early rat mother nurture impacts behavior through epigenetic modification of rat pups.

In human mother-infant dyads, continuous breastfeeding is a potential proxy for the HLG rat mother. Mother-infant dyads who breastfed for more than 4 months had similar results to the HLG offspring. The offspring of mothers who breastfed more than 4 months had more cortisol receptors, decreasing blood cortisol levels, and decreased cortisol reactivity compared to the offspring of mothers who breastfed less than 4 months (Lester et al., 2018). Confirmation of similar epigenetic outcomes between rat pups and human infants who have had enhanced maternal caregiving behavior suggests the opportunity for repair of suboptimal in utero environments. For example, Nelson, Zeanah, and Fox

(2019) demonstrated in the Bucharest Early Intervention Study, high quality foster care provided to at-risk infants and toddlers may optimize the opportunity for repair of early traumatic disruptions of care.

Our understanding of the impact of paternal care effects is evolving. Curley, Mashoodh, & Champagne (2011) detailed the routes of environmentally-induced epigenetic changes that can affect paternal spermatozoa. Paternal nutrition, toxic exposures, and age all potentially impact epigenetic changes in the spermline. In addition, evidence suggests that paternal influences extend to male-induced maternal effects including maternal choice of male partners, the mother's prenatal investment and changes in maternal care induced by the offspring.

In prairie voles, monogamous small mammals, caregiving of offspring is shared by mothers and fathers. Rogers, Rhemtulla, Ferrer, and Bales (2018) suggest a pattern of compensatory paternal involvement where mothers initially make high investments in care that decreases through successive generations. Fathers, initially with little involvement in care, increase their involvement and caregiving as mothers' availability to the successive litters wanes.

BEGINNING IN THE PRIOR GENERATIONS

The developing fetus is a product of his own genotype, the experiences of prior generations as they impacted his parents and their predecessors, and the fetal environment including mother's health and available nutrition in the womb. The contributions of both DOHaD and epigenetic influences come into play. For example, let us consider a pregnant white woman, Melissa, who, herself, was born at a low birth weight. Perhaps her low birth weight was related to her mother's severe psychosocial stress leading to homelessness, mental health concerns, incarceration, and cigarette smoking. In early childhood, Melissa began to gain excess weight. By the time she conceives, she has graduated from high school and is working at a minimum wage job. She is very overweight and has developed non-insulin-dependent diabetes, hyperlipidemia, and hypertension, all part of classic metabolic syndrome. Her health trajectory is consistent with the DOHaD framework.

What of Melissa's fetus? Her fetus is vulnerable to the impact of DOHaD because the fetus faces potential overgrowth because of Melissa's high circulating glucose levels. The high glucose levels stimulate the fetus' pancreas to make insulin. High insulin levels causes Melissa's baby to be born large-for-gestational age. Both epidemiologic and animal models suggest the large-for-gestational-age infants born to non-insulin-dependent diabetic pregnant women are also at risk for developing early insulin resistance and later non-insulin-dependent diabetes. Excessive nutrition in the early postnatal period compounds this risk, whereas breastfeeding is protective against obesity.

EARLY LIFE TOXIC STRESS AND ADVERSE CHILDHOOD EXPERIENCES (ACES)

Against a background of fetal programming and epigenetic changes, many infants and young children are exposed to adverse childhood experiences (ACEs). Adverse childhood experiences are any toxic stress of early childhood: "strong, frequent or prolonged activation of the body's stress response systems in the absence of the buffering protection of a strong, supportive adult relationship" (Shonkoff et al., 2012, p. e236). In order to better delineate the frequency of toxic stress in early childhood, Felitti and colleagues (1998) pioneered the Adverse Childhood Experiences (ACEs) survey in a population of insured adults cared for in a health maintenance organization (HMO). The 10 questions explore exposure to childhood emotional, physical, or sexual abuse, experience of love or family closeness, parental alcoholism or substance use, parental separation or divorce, domestic violence, parental mental illness, parental incarceration, and the presence of guns in the household.

In this insured population, only one-third (35%) of adults ≥19 years identified no ACEs. More than one in 10 (10.9%) adults 19–35 years old identified ≥ 4 ACEs (Felitti et al., 1998). Furthermore, for those respondents who acknowledged ≥ 4 ACEs, the odds ratios of health risk behaviors including smoking, severe obesity, physical inactivity, depressed mood, and suicide attempts were dramatically increased. For example, respondents who had ≥ 4ACEs had 12.2 times the risk of suicide attempts as those reporting no ACEs (Felitti et al., 1998). For individuals with ACE scores > 4, Anda and colleagues (2006) also reported significantly increased odds ratios for panic reactions (2.5-fold), depressed affect (3.6-fold), anxiety (2.4-fold), hallucinations (2.7-fold), and impaired memories of childhood (4.4-fold).

Sonu and colleagues (2019) replicated the ACEs study among 87,000 respondents across nine states. Almost one in five (19.1%) of the youngest groups of respondents, 18–34 years old and (18.3%) of 35–54 years old had ≥ 4 ACEs. Approximately one in 10 (8.9%) of those ≥ 55 years old had ≥ 4 ACEs. The highest disproportionate increase in chronic health conditions attributable to ACEs and the highest proportion of respondents reporting having any days of poor mental health in the past 30 days were both reported in those 18–34 years old. The lifetime impact of high ACE scores that are disproportionately distributed among the youngest adults raises serious public and population health concerns for current and future generations.

As we reconsider Melissa, pregnant in young adulthood, her ACE score, conservatively, is 5. She likely felt unloved, did not have enough to eat or clothes, was abandoned by her mother, and had a parent who had severe mental illness and who was incarcerated. By young adulthood, Melissa already has severe obesity, non-insulin-dependent diabetes, and hypertension, all chronic conditions that increase her risk for cardiovascular disease and premature mortality.

While caravans of risk passageways frequently include low socioeconomic status, poor educational attainment, and disconnected parenting, ACEs are prevalent across all populations. Consider, instead, James, a Black man who went to law school after serving 10 years on the police force. At 44 years old, James has all the outer trappings of success. Unbeknownst to his colleagues, James struggles to manage his alcohol intake, and has symptoms of irritable bowel syndrome (IBS), and high anxiety levels. Lately, James has started using marijuana to manage his anxiety and his IBS. He is fearful if he sought mental health treatment, his firm would find out, and it would affect his employment. James is out of touch with his family. He is the younger child of two teachers who both led after school extracurricular activities that frequently took them away from home on the weekends.

During their absences, James was cared for by his older brother who drank secretly and introduced him to alcohol. James was sexually molested by one of his brother's friends, an incident he never acknowledged to anyone. James learned to keep his distance from men, impacting his male friendships. While he feels more comfortable with women, his relationships typically end whenever questions of permanence or long-term relationships arise.

Like Melissa's, James's ACE score from childhood is high. His ACE score is at least 3 (feeling unloved, experiencing sexual molestation, and living with an alcoholic). His risk for pervasive physical and mental health concerns impacting his long-term health, well-being, and mortality is extremely high.

HOW ACES IMPACT INFANT, CHILD, AND ADULT HEALTH OUTCOMES

What are the potential mechanisms through which Melissa's and James's adverse childhood experiences predispose them to obesity, metabolic syndrome, mental health concerns, IBS, and substance misuse? Their caravans of risk passageways include combinations of transgenerational transmission of stress, epigenetic changes, alterations in the HPA axis and immune responses, and complicated neuroendocrine pathways resulting in chronic inflammation. The impact of these neurobiologic, physiologic, and epigenetic changes also has significant implications for other developmental processes that set the stage either for social connectedness or isolation or loneliness. A unifying hypothesis suggests alterations of early nurturing patterns beginning in pregnancies of earlier generations and converging on Melissa's and James's earliest years. Both Melissa's and James's mothers experienced stressors that potentially influenced their caregiving.

Racism and discrimination are associated with increased poor birth outcomes including low birth weights and preterm births in a dose-response manner (Black, Johnson, & VanHoose, 2015). Additionally, according to Nuru-Jeter and colleagues (2009), African American women report they are most sensitized by racial discrimination experiences in childhood. For example, one respondent discussed an episode when a child told her Black friend that her parents said, "we can't allow anybody (Black) in the house" (p. 32). Included are the pervasive nature of their experiences across community, school, and health domains; their later hypervigilance and anxiety about their own children's experiences of racism; and their attempts to protect their children (Nuru-Jeter et al., 2009). Later in this chapter, we will discuss the impact of systemic/institutional racism and structural stigmas, both of which result in reduced life expectancy and adverse health outcomes.

At the same time, Melissa's and James's mothers' neurobiology was likely affected by their own nurturing in childhood. Their mothers' nurturing patterns may have approximated the low licking and grooming rat mother. Perhaps their grandmothers' stresses took them away from their child frequently. Perhaps when present, they were less engaged with their children due to their own stresses and health needs.

Consistent with the impact of the DOHaD framework, Melissa, who is now grown and pregnant, potentially experienced childhood stresses that resulted in epigenetic alterations leading to reduced cortisol receptors. With fewer receptors, there is more circulating cortisol that will impact the system at multiple levels. Increased cortisol will result in weight gain in a particularly dangerous distribution around her waist and chest. Melissa's hypothalamic-pituitary-adrenal axis (HPA) may be less responsive to feedback inhibition to cortisol than women who have not experienced toxic stress. Melissa's capacity to manage stress is challenged as she feels more and more sympathetically activated with less ventral vagal input. DOHaD and epigenetics are thus continuously interacting, with the resulting impact potentially becoming exponential rather than additive.

Ulmer-Yaniv and colleagues (2018) conducted longitudinal research over 10 years comparing biomarkers for stress and immune responses in mothers who had perinatal depression and their children versus control mothers and their children. They demonstrated that mothers who had perinatal depression and their children had elevated cortisol levels, a stress biomarker, and elevated levels of secretory IgA (sIgA), an immune response biomarker. Increased sIgA levels were associated with decreased maternal sensitivity and increased prevalence of child anxiety disorders. At 10 years old, children with depressed mothers had increased psychiatric disorders and higher sIgA levels. The association of chronic trauma with increased sIgA levels suggests the long-term impact of trauma on the immune system.

PERSISTENT STRUCTURAL STIGMA

Social scientists Hatzenbuehler and Link (2013) expanded the understanding of stigmatization and discrimination beyond the individual level to a societal level. They further hypothesized that structural stigma is a risk indicator for adverse health outcomes including premature mortality. Persons with mental illness, sexual minorities, and persons who have HIV/AIDS are among those who are frequently stigmatized. Hatzenbuehler and Link define structural stigma as "societal-level conditions, cultural norms, and institutional policies that constrain the opportunities, resources, and wellbeing of the stigmatized" (p. 2). For example, persons who are sexual minorities and reside in high structural stigma communities die 12 years earlier on average than persons living in low structural stigma communities (Muennig, Fiscella, Tancredi, & Franks, 2010). Furthermore, as risk factors often converge together in caravans of risk passageways, the impact on health and well-being may grow exponentially over time. Because structural stigma constricts stigmatized people's opportunities, resources, well-being, and even their lifespan, we might better call it structural oppression. Marginalized groups aren't only disparaged and scorned. They are unjustly maltreated and injured as well.

Deeply embedded in the structural stigma—structural oppression frameworks are powerful hierarchies of historical control of cultural, political, and religious institutions that are dominated by white people, particularly males.

SYSTEMIC RACISM AFFECTS HEALTHCARE AT ALL LEVELS

Typical health disparities research is focused exclusively on health outcomes. Feagin and Bennefield (2014), however, addressed the persistent power hierarchy among the decision-makers in health care including public health, medical schools, hospital, and pharmaceutical executives. As of 2018, 56% of US active physicians were white; 17% were Asian; 5% were Black; and 5.8% were Hispanic. (American Association of Medical Colleges, 2019). By contrast, in 2019, 60.1% of the US population were white; 5.9% were Asian; 13.4% were Black; and 18.5% were Hispanic (U.S. Census Bureau, 2019).

When exploring the diversity of the National Institutes of Health (NIH) leadership including senior investigators, clinicians, and scientists, 78-85% were white and 10-23% were Asian. A small number were Black or Hispanic (National Institutes of Health, 2018). So, a majority white or Asian physician workforce and leadership at the NIH provide the clinical care, develop the research agenda, and perform the research.

Feagin and Bennefield (2014) describe how "white-framed language" (p. 8), which uses euphemisms and focuses on Black experience without mentioning white people, conceals the role white people play in institutionalized racism in healthcare. White-framing, along with the disproportionate number of physicians and researchers, presents a major challenge to identifying, studying, and addressing the impacts of systemic racism. The authors detailed a long history of persistent systemic racism in medicine of shameful experimentation without consent, including performing surgical techniques on Black women that were only later offered to all women once standardized (Washington, 2006) and injections of plutonium in Black persons to observe the natural history of radiation exposure (Washington, 2006).

On top of such blatant medical abuse, Feagin and Bennefield (2014) elaborated the inequalities resulting from differential approaches to treatment by race that document Blacks are less likely to receive pharmacologic therapy, angiography and catheterization, and surgery for heart disease than white patients (Mayberry, Mili & Ofili, 2000). They are less likely to receive surgery for lung cancer (Bach, Cramer, Warren, & Begg, 1999) and less likely to be referred for kidney transplantation (Ayanian, Cleary, Weissman, & Epstein, 1999).

In addition to the substandard care that the U.S. health system delivers to Black people and the medical abuse described above, the stress of racism impacts the bodies of Black people in other lamentable but biological explainable ways. Harrell and colleagues (2011) detailed the potential pathways through which individual, institutional, structural, and cultural racism result in poor health outcomes. They point out how both conscious and unconscious racial stress disrupt the HPA and sympathetic adrenal medullary axes. Racism also increases allostatic load, which, as we saw in Chapter 4, is a measure of how severe circumstances produce extensive changes in biology and physiology, which can wear out the brain and other organs. Neblett and Roberts (2013) showed racial stress in African American university students can activate autonomic changes as predicted by the Polyvagal Theory. As students heard vignettes of blatant, neutral, and subtle episodes of police racism, changes in RSA indicated removal of the vagal brake, and changes in cardiac preejection period indicated activation of the sympathetic nervous system. When evoked repeatedly, these autonomic reactions can disrupt the physiology of the stress response.

EPIGENETICS AND SYSTEMIC RACISM

As understanding and acceptance of the life long impact of systemic racism increases, neuroscientists continue to seek the final common pathways responsible for changes at the cellular level. As discussed earlier in this chapter, epigenetic changes function like the software of a computer directing protein production that alters cellular metabolism. Structural and systemic racism result in chronic stress that affects health and well-being. Barcelona de Mendoza and colleagues (2018) confirm the epigenetic changes associated with perceived racial discrimination in reproductive-age African American women. Women who scored higher on the Major Life Discrimination scales had increased DNA methylation at nine sites associated with increased risks for adverse health outcomes, including schizophrenia, bipolar disorder, and asthma.

Applying this paradigm shift to the story of James and his mother, we see that despite James' financially secure, middle class upbringing and his apparent professional success, the transgenerational impact of chronic stressors experienced by his mother and grandmother are potentially a critical component of James' life-time experience.

THE IMPACT OF PARENTAL MENTAL HEALTH CONCERNS ON STRESS REACTIVITY

Depression and anxiety are the most frequent mental health disorders seen in pregnant and postpartum mothers and fathers. Rates of postpartum depression (13–25% vs. 8.4–10%) and anxiety (10–18% vs. 5–10%) are higher in mothers than fathers. The disorders are also often co-occurring (Aktar et al., 2019). Unfortunately, there is little research on the impact of paternal depression and anxiety on children. There are, however, two likely pathways:

direct effects upon children and indirect effects through influencing maternal well-being. Most studies are observational, as researchers cannot randomly assign pregnant and postpartum women to stress versus no stress.

In addition to changes in HPA axis reactivity, infants whose parents have depression or anxiety likely also have changes in their vagal tone, manifested as alterations in their respiratory sinus arrhythmia (RSA). They may also have alteration in structural and functional development of their limbic system, especially the amygdala.

Higher respiratory sinus arrhythmia or RSA is associated with more emotional flexibility and ability to manage unexpected disruptions. The first year after birth is associated with significant changes in maturity of the parasympathetic nervous system that typically result in increases in vagal tone and RSA (Field, 1998). Infants of depressed mothers have altered vagal maturity leading to less than expected increases in vagal tone and RSA. The result may be infants' diminished facial reactivity and ability to send the signals to providers that convey their needs and responses (Field & Diego, 2008). Thus, depressed or anxious mothers may have babies who are both less able to show them their needs and less able to respond with signals of pleasure that engage parents with their babies in the dyadic dance so critical to development.

Clues of danger may include low-pitched threatening sounds of a presumed predator, loud sounds that disrupt the immediate environment, or facial expressions of a caregiver that may signal likelihood of withdrawal from essential caregiving. In studies of adults with post-traumatic stress syndrome (PTSD), Shin, Rauch, and Pittman (2006) showed exaggerated amygdala responses to emotional stimuli.

In animals, chronic stresses are associated with changes in the structure of the amygdala. The fetal human amygdala is rich in cortisol receptors, making it particularly vulnerable to the elevated maternal cortisol levels seen in depressed pregnant women. Depression in pregnant women may affect the structure and connectivity of the fetal amygdala. Together, the enhanced maternal cortisol and increased amygdala connectivity potentially increase the risk of affective disorders in infants and children (Herman, Ostrander, Mueller, & Figueiredo, 2005; Rifkin-Graboi et al., 2013).

The neurobiologic, physiologic, and epigenetic changes that impact early caregiving are complex, multidimensional, and dynamic. Transgenerational transmission of stresses, such as institutionalized racism or poverty, may impact stress reactivity in pregnant women through epigenetic changes that increase their cortisol levels and diminish their capacity to manage their stress reactivity. The diminished stress reactivity is reflected in increased cortisol levels that are transmitted to the fetus either by placental mechanisms or the fetus' own HPA axis. The resulting elevated fetal cortisol levels affect the structure and function of the amygdala, postnatally heightening the infant's reactivity to stress. The increased fetal and infant cortisol diminishes the development of vagal tone maturity, with a delay or reduction in expected increases in RSA. The fetus, now infant, is less equipped to manage stress and to be co-regulated by an adult caregiver.

The adult caregiver who has elevated cortisol perhaps often engages either in intrusive (sympathetically activated) or withdrawn (dorsal vagal) interactions with the vulnerable infant. The stage is now set for reduced co-regulatory activities between the infant and adult caregivers, delayed or diminished infant self-regulatory capacity, and the increased risk of affective disorders in childhood and adolescence. Furthermore, the persistence of elevated cortisol and sIgA levels throughout early and middle childhood suggest these changes may lead to lifelong dysregulation and more emotional challenges. Thus, the vulnerable child now faces an adult caregiver who is less able to scaffold the young infant and child to manage challenges with resilience.

On a more hopeful note, research indicates that as a parent's state of mind changes, their child's does too. In a study examining the relationship between parental and child depression, Garber and her colleagues (2011) started with the observations that "offspring of depressed parents had higher levels of depressive symptoms, lower functioning across multiple domains, and lower perceived competence compared to children of nondepressed parents" (pp. 237–238). When parents' depression improved, however, their children's symptoms did too, even though the children received no specific treatment themselves. When parents' depression lifted, they often became more accepting of their children, and parental acceptance was considered to be one factor mediating their children's improvement. From a polyvagal perspective, acceptance likely functions as a signal of safety, bringing the child into the improved mood and functioning associated with the social engagement system. From these findings, the authors suggest that coaching depressed parents to support and accept their children might decrease the children's risk of developing depression. Studying how parent and child states are linked informs our ability to guide both parents and children toward ventral vagal engagement and health.

THE DOWNSTREAM EFFECTS OF IMPAIRED STRESS REACTIVITY

The impaired stress reactivity beginning in the fetal period potentially extends into adulthood through multiple pathways and often through persistent affective disorders, for example, depression. According to the World Health Organization, the disease burden of depression will be exceeded only by cardiovascular disease in 2020, and by 2030, the disease burden of depressive illness will be the most significant of all chronic medical conditions (Lepine & Briley, 2011).

Decreasing parasympathetic (PNS) or vagal tone and increasing the sympathetic nervous system (SNS) sets up a cascade of proinflammatory factors. When the SNS is activated, epinephrine (adrenaline) and norepinephrine (noradrenaline) are released preparing the body for fight-or-flight reactions. The resulting flood of epinephrine and norepinephrine results in activation of the HPA axis and production of elevated cortisol. From an evolutionary perspective, the rush of epinephrine and cortisol was adaptive and protective. Earlier humans needed to protect themselves from predators by being able to alert and flee. There are still times when a rush of stress hormones is critical for survival. For example, you see a young child headed toward a busy street. Your amygdala immediately signals danger, and you quickly move to catch the child. For a while, your heart will race and pound, and your body will shake. This is all good for you and the child.

In typical stress reactivity, as the surge of stress hormones diminishes, your cardiovascular system responds appropriately as your heart rate declines; your heart ceases pounding; and the shakes go away. If, however, your stress reactivity is heightened, the surge will continue; your heart rate remains elevated; and you do not return to calm. Even when the danger is gone, your brain continues to signal danger.

Persons with depressive illness and baseline elevated cortisol levels experience persistent, altered stress reactivity. The concomitant decrease in parasympathetic activity affects their immune responses. Interleukins are a group of proteins produced by blood cells that regulate immune responses. Their activated immune system continues to produce inflammatory biomarkers such as

Interleukins 2 and 6 and decreases in anti-inflammatory cytokines such as IL 4 and 10. Prolonged expression and secretion of inflammatory cytokines and elevated cortisol levels are associated with dysfunction of multiple organ systems, including the heart and the intestines (Felger & Lotrich, 2013). The relationship of chronic inflammation to cardiovascular disease is so strong that some suggest monitoring inflammatory markers in people at risk for heart disease to drive treatment (Mattina, 2019).

There is also a strong relationship between ACEs and development of functional gastrointestinal disorders such as irritable bowel syndrome (IBS). Persons with IBS are more likely to have increased ACE scores compared to a control population. For example, patients with IBS compared to controls (35% vs. 14%, $p < 0.0001$) were significantly more likely to report their parents often failed to understand their needs (Bradford et al., 2013). IBS patients also had higher cortisol levels following stress and slower return to baseline cortisol levels than controls. The time of return to baseline levels of cortisol levels was related to symptom severity (Videlock et al., 2009).

The presumed mechanism of elevated inflammation is related to transgenerational epigenetic changes in stress reactivity that alter early caregiving responses and result in infants and children who have elevated stress reactivity (Bradford et al., 2013).

For Melissa and James, the resulting adult impacts of poor stress reactivity and early onset of chronic medical conditions that impact their quality of life and predicted lifespan began in prior generations. Their cycle is unbroken. How can we break the cycle for future generations to enhance the quality of their day-to-day lives, build social connectedness that will sustain them throughout their lifespans, and relieve them of the disease burden of chronic medical conditions?

SECTION III

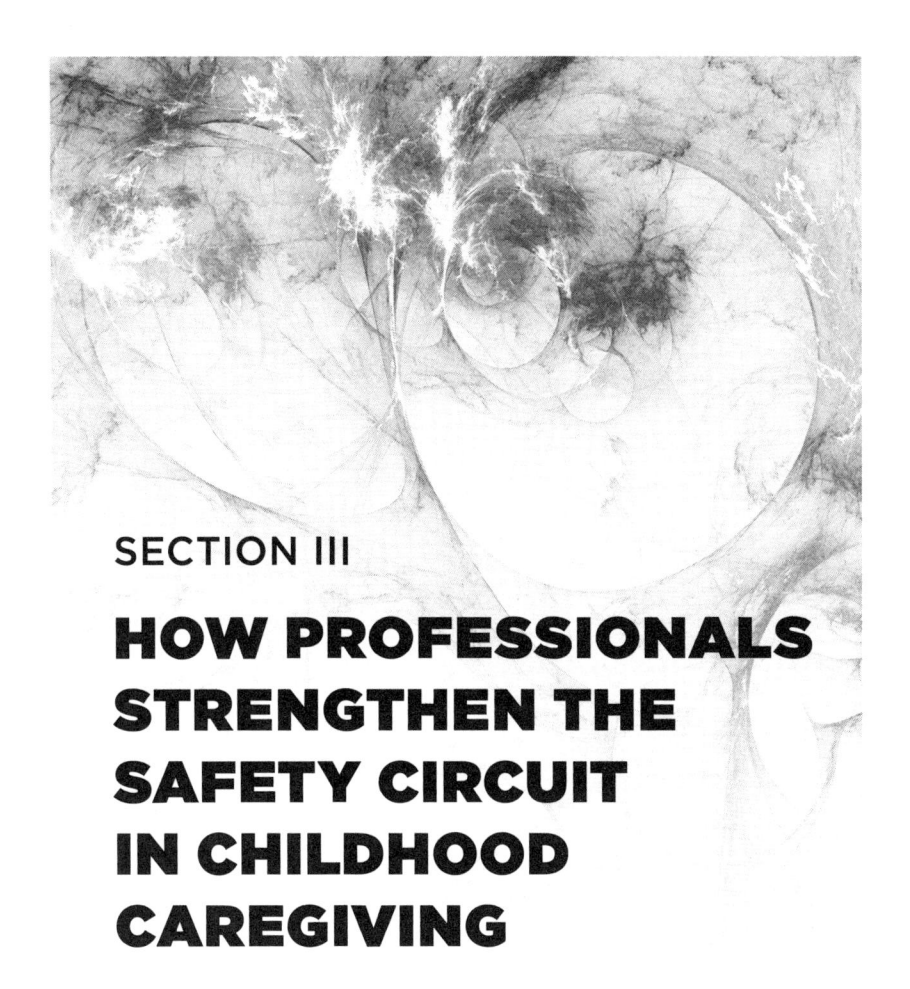

HOW PROFESSIONALS STRENGTHEN THE SAFETY CIRCUIT IN CHILDHOOD CAREGIVING

CHAPTER 6

Take Your Own Pulse: Self-Regulate to Co-Regulate Children, Families, and Colleagues

The state our body is in sends a message to the children around us. Bodies communicate. The children subconsciously know we are not OK and things are not OK—and therefore, potentially, they are not OK, either . . . and their survival make-myself-safe behaviours begin.
—CLAIRE WILSON, 2018

A large world of *child-serving professionals* participates in the care of infants, children, and adolescents. Early in a child's life, healthcare providers, early care and education staff, social workers, care coordinators, and child welfare workers interact regularly with children and their families. As children age, teachers, coaches, clergy, other parents acting in organizational leadership roles, and mental health clinicians come on board. Sadly, our most vulnerable children and adolescents are often involved with police, the criminal justice system, and immigration or border patrols (National Child Traumatic Stress Network, 2011).

Ideally, child-serving professionals are in ventral vagal states as they engage with children and their families. These professionals give messages that the children are safe, and children recognize the green light and approach them to get their needs met. However, as therapist Claire Wilson (2018) highlights, if we are not ourselves okay, children will sniff it out and by contagion catch the adult's dis-ease. The child's nervous system will then default to its survival-seeking behaviors of sympathetic mobilization or immobilization and collapse.

Alternatively, child-serving professionals can channel their autonomically driven states to facilitate similar states in infants, young children, families, and each other. To do so, professionals must first recognize their own states in the moment and strategize to alter their own and others' autonomic states. In doing so, professionals provide both clinical and emotional leadership to children and families. Effective leaders are those who bring competence, calm, and security to any setting, no matter how challenging and unpredictable.

However, there is a personal cost to professionals serving children and families who experience traumatic disruptions. In the short run, disquieting events may unmoor us from our ventral vagal engagement and trigger our sympathetic activation. Depending upon our own trauma histories, these shocks may drop us into a state of shutdown or freeze. We hope that other colleagues will notice and reach down a steady hand to prevent a free fall.

NURTURING THE CHILDREN AND FAMILIES WE SERVE: WHAT IS SAFETY AND WHERE DO YOU FIND IT?

Millions of U.S. children and their caring adults live in environments where they have daily exposure to violence and danger. These children and their adult caregivers are on high alert for any signs they are in physical danger.

Shawn, a white woman, is a recent college graduate who teaches in an elementary school in a large urban area. These young school-aged children are frequently angry and dysregulated. The school system attempts to manage their behaviors by having rigid expectations and using loud voices to quiet the upset children. Shawn says this year seems different, and the children are angrier. The day before, Shawn saw an 8-year-old girl, Kendra, punch another 8-year-old girl named Alexis in the face because Alexis had inadvertently bumped her when she sat down. Shawn is distressed by the behaviors and the strategies she is expected to use when facing challenging behaviors. Shawn doesn't believe it is helpful to the children to simply yell louder. Yet, the only thing the children seem to respond to is adults who are loud and keep kids in line. Shawn enters the scene with a loud angry voice and her adult body looming over the two girls and separates them. Shawn recently had a performance review with her supervisor, a white woman named Ginger. Ginger told Shawn that she had many talents but needed to work harder at controlling her classroom. So, Shawn's autonomic nervous system was on high alert after her performance review.

For Kendra and Alexis, danger in their daily environments primes their limbic systems to alert the body to risk and to prevent injury. Even a friendly or inadvertent bump in line may be read by the other's amygdala as a hostile attack. The amygdala is sensitized by embedded memories of prior harms stored in the hippocampus. When risk is sensed, the sympathetic nervous system springs into action with full force. What may have started out as two children preparing for a circle activity deteriorates into a fist fight.

Polyvagal-informed therapist and writer Deb Dana (2018) describes the movement between autonomic states (safety, danger, life threat) as akin to moving up and down the rungs of a ladder (see Figure 2.3). Kendra may start the day already halfway down the ladder. If she lives with daily violence, she is always on the lookout for danger and is prepared to defend herself. Kendra's survival strategy causes her to strike out when her neuroception says danger lurks. Shawn had worked hard to engage both girls, to interest them, and to be a positive and affirming adult presence. She particularly enjoyed Alexis, a quiet, self-contained child who only recently had started participating more actively. Suddenly Shawn, formerly a safe and calming presence for Alexis, is large and threatening. Previously, Shawn reached down from the top of the ladder to connect with Alexis and pull her up the ladder. However today, Alexis's autonomic nervous system senses danger in Shawn's presence. She becomes extremely quiet, will not answer questions, and keeps to herself for the rest of the lesson. Shawn was not aware that Alexis experienced frequent anger outbursts by other members of her household. Alexis's autonomic nervous system learned early that survival depended upon disappearing and trying to become invisible to avoid physical or emotional injury. For the next few days, Alexis ignores Shawn. Shawn tries to approach her, expecting to resume their usual relationship, but Alexis is at the bottom of the ladder with no place to go. Shawn tries to ask her what is wrong, but Alexis shrugs, says nothing, and walks away.

Three autonomic nervous systems sensed danger. There were three different responses to stress. Shawn went from safe, social, and calm to sympathetic activation after her performance review. Kendra, who is always on high alert, became highly mobilized when Alexis bumped her, and she attacked. Alexis, whose position was most precarious, collapsed into immobilization when Shawn became angry. Shawn will need to work hard to regain Alexis's trust. She will need to apologize for frightening Alexis, then show Alexis that she will remain regulated and help Alexis to regulate herself. If Shawn does slip up and become dysregulated again, once more she will need to apologize, repair the relationship, and recommit to staying regulated as much as possible.

Developing the ability for self-regulation, to keep oneself in a ventral vagal state even under difficult circumstances, is a part of what it means to be a professional (Arnold & Thompson, 2010; Thompson, 2018). The capacity for self-regulation is important in professionals' relationships with the children with whom they work. Staying emotionally regulated with one's colleagues is equally important.

SAFETY IS MORE THAN THE ABSENCE OF DANGER OR RISK OF INJURY

The Institute of Medicine (IOM, 2000) report, *To Err is Human*, defined safety as "freedom from accidental injury" (p. 4). The report recognized that, although healthcare providers enter the profession with the intention to provide quality care, they sometimes make mistakes that endanger patients. The IOM stressed the importance of layered systems of care to prevent errors. In the following decades, health care focused on developing algorithms and safeguards to prevent adverse outcomes including preventable complications and deaths. While the IOM report identified straightforward and timely communication as an important step, less time was spent discussing the role that interpersonal safety in professional relationships plays in preventing errors. Consider the following example from a hospital setting:

- Dr. Gabrielle Smith, a newly-arrived white pediatric resident, was working hard to meet the needs of her patients. One of her patients, Matthew, a Black child, was admitted to the hospital to treat an asthma flare-up. He had been running hard during basketball practice then started wheezing and couldn't catch his breath. Dr. Smith visited Matthew at his bedside with his mother and Donna, an experienced white nurse. When Dr. Smith finished her exam, she went to the physicians' computer to order the medication. After a few minutes, Donna approached Dr. Smith, made eye contact and pleasantly asked, "Dr. Smith, is this the dose you want me to give? I usually see the doctors here give a different starting dose." Dr. Smith realized that she had indeed written the incorrect dose for the patient. She returned Donna's eye contact and apologetically said, "Thank you so much. You are absolutely correct. That is not the dose I intended to write. I will correct it immediately." Donna gave her a gentle smile and said, "Thank you. I really appreciate how open you are to input from nurses."

Without Donna's willingness to speak up, Dr. Smith could have made a medical error that would have harmed her patient. What factors facilitated Donna's courage and Dr. Smith's openness? Why did this communication work so well to prevent an error? How was Dr. Smith able to readily acknowledge and correct her mistake? Although Donna was sensitive to how Dr. Smith might take being corrected, she knew she needed to ensure that their patient received the right dose of medication. So, she told herself that no matter Dr. Smith's reaction, she needed to let her know of the mistake. Furthermore, she knew from Dr. Smith's first two months on the service that Dr. Smith was dedicated and approachable by families and staff alike. Even though it made her uncomfortable, Donna sought Dr. Smith out, made sure she had her attention by making eye contact, and calmly delivered her message. Donna saw a flicker of fear on Dr. Smith's face, but because Donna's tone and facial expression conveyed a collegial concern for the patient's well-being, Dr. Smith took a deep breath and heard her message. Donna's stable sense of security in her nursing role anchors her at the top of the autonomic ladder, enabling her to stay emotionally regulated even though she is uncomfortable. She recognizes the level of responsibility she has for her patients. She also understands the importance of her role in training physicians. She enjoys their presence and communicates her enjoyment to them. She believes her job is enriched by their presence. Because Donna is anchored in ventral vagal safety, she is self-assured enough to get Dr. Smith's attention, point out the doctor's mistake, and facilitate the doctor's feeling of safety in the interaction. Dr. Smith enjoys working with Donna, too. She appreciates Donna's professionalism and steadiness under pressure. They share some interests and chat from time to time. As a diligent resident, Dr. Smith was initially sympathetically activated when she realized her mistake; her heart started beating faster, and she felt short of breath. She could easily have moved down the autonomic ladder, but Donna's warm appreciation felt to Dr. Smith as if she was being hoisted up by a benevolent rescuer. She was co-regulated by Donna's own calmly confident style.

CREATING PSYCHOLOGICAL SAFETY REDUCES MEDICAL ERRORS

In recent years, organized medicine has broadened its consideration of safety beyond the IOM report to include emotional and relational factors involved in the prevention of accidental injury. In 2019, the Association of American Medical Colleges (AAMC) invited Harvard Business School researcher Amy Edmondson to discuss the value of *psychological safety* during its closing plenary session. Edmondson told attendees: "Creating an interpersonal climate in which all employees feel empowered to speak up will lead to fewer errors and better performing teams" (Redford, 2019, para. 1). Edmondson also suggested leaders acknowledge that errors are bound to happen in an endeavor as complex as medicine. She recommended that they cultivate an atmosphere in which team members feel free to point out errors, even when made by leaders. Furthermore, leaders can facilitate team members' expressed understanding that they each have a unique contribution to make to the common purpose of healing. Edmondson is hopeful health care providers will create psychological safety with their colleagues because good clinicians already relate to their patients with curiosity and humility. Clinicians need to recognize that their collective psychological safety is essential for good patient outcomes.

How does Donna create psychological safety for Dr. Smith? Dr. Smith, realizing the seriousness of her mistake, could easily have continued down the ladder into further sympathetic mobilization or even immobilization and collapse depending upon her own embedded experience. But Donna understood this risk and didn't want that to happen. To that end, Donna deliberately maintained her composure to help Dr. Smith stay emotionally regulated in a potentially challenging situation. Dr. Smith did her part too, by embracing and making use of Donna's efforts to help her stay regulated, which in turn supported Donna's regulation. Absent Dr. Smith's grateful responsiveness to Donna, or worse yet, if Dr. Smith had replied with dismissive or belittling anger, Donna could have also tumbled down the ladder. Instead, the two colleagues used their clinically-acquired relationship skills, in accord with Edmondson's advice, to create psychological safety for each other.

ESTABLISHING A DOCTOR-PATIENT RELATIONSHIP IS AN INTERVENTION

Conveying a compassionate equanimity may be the art of the doctor-patient relationship. It entails establishing the same kind of person-to-person attunement that is essential to the development of the newborn and remains a vital social support throughout the lifespan of higher animals.
—HERBERT ADLER, 2002

How do patients and families find safety and security in a relationship with a healthcare provider? We often find ourselves autonomically challenged when we are ill or caring for a loved one who is ill. Even those of us who are well self-regulated and maintain a ventral vagal state when healthy can feel off balance when we are sick. When we are sick, we are vulnerable and feel our well-being is endangered. When we are in danger, we will seek safety using the mechanisms most readily available to us. Those mechanisms will be influenced by our own histories, experiences of social connectedness, and attachments.

Social connectedness is an evolutionarily embedded requirement for optimum health and well-being. Social connections are more protective against premature mortality than stopping smoking, decreasing alcohol consumption, flu vaccine, or physical activity to control obesity (Holt-Lunstad, Robles, & Sbarra, 2017; Holt-Lunstad, Smith, Baker, Harris & Stephenson, 2015). As social connectedness increases, so does vagal tone. Individuals who have increased vagal tone are more flexible and resilient, better able to maintain positive emotions even in the face of challenges, and more likely to engage in affiliation/approach behaviors (Kok & Fredrickson, 2010).

For young mammals, a protective adult caregiver is essential to survival beyond birth. Like the adult caregivers in proximity to babies, healthcare providers who are emotionally available, sensitive, responsive, and timely in their responses can become a secure base for the patient who seeks care because of an illness or health concern. Oncologists Gerretsen and Myers (2008) describe what happens when things go well:

> Paralleling the infant-caregiver dynamics, the patient develops a model of the practitioner-patient relationship in which the self is viewed as valuable and worthy of care and the health care provider is regarded as available and compassionate. The perception of availability instills a profound sense of security thus potentially alleviating anxiety and establishing a secure doctor-patient relationship. (p. 5295)

Gerretsen and Myers (2008) discuss the doctor-patient relationship through the lens of attachment theory. Sickness, risk, or uncertainty activate attachment behaviors that cause the patient to look for help, an intervention to make him feel better or less worried. The family has done what it can to provide support, reassurance, or simple remedies. The patient then looks for another attachment figure, the doctor or other healthcare provider, who is knowledgeable, trustworthy, compassionate, available, and attuned to his needs.

THE NEED TO KNOW AND BE KNOWN

The interpersonal engagement required in the clinical realm rests on complementary and basic needs, especially the need to know and understand and the need to feel known and understood.
—GEORGE ENGEL, 1992

In an environment of abundant technology and expectations of productivity, algorithms and pathways often substitute for a relationship-nurturing, patient-centered interview when the healthcare provider first meets the patient (Thompson, 2018). The electronic medical record templates are check boxes, with yes/no responses that discourage elaboration of detail. The computer screen often stands between patient, family, and healthcare provider. The typical pediatric well-child visit lasts less than 20 minutes. About one-third (33%) of parents report spending less than 10 minutes on their last well-child visit (LeBaron, Rodewald, & Huniston, 1999). The typical adult well care visit lasts 17.5 minutes (Gilchrist, 2005). How can a healthcare provider help the patient and family know and feel known during such brief visits?

The likelihood that the patient knows and feels known is potentially disrupted by the reductionist view of the patient as a collection of symptoms and lab values. In a reductionist view, when a 12-year-old is repeatedly hospitalized for diabetic ketoacidosis, the relapses are often seen as the result of deliberate misbehavior, noncompliance, and parental neglect of diet and nutrition. "What's wrong with them?" broadcasts in the background when the provider, patient, and family talk. When providers instead consider "What is happening to them that this keeps happening?" the patient and his mother feel known by us, and the complexity of their larger environment is revealed. Now we learn about poor access to nutritious food, lack of green space for play and exercise, community violence, and an adolescent striving for acceptance in his peer group.

Engel (1992) eloquently states that "dialogue is truly foundational to scientific work in the clinical realm" (p. 8). Dialogue enhances the provider's knowledge of who the patient is, who he wants to be, how he suffers, how he hopes and aspires. According to Engel, the things a patient most wants to know about their provider are "do they sense my personhood and my individuality? Do they acknowledge my humanity? Do they care?" (p. 11). Engel referenced the patient's need to know and understand as representative of the self-organizing and regulatory capabilities necessary to assure growth in a changing environment.

Needing to feel known and understood relates to the transition from the duality and mutuality of fetal life to the need for social connection in neonatal life forward. Engel (1992), like Porges, acknowledged the biological imperative of social connectedness to permit survival. However, he stopped short of understanding how the sympathetic nervous system and parasympathetic nervous system work in tandem through the release or application of the vagal brake.

PROFESSIONALS CONVEY SAFETY TO PATIENTS WHEN THEY ARE OPEN WITH EACH OTHER

On daily rounds, Dr. Nguyen, a Vietnamese physician, and Karen, a white advanced practice provider, were discussing Josiah, a biracial preterm infant. Josiah's mother, Miranda, a Latina woman, attended rounds daily. Karen presented her understanding of Josiah's medical concerns. Dr. Nguyen asked a number of thoughtful questions and indicated she did not understand some of Karen's assumptions and conclusions. Miranda quietly listened but did not voice any comments or questions as Karen answered Dr. Nguyen without becoming defensive.

When Dr. Nguyen circled back to the bedside later in the day, Miranda said, "I like hearing you ask Karen hard questions about my baby's care. It makes me feel that my baby is in good hands."

It would have been easy for Dr. Nguyen to avoid any hint of conflict by accepting Karen's clinical assessment of Josiah without question or waiting until later to clarify her concerns. Instead, Dr. Nguyen openly explored Karen's thought processes about Josiah in front of Miranda, and Karen freely engaged in an earnest and visible inquiry into the baby's condition without any self-consciousness. In such interactions, the patient and family are looking for signs of approach versus avoidant behaviors (see Table 6.1). These colleagues readily approached the task of developing a shared clinical understanding, and their willingness to set ego aside for the well-being of the baby conveyed how seriously they took their medical duty. Miranda noticed them leaning into the process of answering important questions about Josiah's condition and concluded that her son was in good hands.

TABLE 6.1 Approach or Avoidance Behaviors

BEHAVIOR	APPROACH	AVOIDANCE
Speech	Modulated	Monotone
Facial expression	Engaged	Distracted or flat
State	Alert or engaged	Hypervigilant or shutdown
Gestures	Open	Tense or absent
Posture	Open	Rigid or withdrawn

It's essential for caring professional teams to build the sense of safety that makes Miranda and other parents feel confident that their babies are receiving high-quality care. Situations like this one can otherwise trigger our earliest relationship and attachment histories, which impact our capacity to form trusting relationships throughout our lifetime. Add to this the anxiety and anguish most parents feel when their newborn's health is threatened, and it becomes even more important for practitioners to employ safety-promoting strategies.

A recent meta-analysis of healthcare workers' attachment histories suggested providers with a secure attachment history may have a positive influence on both patient perceptions of their relationship and outcomes over the long run. However, there is little influence in short-term outcomes (Mimura & Norman, 2018). Given the variable attachment histories providers and patients bring to their relationships, the lack of short-term influence is not surprising.

ATTACHMENT HISTORIES, PROVIDER-PATIENT RELATIONSHIPS, AND THE POLYVAGAL THEORY

Likewise, patients' attachment histories have an impact on their medical outcomes and impact their perceptions of their communication with the provider as well. Particularly concerning are the implications of attachment history for provider-patient collaboration in the management of chronic diseases. Both in adult medicine and in pediatrics, preventive, curative care is often sidelined by the morbidity associated with obesity, chronic diseases of adulthood (e.g., diabetes and cardiovascular disease), and behavior and mental health concerns. An understanding of the patient's attachment history offers a valuable window both into establishing the healthcare provider as a secure base and developing a collaborative style that is consistent with the neuroceptions that derive from the patient's attachment style.

Bartholomew and Horowitz (1991) identified four adult attachment styles that are a useful model for conceptualizing the ease or demands of the caregiver-patient relationship. Their model includes both the adult's self-concept and the regard with which they view others. For example, a person with a *secure attachment* has both a positive model of self and of the other. The secure adult functions autonomously and because of their high regard for others is comfortable in relationships and with intimacy.

When patients have secure attachments, they are open and trusting and have internal working models of self that reinforce both their own self-worth and their worthiness of the provider's attention and care. They are primed for social engagement, can readily accept reassurance from the provider, and can hear that the provider will stick with them and be available when there are challenges in care. They expect to be treated well because their earliest experiences were warm, caring, and attuned to their needs. They go forward in the world treating people well and expecting to be well treated in return. When there is an exception to their expectations, they may rationalize that the provider was having a bad day or had something on their mind. Except under extreme conditions, these patients are unlikely to become significantly dysregulated in the relationship with the provider.

Adults with *dismissive-avoidant* attachment styles often experienced distance or rejection in their early care, leading them to develop an excessive reliance upon themselves alone. They see themselves as independent and view dependency as a character weakness or flaw. They will go it alone irrespective of the physical and emotional cost to them. This personality style is manifested in their neurobiologic responses to pain. For example, persons with dismissive-avoidant attachment styles report experiencing less pain when they are alone than when someone else is observing them (Sambo et al., 2010). Because they mistrust others, they feel threatened by others' presence and safer when they are on their own.

Adults with dismissive-avoidant styles are at particular risk of poor health outcomes as they may provide less information to providers, miss appointments, and be less compliant with recommended treatments. The impact of their dismissing attachment styles can, however, be mitigated by good communication and a good working alliance with the provider (Bennett et al., 2011; Ciechanowski et al., 2001).

Across a typical population, about 59% of adults exhibit a secure attachment style; 25% exhibit avoidant attachments (including both avoidant-dismissing and avoidant-fearful attachment styles) and 11% exhibit anxious or preoccupied attachment styles (Mickelson, Kessler, & Shaver, 1997). The distribution of attachment styles varies widely across clinical populations. For example, only 25% of patients with somatoform disorders (Waller, Scheidt, & Hartmann, 2004) and 20% of patients with psychiatric disorders (Mason, Platts, & Tyson, 2005) have secure attachment styles.

How, then, does the polyvagal-informed healthcare provider establish effective working relationships and optimize patient outcomes across this broad range of early experience and attachment histories? As a skilled provider, do you begin by assessing your own place on the autonomic ladder when you walk in the door? Are you bringing a ventral vagal presence to promote safety for the patient or, are you sympathetically activated because you awakened late, had to drop your children off at school, and rushed to the office? Are you nearing the bottom of the ladder because your own trauma history is activated by the patient about to be before you? If you are sympathetically activated or moving toward a dorsal vagal state, the patient will sense your own neuroception of danger and begin moving to his own survival strategies to protect himself. Depending on his attachment history, the patient with a preoccupied or anxious history may become derailed in his need to make you feel better. The patient with a dismissive-avoidant attachment may become quiet or sullen, knowing that he could never count on you, anyway. The patient with a fearful-avoidant style may worry that your intentions are malicious and that you are a bodily threat to him. Your own dysregulation thus looms large and may occupy the room if you don't take corrective steps. Your patient will respond with their version of make-myself-safe behaviors. Next we will see how implicit biases activate make-myself-safe behaviors in professional relationships.

IMPLICIT BIASES THWART PROFESSIONALS' EFFORTS TO CREATE INTERPERSONAL SAFETY

> *Uncertainty is the biggest trigger for human anxiety. Our brains work hard at making life more predictable, at making quick sense of what is going on so we can decide what action we need to take. We see every day that fear tends to turn us all into either/or thinkers, for us or against us, us versus them.*
> —JON BAYLIN AND DAN HUGHES, 2016

Implicit biases are the automatically arising, nonconscious, negative attitudes and stereotypes people hold about others. For example, people may see others as more dangerous, or as less cooperative, responsible, intelligent, or worthy, based solely on their race, gender identity, sexual orientation, or ability status. As we saw in Chapter 3, negative implicit biases promote automatic reactions as well. As professionals, when we *act* from our implicit biases, we cause our patients, clients, students, and colleagues untold suffering and harm, in direct opposition to our explicit values and professional oaths. Our implicit biases are hidden barriers to creating interpersonal safety so important to a polyvagal-informed practice. To stop causing harm and to ensure that we treat people equitably, we must take responsibility for learning to identify and manage the ways we act from our implicit biases. Polyvagal Theory gives us a neurobiologically-grounded understanding of long-discussed perspectives and strategies as we take charge of these automatic reactions and communicate safety and respect instead.

Implicit bias of healthcare providers signals danger to patients in the same way that caregivers warn their children: through body language, facial expression, and voice tone, volume, and prosody (Hagiwara et al., 2020). From a polyvagal perspective, we understand that our patients, clients, and students react to this nonverbal expression of our biases through the nonconscious process of neuroception. While explicit bias and discrimination exist and damage the health and well-being of stigmatized people, because implicit biases act outside of awareness, they have the potential to leave both parties wondering what happened when professional relationships are disrupted.

The amygdala is a central actor in both implicit bias and the Polyvagal Theory. The amygdala mediates neuroception (Porges, 2011) and also plays a key role in social decision-making related to unconscious biases (Reihl, Hurley, & Taber, 2015). Again, in Chapter 3, we saw that caregivers socialize their children toward manageable risks and away from hazards at least in part by activating the amygdala's fast, nonverbal assessment of danger. The cumulative experiences of neurocepting danger socialize children and shape neural circuits encoding implicit biases about the people they encounter. Because our implicit biases were created outside of awareness when we were children, we are not responsible for creating them. But we can take responsibility for how they show up now and in the future.

To begin addressing one's implicit biases, Nancy Michael (2020b) recommends attending to the feeling of one's autonomic state, looking in particular for reactions that do not match our stated values. Further, she urges us to appreciate unconscious bias as a byproduct of socialization, a natural process which encodes learning about danger in Hebbian synapses through long-term potentiation. Once we recognize and respect our automatic responses, as Dana also advised (2018), we can use higher cortical reflective processes for regulation and re-storying. Devine and colleagues (2012) added that deploying concrete strategies could break habits of implicit prejudice. Their strategies included replacing stereotypical responses with unbiased acts, taking first-person perspectives of stigmatized people, and getting to know specific information about them. Hagiwara and colleagues (2020) point out that healthcare providers' chronic stress might impede their ability to use cognitive strategies like those recommended by Devine's group. They suggest that training professionals to use positive nonverbal communication might also curb automatic bias to some extent in these situations.

Implicit biases and neuroception are both part of a fast system to detect threat and activate defense. But when the speed of our thinking or reactions indicate that this fast system is engaged, we have the opportunity to change our brain state for the benefit of those whom we serve. Slowing down to understand a person's uniqueness turns on *our* cortical systems that suppress the subcortical defense systems, which drive *our* implicit bias. When our clients are particularly nervous, uncertain or confused, we can take extra care to use positive nonverbal communication along with asking about their experiences and their lives. Though fully integrating our implicit bias takes an investment of time and effort, taking a few extra minutes in those particular moments opens the door for us to see the client as a person, and for the client to feel seen and respected for who they are.

A RELATIONSHIP WITH THE AUTONOMIC NERVOUS SYSTEM THAT CHANGES EVERYTHING

It should now be clear how important it is for professionals—in their dealings with patients, families, and colleagues—to stay emotionally well-regulated. It should also be clear that good-enough early childhood caregiving relationships build a person's capacity for self-regulation. But how do we enhance our own abilities for self-regulation so that we can use our self-regulation to co-regulate others? Deb Dana's application of Polyvagal Theory to psychotherapy offers useful approaches.

Dana, a trauma therapist who works collaboratively with Stephen Porges, constructed both a polyvagal-informed conceptual framework for change (2018) and a set of exercises to bring about that change (2018, 2020). Dana (2018) outlines the process she utilizes for polyvagal-informed therapy in what she calls "the four R's:"

- Recognize the autonomic state.
- Respect the adaptive survival response.
- Regulate or co-regulate into a ventral vagal state.
- Re-story (p. 7).

Following these four steps and using Dana's exercises can transform a person's relationship with their own nervous system. Instead of being driven by our automatic responses to events, Dana shows us how to take our place in the driver's seat, steering our way through the autonomic landscape with more skill and confidence.

Using the autonomic hierarchy ladder found in Figure 2.3 of this book, we can start to map how we feel, think, and see the world when we are in a ventral vagal, sympathetic, or dorsal vagal state (Dana, 2018, 2020). Dana recommends deliberately calling up each condition so that we can *recognize the autonomic state* as it occurs in our lives. She says, "For each state, fill in the section by writing what it feels like, looks like, sounds like. What happens in your body? What do you do? What do you feel? What do you think and say?" (2018, p. 61). Each of us has a unique set of responses to become familiar with, what Dana calls our "individual autonomic profile" (p. 54). Knowing where we are on the ladder is the first step toward taking charge of our autonomic reactions.

Next, Dana (2018) recommends that we identify those circumstances that trigger us to go into fight-or-flight and freeze-shutdown states and map those triggers onto a second autonomic ladder diagram. We should also list on the diagram those events and conditions that evoke a ventral vagal state. Charting the precursors to our autonomic states enables us to more readily see them coming. Understanding this process and predicting its sequence of events increases our sense of safety and control. It also provides us with an opportunity to *respect the adaptive survival response* inherent to the autonomic nervous system.

We have built-in neurobiological mechanisms organized to switch our physiological state rapidly in response to changes in our environment. Even though this system may produce inappropriate responses at times, Dana (2018) suggests we develop a compassionate appreciation for how these states protect us and steer us toward connection with others when we feel safe. She asks us to consider how feelings of respect and appreciation for our neurobiology might balance the other reactions we may have had towards our sympathetic and dorsal vagal states. If we have been critical of our reflexive reactions or if others have criticized our reactions, we can find relief by adopting a respectful attitude toward the adaptive functions of each state. Seeing our neurobiology in this new light is a second step toward mastering our ANS.

Because none of us likely spends 100% of our time in any one autonomic state, we can see shifts in state, no matter how small, as opportunities to observe what preceded movement up or down the ladder. In following Dana's (2018) recommendation to identify what propels us out of freeze-shut down and out of fight-or-flight toward the ventral vagal state, we can focus on what helps us feel less afraid and defensive and what helps us feel safer and more open and connected. In addition, we can determine what things we do on our own to move ourselves up the ladder, and the assistance we need from others. Once identified, these factors become resources that we can deliberately practice as we *regulate or co-regulate into a ventral vagal state*. Creating this "Regulating Resources Map" (p. 76) shows us our unique opportunities for moving up the autonomic ladder, either by ourselves or with the help of others we trust. In making this map, we can use additional ways to move into ventral vagal, such as yoga or various breathing techniques.

Learning self-regulation skills is the third step toward taking our place in the autonomic driver's seat, and *re-story* is the fourth of Dana's four R's, in which we create different narratives about our ANS. Dana (2020) provides five writing prompts to begin to notice how we describe our autonomic states, so that we can change the stories we tell ourselves about what is happening:

- My autonomic state is . . .
- My system is responding to . . .
- My body wants to . . .
- My brain makes up the story that . . .
- When I review my short story, I notice . . . (pp. 74–75)

Taking time to answer these prompts when we notice that our physiologic state has changed builds our awareness of what is happening in our bodies. Using narrative to clarify our experiences prepares us to steer our autonomic nervous systems as well as alter both our states and the stories we tell about them. In turn, we have greater capacity to co-regulate others when the demands of the moment have overwhelmed their ability to regulate themselves.

One child behavioral health agency led their therapists through this series of exercises to give them experiential clarity about how autonomic states affected them and the children with whom they worked. The therapists immediately saw, through these exercises, that if they were in a defensive state, the world loomed threatening and dangerous for them. They clearly understood that nothing they would say to a child or family from this frame of mind could possibly be helpful. From this exercise, they realized, when they were triggered, their first order of business was to bring themselves back up the ladder. Only when they were open and connected again would it be safe for them to speak. They developed a more compassionate attitude toward their own trips down the autonomic ladder as well as towards the defensive behavior of their co-workers, and the children and families who were their clients.

The therapists enjoyed sharing their triggers as well as their resources for moving themselves back up the ladder. They discovered that one person's trigger was another person's resource. For example, some therapists really liked when a colleague noticed that they were struggling and asked how they were doing. Others found that they moved down the ladder if a colleague put too much attention on a perceived struggle they were having. Still others moved up the ladder when colleagues noticed their distress, but only if it was a colleague that they particularly trusted. These insights gave them a more intimate working knowledge of the Polyvagal Theory and increased their awareness of their own and others' autonomic states. From a heightened awareness and enhanced self-efficacy, they told new stories that contained words like neuroception and dysregulation and included the perspective that autonomic states are changeable and temporary.

NURTURING OURSELVES: THE TRAUMA OF WORKING WITH AND THROUGH OTHERS' TRAUMAS

Every morning the Memorial General hospital staff meets to review what is expected for the day. Although anything can happen, the morning huddle discusses what they know or anticipate now before inviting staff to share acknowledgements or comments. One morning, the physician, Dr. Nelson, invites the staff to think of themselves on the autonomic ladder. Where are they now, in the moment? Are they secured in ventral vagal safety, pitched into sympathetic activation, or collapsed at the bottom of the ladder? As the physician finishes, a senior nurse puts her hand on Dr. Nelson's forearm and warmly comments: "Oh, Dr. Nelson, I would never leave you at the bottom of the ladder." This is what connectedness and co-regulation look like on a health care team. Team members notice each other's emotional states, empathizing with their distress and addressing states that might get in the way of their performance. Over time, team members come to trust that their teammates have their best interest at heart, which increases their willingness to reveal their struggles and receive their colleagues' support. To stay emotionally healthy, healthcare providers need social connectedness, both within their work setting and in their lives away from work.

Without social connectedness to buffer the stresses and challenges of increasingly heavy clinical workloads, clinicians are at high risk for burnout. "Burnout is a psychological syndrome emerging as a prolonged response to chronic interpersonal stressors on the job. The three key dimensions of this response are overwhelming exhaustion, feelings of cynicism and detachment from the job, and a sense of ineffectiveness and lack of accomplishment" (Maslach & Leiter, 2016, p. 103). According to Southwick and Southwick (2020), burnout is frequently associated with social isolation; lack of respect, community, and adequate support systems; fewer long-term mentoring relationships; high levels of competition; frequent humiliation; decreased time for patient care experiences; poorly functioning teams; and little to no appreciation of clinician efforts.

There is a cost to working with others' traumas, often causing caregivers secondary traumatic stress, which is the "presence of PTSD symptoms caused by at least one indirect exposure to traumatic material" (National Child Traumatic Stress Network, 2011, p. 2). Trauma therapist Laura van Dernoot Lipsky (2009) uses the alternative term "trauma exposure response" (p. 41), which she describes as the "transformation that takes place within us as a result of exposure to the suffering of other living beings or the planet" (p. 41).

Whether the patient has suffered abuse, neglect, a failed resuscitation, or escalating medical care viewed as nonbeneficial by the team, the caregiver's autonomic nervous system is injured. Just as in a physical wound, there are the immediate impact of the wound, the subsequent inflammatory response, and the degree of long-term impairment. A burned-out or traumatized healthcare provider can't muster the imperturbable self-possession required to move unnerved children, families, or colleagues up the autonomic hierarchy (Thompson, 2018). Hence, the traditional dictum, *physician heal thyself.*

According to Dalia and colleagues (2013), symptoms of posttraumatic stress disorder (PTSD) are seen in up to one in six (17%) pediatric critical care staff, and two in three staff (65%) report concerning symptoms of acute stress disorder (ASD) that do not reach the level of PTSD. One in five staff (22%) report some level of depersonalization, which is a profound sense of disconnection from oneself. Not surprisingly, higher staff resilience is correlated with lower risk of PTSD/ASD and negatively associated with risk for burnout. The National Traumatic Stress Network (2011) notes that other child-serving professionals who are at significant risk for secondary traumatic stress include therapists and child welfare workers.

Symptoms of secondary trauma (van Dernoot Lipsky, 2009) may include signs of sympathetic activation, e.g., hypervigilance, fear, sleeplessness, and anger or dorsal vagal collapse, including avoidance of patients or clients, chronic exhaustion, hopelessness, or inability to embrace complexity. Providers' secondary traumatic stress (National Traumatic Stress Network, 2011) may place patients at risk due to provider inattention or suboptimal performance and can result in providers' transition to other professions, depleting the already small pool of those with skills to care for newborns, children, and adolescents who experience trauma.

Professionals who are at high risk for secondary traumatic stress benefit from understanding their own vulnerability and participating in organizations that promote a "culture of awareness" (Steinberg & Kraemer, 2010, p. 17). A culture of awareness brings attention to both the explicit and implicit communication among staff and families, staff peers, and staff across healthcare disciplines (e.g., doctors, advanced practice providers, nurses, and others). Embedding mental health clinicians in the medical setting assists families and staff alike in attending to their neuroceptions of safety or danger. Mental health clinicians are interpreters who bridge communication gaps when other professionals, involved in the medical "culture of action" (Steinberg & Kraemer, 2010, p. 16), are challenged to listen both to their own neuroceptions and those of other staff and families as well. Because they are not members of the medical and nursing team, embedded mental health clinicians can have a vital and irreplaceable role promoting safety, security, and connectedness among other stakeholders (Steinberg & Patterson, 2017). The National Perinatal Association (Hynan & Hall, 2015) recommends including an embedded mental health clinician in the newborn intensive care unit.

Ideally, secondary traumatic stress can be prevented or at least mitigated by developing a microculture of individuals who support each other through both encouragement and accountability. As van Dernoot Lipsky (2009) comments, "Its members must be people we can debrief with, laugh with, brainstorm with, consult with, cry with, and become better people with" (p. 185). Members of our microculture are those with whom we can share our neuroceptive states without shame and who will reach down to grab us as we lose our footing on the autonomic ladder. On another day, we may be the ventral vagal anchors who co-regulate other members of the microculture. Within our microcultures, we set aside formal administrative and reporting responsibilities from time to time as we support and re-regulate each other. Within an organization, it is critical for younger staff at earlier stages of their careers to know who is available to them for consultation, consolation, and encouragement.

When first responders, healthcare workers, or school staff contend with disasters, the recognized evidence-based standard of care is to provide them with psychological first aid (PFA). The message across settings acknowledges the importance of the autonomic nervous system's message to both provider and survivor. Universal recommendations to first responders include (Hobfoll, Watson, & Bell et al., 2007):

1. Promote safety.
2. Promote calm.
3. Promote connectedness.
4. Promote self-efficacy.
5. Promote hope.

Embedded within the recommendations are acknowledgments of the steps of the autonomic ladder:

1. **VENTRAL VAGAL ANCHOR:** promote safety, self-efficacy, and hope.
2. **SYMPATHETIC ACTIVATION:** promote calm to diminish sympathetic activation.
3. **DORSAL VAGAL COLLAPSE:** promote connectedness to interrupt isolation and despair.

Debriefing sessions both for bereavement and critical incidents are helpful in preventing secondary traumatization. While their structure may vary, debriefings focus on exploring and providing support for staff and in metabolizing the grief and loss experienced. Debriefings afford staff a voice to explore the unspoken (e.g., guilt, shame, or failed self-expectations) in a supportive setting. Staff who participate in bereavement sessions report better management of their grief and better ability to maintain their professional integrity (Keene, Hutton, Hall, & Rushton, 2010). Timely critical incident debriefings by an experienced provider can be useful, especially after an unexpected tragedy. Debriefings ideally occur within a time frame to include the participants and focus upon the events and timeline, embracing recognitions and interventions that went well and opportunities for improvement. As the team reflects upon their collaboration and individual members are recognized for their contributions, growth can occur for team members irrespective of the outcome of the incident prompting the debrief. Staff members may also self-identify (or be identified) if it appears they will benefit from individually targeted support.

While staff members express interest in critical incident debriefings, challenges are noted in finding time during a busy shift, lack of training available to facilitators, and potential negative impact upon participants (Sandhu et al., 2014). Development of simulation models for debriefing may offer new opportunities to explore training, content, and efficacy (Zigmont, Kappus, & Sudikoff, 2011).

AN OPTIMAL RESPONSE TO CRISIS: LIFTING THE VAGAL BRAKE AND BOOSTING SOCIAL ENGAGEMENT

First responders, intensive care staff, and emergency department staff are bombarded with signals of danger that make it essential for them to work collaboratively to accomplish their missions and directives. The tempo of their work may change in a moment, going from calm to chaos. Where do they get the energy that such challenging work requires? The Polyvagal Theory provides an answer that also explains a mobilization tightrope that our nervous systems walk as we negotiate the dangers of the world.

In Polyvagal Theory, we see that mammals have developed the capacity to neurocept the security of their environments and then activate states that prepare the body physiologically for various situations. Friendly environments activate the Social Engagement System. Dangerous environments activate the high-energy fight-or-flight response. Life-threatening environments activate an energy-conserving shutdown. But when trained first responders meet danger, they require a different physiological response. First responders need to access both high-level energy and their ability to coordinate skillfully. They do that through a process that has come to be known as lifting the vagal brake (see also Chapters 2 and 3).

The sympathetic nervous system almost never shuts off completely; it has a resting activity level, analogous to a car's engine idling when the car is not in motion. If your car is running and in *drive*, you have to keep your foot on the brake to keep the car stationary. Lift your foot from the brake, and the car will move forward. The vagus nerve serves as a brake to keep resting levels of sympathetic energy from driving the body forward. Lifting the vagal brake allows sympathetic energy to recruit the heart to pump faster and stronger. As Porges (1996) said, "By transitory downregulation of the cardioinhibitory vagal tone to the heart (i.e., removal of the vagal brake), the mammal is capable of rapid increases in cardiac output without activating the sympathetic-adrenal system" (p. 68). He explained that the autonomic nervous system provides the energy required in high-stakes situations by almost completely lifting the vagal brake (personal communication, 2019). For example, when a physician leads a resuscitation effort (i.e., when she "runs a code") her heart beats faster and harder as her vagal brake withdraws but doesn't disengage totally. She has the energy she needs to make observations, direct people, and give orders. This added energy empowers the doctor to function at higher than usual levels—with greater strength, concentration, and endurance than she could muster during more ordinary circumstances.

Lifting the vagal brake is not a volitional process that a person can decide consciously and deliberately. Porges explains that the application and removal of the vagal brake is an out-of-awareness reflex in response to changing circumstances (personal communication, 2020). To understand this reflex, Porges says that we can look at what happens physiologically when blood pressure drops as a person stands up. When arterial sensors detect the drop in pressure, they cause the vagal brake to lift, increasing sympathetic output, thereby causing the heart to beat faster and stronger, thus returning blood pressure to the level needed to maintain proper blood flow to the brain and other organs.

Porges (personal communication, 2020) says that similar sequences may be activated in other situations where an increase in energy is needed, like in our example of the physician running a code. However, he points out, lifting the vagal brake to this extent narrows the gap between ventral vagal stability and fight-or-flight mobilization. It puts the physician closer to sympathetic dysregulation, in which unleashed sympathetic neurotransmitters and mobilization hormones like cortisol could flood and overwhelm her system. This combination may push the physician down the autonomic ladder into a full-blown fight-or-flight state. How can people get the energy they need to handle critical situations without going over the brink into dysregulation? Porges says that anything that bolsters social engagement or ventral vagal safety will increase people's capacity to tolerate and constrain a higher level of sympathetic energy, preventing them from getting flooded. For example, in daily life, coherent breathing strategies with a prolonged expiratory phase activate the ventral vagal. Visualizing loved ones does too.

When running a code, the physician, more than ever, needs to energize her team's social engagement system to keep her team in a ventral vagal state. She can help them maximize social engagement by increasing the quantity and frequency of their verbal, non-verbal, and face-to-face communications. A simple nod of the head or brief direct eye-to-eye contact with another team member signals a well-functioning team. The team communicates and collaborates in a highly coordinated fashion. Team members maintain their face-to-face and face-to-heart connections, continuing to tend to the safety of the relationships while simultaneously going full speed (e.g., Porges and Furman, 2011).

On the other hand, Porges observes that not everyone's vagal brake is in good working order (personal communication, 2020). Sometimes the brake comes off too soon or does not get reapplied when the need for energy has passed. When a team leader or other member becomes sympathetically activated, a neuroception of danger plunges the person into the emotional dysregulation of the fight-or-flight state. What we think of as a disruptive physician, nurse, therapist, or teacher may actually be a dysregulated professional whose untempered vagal brake disengages suddenly. Understanding this neurophysiology explains why the behavior of dysregulated professionals is so fraught with danger both to the patient or client and to colleagues. When dysregulated professionals are in sympathetic overdrive, they lash out at those around them, frightening and intimidating them. Their teammates can't relax into social engagement because they must stay on guard to protect themselves. When team members have to keep one eye on a dysregulated teammate, they can't keep both eyes on their mission. All too often dysregulated providers and their staff endure this survival-struggle dynamic without definitive resolution until something tragic occurs.

A polyvagal-informed organization, as described in Chapter 8, educates staff to attend to their own neuroceptive states and those of their colleagues. The organization both sets clear expectations that professionals stay regulated and provides the structure to contain the individual's dysregulation while providing support to move toward more regulated states. Ultimately, the polyvagal-informed organization recognizes that the function of the team and collective staff supersedes the value of an individual member, no matter how otherwise high performing the individual team member is.

EFFICIENT AND EFFECTIVE COMMUNICATION PROMOTES SOCIALLY-ENGAGED TEAMWORK

Brindley and Reynolds (2011) adapted practical communication methods from the aviation industry for use in critical care medicine that promote effective teamwork and convey confidence and competence. They recommend that critical care providers, like those on our physician's team, do the following things:

— Build shared mental models by explaining one's understanding of the situation and the clinical rationale for action, as in, "the patient has no pulse and we are going to begin advanced cardiac life support."
— Create a culture that permits and expects everyone to speak up, for example, through the use of preoperative checklists: "We will not move forward until everyone in the operating room agrees on the patient, the site of the surgery, and the type of operation we are doing."
— Learn to "resuscitate by voice" (p. 157), meaning to state observations, concerns, and intended actions explicitly and openly. "Blood pressure is dropping despite the medications we have given. What else could be causing the drop?"
— Use straightforward and direct language, which is neither overly aggressive nor overly polite: "Get me the intubation kit now."

- Structure critical patient care conversations by using strategies such as SBAR: making brief statements that address the Situation, Background, Assessment, and Recommendations.
- Close the loop in communication by giving an order and asking to be informed when it is completed, or by repeating back an order that one has been given: "Okay, I have just given 10 mg into the peripheral IV."
- Limit communication during critical moments, such as when intubating the patient. Brindley and Reynolds point out that, in aviation, only essential communications are allowed when the plane is below 10,000 feet.

Consideration of Brindley's and Reynolds' recommendations from a polyvagal perspective show that, in addition to coordinating team members' actions and providing much needed information, these communication strategies will increase team members' sense of safety. Taken together, these strategies create a common understanding and purpose, explain when and why things are being done, and confirm that actions were taken. This type of communication affirms that each member is important and that they are working together to meet the critical challenges they are facing.

COVID-19 IS REWRITING ALL THE RULES

Historically, most United States' healthcare providers experience traumas that are limited in numbers and durations of disruptions of connectedness. However, the advent of the COVID-19 pandemic thrust our country and the global community into disruptions of social connectedness with no end in sight. Exhausted healthcare providers, first responders, therapists, teachers, and other essential workers toil heroically to address the work in front of them on a daily basis. Nothing we have previously experienced prepared us for the disruption and accompanying dysregulation that infiltrate our professional and personal lives. In Chapter 9, we speak specifically about how the pandemic reframes our lives with patients, families, and each other as uncertainty and fear cloud the path forward.

CHAPTER 7

Supporting an Emerging Humanity: Polyvagal Theory for Physicians, Therapists, Teachers, and Other Providers

> *"Tell us please, what treatment in an emergency is administered by ear?"* . . . *I met his gaze and I did not blink. "Words of comfort," I said to my father.*
> —ABRAHAM VERGHESE, 2009

Once healthcare providers, therapists, teachers, and other professionals who work with children learn about the Polyvagal Theory, they recognize that the particular state of people's autonomic nervous systems shapes their behaviors, performances, and relationships. Professionals know that these states dramatically influence people's view of themselves, others, and the world. However, this knowledge is not enough. To take full advantage of the theory's power, professionals need to apply their understanding across different settings. They also need to help people shift their states from shutdown or fight-or-flight into social engagement, so that they're able to engage in health, therapy, and education.

This chapter explores what the Polyvagal Theory looks like when healthcare providers, therapists, teachers, and other professionals apply it to their work with children, particularly when the children or their parents are scared, dysregulated, or shut down. This chapter provides a sense of what it is like to apply the Polyvagal Theory in practice. By looking at how professionals use a polyvagal perspective to respond to the challenges that a dysregulated child presents, we can better see the value that the Polyvagal Theory delivers.

THE POLYVAGAL-INFORMED MEDICAL PROVIDER: PHYSICIANS, NURSES, AND ESSENTIAL OTHERS

Physicians, nurses, and other healthcare providers can use the Polyvagal Theory in many settings and situations, from private practice to hospital intensive care units to drop-in clinics. Incorporating the theory into practice equips us to appreciate the suffering inherent in emotional dysregulations, rather than simply seeing distressing behaviors. Looking past behavior to the underlying physiology and experiences initiates a culture of care, but implementing and sustaining such a culture of care requires that we consider various scenarios and practice appropriate strategies. For this caring perspective to take root, we need both to have a cognitive understanding of the theory and to embody it by acting on its insights.

Embodying Polyvagal Theory changes the stories we tell ourselves about what is happening in our environments and with our patients. These new narratives play important roles in how we respond to the intense emotions that may erupt suddenly in healthcare settings. These dysregulations present opportunities to strengthen the doctor–patient, advanced practitioner–patient, and nurse–patient relationships through co-regulation of the affective intensity, which in turn serves as a good model from which children and their parents can learn.

EMOTIONS RUN HIGH WHEN THE STAKES ARE HIGH

Because hospitals and clinics are the settings for many life-and-death situations and conversations, it's common for patients and their families to encounter signals of danger and life threat when they see the doctor. Frightened patients may become dysregulated enough to disrupt the medical and healing process. Even though physicians, nurses, and other providers may see their job as tending to physical rather than emotional issues, skillfully managing patients' emotions and behavior is essential to successful medical treatment.

We have all seen people's emotional states managed poorly, with people ending up at the bottom of the autonomic ladder, agitated, distressed, or immobilized. There's another approach that leaves people higher up the ladder, more regulated and engaged, and more able to collaborate with providers in the goal of healing.

Imagine a pediatric intensive care unit. Avery, a white man whose little girl is in critical condition is standing at the nurse's station, pounding his fist on the counter and yelling to no one in particular, "I need some answers now!" His hands and jaw are clenched. His arms and legs are trembling, and he is looking around to find someone who will listen to him. Consider two different ways this exchange can play out:

- Jeremy Jones, a white nurse practitioner who is walking by, says, "Sir, you really need to keep it down. This is an intensive care unit. You're going to upset people, and that's going to have an impact on their recovery. I need your cooperation."
- Avery then says, "You people are all the same. No one cares about anybody anymore. You're all just interested in making money and being big shots."
- Jones says, "That's really inappropriate, sir. If you can't calm down, I'm going to have to call security."

Neurocepted danger sends them both down their polyvagal ladders.

Now consider a PVT-informed way the nurse practitioner could respond to the father and shape the outcome differently:

- Avery yells, "I need some answers now."
- This time, Jeremy Jones says, "Sir?" loudly enough to get his attention, but with a suggestion of curiosity in his voice. When the father turns toward him, the nurse practitioner spreads his arms wide with his hands open and at belt-level and sings out, "You're really upset."
- "You're damn right I am. Everybody's just giving me the runaround here."
- Jones says, still way louder than usual, "That must be extremely frustrating. It's obvious that there's something very important to you that you're not getting answers to." His hands now cover his own heart, one on top of the other, and with a sigh his voice softens. "How about we step into the conference room so that I can understand what's happening and see if we can get you the answers that you're needing?"
- Avery inhales deeply, looks down briefly, then follows Jones down the hall to the conference room.

Ignorant of the neurobiology that is triggered by something frightening, Jeremy Jones in the first scenario focuses on changing the father's behavior, as if the father was in control of his reaction. Without a working comprehension of Polyvagal Theory, Jones is left to manage the behavioral aspects of sympathetic and dorsal vagal states without awareness of their root causes. His options are determined by his understanding. He can try reasoning with the father or demand that he calm down, but these approaches just worsen the situation by stirring him up more. Because the father's nervous system is defensively engaged to respond to peril, it will neurocept both intellectual discussion and insistent demands as threats to his daughter's well-being.

What the father needs to regulate his nervous system at this point is an ally in addressing the threat. That ally must understand who or what is being threatened, how it is being threatened, and what might be done to repel the threat. Therefore, Jones's first task is to convey that he understands that something of vital importance to the father is at risk of imminent harm. He must send a signal to the father's nervous system that says, "I get it! There's something terribly wrong here that requires immediate action." Even though Jones doesn't yet know the father's daughter is a patient in the pediatric intensive care unit, Jones is acknowledging Avery's state of alarm. If Avery feels that people don't get how urgent things are, he will need to keep intensifying his efforts to communicate the gravity of the situation until they do. The more intense his communications become, the more likely the unit staff is to respond to the threat that they feel he represents, rather than to the need he is attempting to express.

Focusing only on behavior without addressing the physiologic underpinnings and emotional dysregulation is not productive. It is like trying to put out a fire by aiming the hose at the smoke. The nurse practitioner matches the father's affect, responding with the same emotional intensity that the father used, but without becoming dysregulated himself. He makes his face and vocal inflection more animated, his gestures bigger, his voice louder. Matching affect, the energetic aspect of emotion, is a nonverbal means of communicating understanding of and attunement with the father's experience (Baylin & Hughes, 2016). In addition, the practitioner accepts that the father is agitated without judging him or trying to change his experience. Accepting someone's experience without evaluating it signals psychological safety, which Edmondson (1999) defines as "a sense of confidence that [others] will not embarrass, reject, or punish someone for speaking up."

In responding to the father in these ways, Jones shows that he has more than a cognitive understanding of the Polyvagal Theory. He *embodies* Polyvagal Theory with his nonverbal cues and voice. He recognizes and appreciates that "every response is an action in service of survival" (Dana, 2018, p. 6). This perspective fundamentally reorients the way he relates to those around him. A humane compassion emerges from Jones's comprehension that dysregulation originates from people's suffering and vulnerability. Grasping this bigger picture and acting from its insights is part of what it means to change the stories we tell by embodying the Polyvagal Theory.

STORIES AND LANGUAGE MATTER

Deb Dana describes consulting with a healthcare provider who asked how to handle a disruptive patient (personal communication, 2016). Dana suggested that, as a start, the provider use the word "dysregulated" when referring to the patient instead of the word "disruptive." The repercussions of that shift in language are notable. Calling someone *disruptive* implies they have a stable, negative trait, which is not likely to change over time. It implies a defect in their character. Calling someone disruptive doesn't produce any insight into what might be helpful in the situation. Your only option is to tell them to control themselves, which they won't be able to do. When the patient does not regulate himself after you have asked him to, it's further evidence that there is something fundamentally wrong with him. Case closed.

On the other hand, calling someone *dysregulated* implies that their behaviors and emotions are representative of a temporary state that can and will change. It implies that they were once regulated and that something happened to cause them to become dysregulated. The word dysregulated elicits a sense of curiosity about what has happened to upset them so. That curiosity steers the provider to inquire about what caused their upset and suffering. Now a discussion can emerge about how to restore the patient's emotional regulation.

This shift in perspective assists a healthcare provider to send more signals of safety and stokes a virtuous cycle, creating a positive feedback loop. A person treated with compassion will neurocept the compassion as a signal of safety that supports them to re-regulate. When they get their composure back, it gives the provider evidence that the dysregulation was indeed transient. The provider's understanding of the patient's experience increases; he feels more compassion for the patient, and the patient neurocepts this understanding and compassion as additional signals of safety. Then the provider and patient can move up the autonomic ladder together.

HANDLING INTENSITY IN THE EMERGENCY DEPARTMENT

Hospital emergency departments are designed to care for people in a medical crisis, and the life-and-death atmosphere can drive the autonomic nervous systems of everyone involved towards sympathetic activation. Even when the patient's condition is not life-threatening, the pressure of this environment can cause ED providers to skimp on communication in order to speed up treatment. But good communication is even more important in an emergency, when the task of the provider is to "connect quickly with the patient and family, help to calm them as much as possible, and provide the necessary information clearly, succinctly, and compassionately" (Thompson, 2018, p. 139). Taking a breath, accepting the state of the patient, and attending to the patient's needs will send the signals of safety needed to quiet jangled nerves. The ED provider connects with the patient in a moment of professional intimacy. Acting in ways that foster greater connection and communication can provide a restorative balm to physicians and other providers as well. Consider, for example, the experience of a young child in the ED.

> Jaxson, a 9-year-old Black child, was horsing around, excited that tomorrow was the last day of the school year. Although he enjoyed school, for him being outdoors was a special kind of heaven. Happily stirred up and silly, Jaxson was chasing the cat around his bedroom, and it wasn't clear whether the cat was enjoying the chase or was simply trying to evade Jaxson's grasp. When the cat ran under the bed, Jaxson dived to catch it before it could disappear. He hit his head on the bed frame, rolled on his side, and yowled so loudly that his mother came running, summoned by the dramatic change in the types of screams coming from the room.
>
> Jaxson was now holding his head with one hand, while he stared wide-eyed in terror at the blood that covered his other hand. When his mother coaxed him to let her see what had happened, she found an L-shaped laceration above his right eyebrow, oozing blood at a brisk clip. Lifting the bedskirt, she saw that the steel side rail was an L-shaped piece of metal, and she knew what had happened.
>
> When she turned back to Jaxson, he was still wide-eyed, breathing deeply and hard, and saying over and over, "What have I done? What have I done!" He was only a little calmer when they arrived at the local emergency department and were quickly checked in.

Four years out of residency, Dr. Norah Austin, a Black physician, was staffing the ED that afternoon. She had attended training on the Polyvagal Theory 6 months earlier and was practicing some of the techniques she had learned. A quick glance at Jaxson told her that he was between fight-or-flight and a chaotic and emotional shutdown state. Mom was taking deep breaths to stay as calm as she could. She was holding Jaxson's hand and looking up at Dr. Austin earnestly. Her facial expressions spoke clearly to Dr. Austin, saying, "Help my son. Make things okay."

Dr. Austin practiced expressing a mixture of empathy and confidence, to convey both that she got how scary this was for them and that she knew how to make it all better. She matched the rhythm of Jaxson's breathing, and heard him say under his breath, "Oh, my God, oh, my God, oh, my God," over and over. In a sort of hoarse whisper, she repeated, "Oh, my, oh, my, oh, my" in time with him, matching his rhythm and intensity. She got down on his level, looked into his eyes and then at his head, keeping up her "Oh, my's." Roger, a white ED nurse, was at her side, ready with a basin of warm saline solution and plenty of sterile gauzes. Using forceps, he picked up a couple of gauzes and gave them to Dr. Austin when she nodded to him. She had told him about her polyvagal training, and he knew to be on the lookout for her to include him in a conversation about Jaxson any minute now.

"This is a brave boy," Dr. Austin said to Roger in a tone of voice that conveyed empathy.

"Sure is," replied Roger, briefly glancing at Jaxson.

"That was a nasty collision he had with his bed," said Dr. Austin. "He was so excited about tomorrow being the last day of school."

"He is so worried that he seriously damaged his head," said Roger empathically.

"Well, and it happened all of a sudden, too," said Dr. Austin. "It must have come as quite a shock! He probably lost his sense of connection with his body. I am glad that it looks like he is reconnecting with himself, now."

"Yes," said Roger. "As you said, he is a brave kid. He made it through the collision with the bed. Now he is making it through getting stitched up, too. He will have lots of stories to tell his friends at school tomorrow."

"Do you think he'll be embarrassed to tell his friends?" asked Dr. Austin.

"Nah, I don't think so. Nothing to be embarrassed about. Sounds like he almost caught that crazy cat, if the bed hadn't jumped out to stop him," said Roger.

By now, Jaxson's breathing had slowed considerably, and a smile was emerging. He watched Dr. Austin and Roger intently as they talked about him and what he was going through.

"Well, ten stitches. And it's all sewn up. Mom, you must be proud of how well your son has done here this afternoon," said Dr. Austin, opening her eyes wide to match Jaxson's.

"I sure am," said Jaxson's mom, as she let out a deep breath. "Thank you both for taking such good care of him."

"We've had a good time with your brave boy," said Dr. Austin. "Take him to his primary care doctor in 7 days so she can take those stitches out."

This situation illustrates that a child may present to the doctor in fight-or-flight for a number of reasons. Jaxson had a combination of mildly dysregulated excitement about the end of school, the sudden pain and shock of hitting his head on the bed frame, and the upset of seeing the large amount of blood that often comes with superficial scalp lacerations. Because he didn't live far from the ED, he was still in fight-or-flight mode when he arrived. Dr. Austin recognized his autonomic state from the training she had received, and she knew that matching the rhythm and intensity of his emotion would communicate to him (and to his amygdala) that she understood his experience on many levels. At this point, he probably paid more attention to her nonverbal communication than to the words she said.

Dr. Austin modeled for her patients and accompanying family members the importance of recognizing their autonomic states and responding appropriately. Responding appropriately means staying emotionally regulated, matching the nonverbal aspects of the patient's experience, and balancing empathy with communication about the seriousness of the situation. Sometimes, allowing the child to seem to overhear a conversation about himself feels safer than being talked to directly. Parents can learn from Dr. Austin just by watching how she handles these situations.

Physicians, advanced practitioners, nurses, and other healthcare providers have many opportunities to show their patients they are safe. They can maintain emotional and physical proximity to the patient, keep an open face, make tolerable eye contact, alter the prosody and cadence of their speech, and if welcomed, use appropriate touch. According to Fenwick and colleagues (2001), even casual chatting at the bedside can affirm the provider's availability and build a sustaining relationship. In addition, the provider anchored in ventral vagal safety can reach down from the top of the ladder and assist the child or parent in interrupting the downward slide and in beginning the climb upward. When there is an ongoing provider-patient relationship, such as in the treatment of a chronic condition like diabetes or cancer, providers may co-regulate patients and parents on multiple occasions, preventing falls down their ladder and helping them move back up. The action of co-regulating another's physiological state exercises and tones their autonomic nervous system. Over time, muscle memory takes over and more time elapses between downward slides, and recovery is faster.

Physiologic state impacts many areas of the doctor-patient interaction. The higher cortical area of the brain works better in the ventral vagal state than in sympathetic or dorsal vagal. Communicating and thinking clearly are crucial activities for patients, parents, and physicians to experience together. If one or more of the parties is down the autonomic ladder, they won't be able to speak effectively, hear accurately, or think clearly. When a physician can help her patient and his parents get into ventral vagal, the physician can better understand what the patient is trying to say and can better help him comprehend the situation. Many people experience going to the doctor with several questions in mind but not remembering half of the questions when they get there. People are often in some degree of fight-or-flight or freeze-shutdown when visiting the doctor, but doctors who put their patients at ease support their movement up the autonomic ladder. Rising into ventral vagal open engagement enhances a patient's cognitive ability to better report symptoms, ask questions, take in data, and understand the implications of what's being discussed. When patients and families are in ventral vagal, they make better decisions.

COLLATERAL DAMAGE: THE PATIENT AND FAMILY TRAUMAS OF BEING THERE

In addition to the sensory overload, medical uncertainties, and suffering of their own child whom they often have to leave, families of seriously ill children are often challenged by the losses suffered by other families with whom they have grown close. Thrown into tight quarters, friendships that would otherwise be unlikely to develop flourish with the common experience of having a sick or distressed child and disrupted family life. When a family one has bonded with under these circumstances loses their child, it's heartbreaking for their medical caregivers. And a bystander family's experience of secondary traumatic stress is distinctly painful and different from the stress of healthcare providers.

Critical care providers often choose their work because they enjoy the high-energy environment. While the agony of failure may loom, they thrive on the frequent successes. Their story arc often peaks after intervention with a healthy child and grateful parents. However, the narrative is different for the parent who learns that someone else's child has died. Bystander parents may be triggered and experience their own challenges attaining a safe place on the autonomic ladder. Some descend into sympathetic activation expressed as survivor guilt, hypervigilance, or heightened anxiety about their own child. Other parents who plunge farther down the autonomic ladder withdraw into hopelessness and despair, beyond the reach of staff or their other supports.

Without violating confidentiality, healthcare providers need to address these potential bystander traumas. A provider, ideally a mental health clinician, can utilize a polyvagal perspective to mitigate the impact of the shock. They can acknowledge the impact of the event for the family members' neuroceptions of danger, empathizing with their sadness for their friends' loss and the fear they have for their own child's well-being. As clinicians help them to cope with their heartache, they can assist the family to understand the pattern of their neuroceptions. Did the event trigger a dive from safety to sympathetic activation? The clinician can then guide and accompany them back up the ladder. Though the clinician can't take their pain away, they can support their return to ventral vagal equilibrium and let them know they are with them in this experience.

THE POLYVAGAL-INFORMED THERAPIST

Therapy starts with the presence of the therapist, which allows clients to neurocept enough safety to embark upon the often frightening journey of self-discovery.
—PAT OGDEN, 2018

Just as the Polyvagal Theory (PVT) informs what happens in healthcare, it has many applications in therapy. PVT can be conceptualized as the framework of a trauma-informed practice, a way of thinking and acting. When therapy is polyvagal-informed, the therapist sees what shuts clients down, what drives their frightened responses, and what, finally, helps them feel safe enough to open up. When clients feel that their environment is safe, they can relax their vigilance enough to direct their attention to what they are experiencing. Sometimes the process of building trust takes minutes; sometimes it takes months. When clients trust the therapist enough to communicate their experiences, the door is open to the psychological change that comes from epistemic trust, which Fonagy and Allison (2014) define as "an individual's willingness to consider new knowledge from another person as trustworthy, generalizable, and relevant to the self" (p. 373).

Deb Dana (2018) describes the science of safety and connection and how to assist clients to identify their unique autonomic responses and view them with compassion. She further demonstrates how to help them learn to tune these responses on their own and with the support of others. Clients end up with "[a]n autonomic nervous system that co-regulates and self-regulates with ease" (p. 191). As they develop an embodied sense of safety, they can discover the profound ventral vagal joy that comes from connecting to loved ones.

Dana's model encourages people to Befriend, Attend, and Shape the ANS (2018, 2020). Dana (2020) says, "*Befriending* [emphasis added] establishes the safety to feel autonomic states, identify individual aspects of each state, and activate and maintain curiosity and compassion during the process" (p. 41). Therapists and other providers can assist children and parents to befriend their autonomic reactions by gently pointing out shifts in their state of mind and asking in a non-judgmental way what they are experiencing now. Sometimes it helps to make an educated guess about the state to get the ball rolling. If a child suddenly gets quiet after chattering joyfully, the therapist might slowly whisper in a conspiratorial tone, "You stopped talking when your mom mentioned that you have a test on Friday. Most kids I know don't really like tests. Tests can be pretty scary, huh?" This brief comment communicates to the child that it's okay to feel nervous and gives them permission to talk about the experience.

As discussed in Chapter 6, when clients start to understand that their autonomic reactions are their nervous systems' attempt to protect them, they can feel empathy and compassion towards themselves for what they have experienced, the process of befriending their own autonomic nervous systems. From this position of self-compassion, they can deepen their awareness of what they feel at this time and in this moment. Emotions and affective states become less bewildering. For example, Roberta is a 5-year-old Native American girl with leukemia who sees a therapist for support. The therapist, Winona Iron Crow, is the member of the same tribe as Roberta. She noticed that Roberta had significant fight-or-flight responses to her treatment procedures. Winona helped Roberta to see that, by slowly breathing through the surges of adrenaline energy, she can actually ride those waves and feel stronger when they subside. *Attending*, the next stage of this model, is the development of a broader awareness of how one's autonomic states change over time (Dana 2018, 2020). Dana (2020) explains, "Helping your clients learn to first notice and then follow the changes that happen as they move within a state or between states brings attention to the ways the autonomic nervous system responds to meet their individual needs" (p. 70). Once Roberta befriended her nervous system, Winona helped her and her mother draw a map of those places where she felt safe and where she felt in danger. Roberta's mom, Adrienne, recognized that Roberta gets nervous every time they reached the freeway because it is the route they take to the oncology clinic. Just knowing that Roberta's fear response was predictable gave both Roberta and Adrienne an increased sense of control.

In the third phase of Dana's model, therapists and parents can help children *Shape* their autonomic nervous systems (2018, 2020). For example, after working with Roberta and her therapist on the map-making activity, Adrienne pretended that the drive to clinic was a roller-coaster ride in an effort to shape Roberta's responses. Roberta's mom makes the clicking sound of an ascending car, then starts a long "Whoaaa" as they get on the freeway. Roberta raises her arms and shouts with delight, "No hands!" She is not afraid of her autonomic responses and can now play with them.

Like the infants in Chapter 1 experiencing opiate withdrawal who had to learn to let their caregivers console them, Roberta has had to learn to let her mother and her therapist accompany her through frightening challenges. Beforehand, when she reacted to challenges with sympathetic arousal and dorsal shutdown, she was alone in her autonomic reactions. Now there is an emotional space in which she can feel her caregivers' and loved ones' presence as a safe and secure base.

Dan Hughes' model (2018), Dyadic Developmental Psychotherapy (DDP), is a polyvagal-informed family therapy approach to treating children whose reactions to early traumas have blocked their ability to trust (Baylin & Hughes, 2016; Hughes & Baylin, 2012). Many of these children also experienced neglect and disrupted relationships, were removed from their homes, and are often now being raised by foster or adoptive parents. Hughes and his collaborator, Jon Baylin, note that traumatized children, often locked in sympathetic or dorsal vagal states, regard most people as dangerous. You don't trust people when you think they're dangerous. These children don't trust their new parents, even when they are good people who wouldn't hurt them, a condition that Baylin and Hughes (2016) call "blocked trust" (p. 46). Hughes (2018) says "The inability of a child to trust even the best parents immeasurably damages the self and the capacity to experience nurturance and a reciprocal relationship" (p. 245). He points out "infants discover who they are—their original sense of self—in the eyes, face, voice, gestures, and touch of their mother and father" (p. 6). However, the fear and anguish that children feel when their caregivers are angry, rejecting, and abusive cause them to shut down, blocking this self-discovery process. Because shutting down enabled them to survive physical and emotional suffering, they resist efforts to change this response, even when they get new caregivers. In a dependable and nurturing home, opening up and allowing themselves to be loved and cared for would be a better strategy, but this requires a complete transformation in their safety-seeking strategies.

Hughes (2018) developed his recommendation for adopting a Playful, Accepting, Curious, and Empathic (PACE) attitude as a powerful antidote to deep-seated mistrust (Baylin & Hughes, 2016). A *Playful* attitude, when used at the right time, communicates that it is safe to engage with others and even experience joy, not to mention serving as a neural exercise (Porges, 2015b). Nonjudgmental *Acceptance* of the child's manifold thoughts, feelings, hopes, and fears (but not necessarily behaviors) creates a psychologically safe space for experiences to be embodied. Through *Curiosity*, the caregiver demonstrates that what the child feels and thinks is important and worthy of consideration and protection. Finally, with *Empathy*, they accompany their child through their distress, comforting them with their regulated presence. In DDP, any ruptures in this understanding and attuned attitude are repaired with additional empathy for the distress that the rupture caused the child. The PACE attitude builds the child's ability to trust that his parents will not harm him but will comfort and support him instead. DDP works because it helps children allow their parents to assist their development, as parents do when a child is not traumatized.

WORKING WITH SHAME AND ANGER

Liam, a white 9-year-old, was sitting on the couch next to Nana, his white paternal grandmother who was his guardian as well. Nana brought him to therapy hoping the therapy could help get Liam's anger under control. Nana had tried to weather the storms of anger as long as she could, but she now realized that it had gotten way beyond what she could manage. She worried Liam would hurt her or someone else.

Liam's father, a white man, was only 17 years old when Liam was born, and Liam's mother, a white woman, was just 18 years old. Both were initially excited to have a baby and raise a son, but the actual responsibility of caring for a child soon overwhelmed them both. Over time their efforts to take care of him diminished, and frequently they left him strapped in his car seat in front of a television while they slept, fought, or did chores.

By the time Liam was three, and his younger brother

Toby was one, social services filed charges of neglect, and the boys were placed in foster care, where they lived for the next 4 years. At age seven, Liam was extremely angry and aggressive, and the foster home gave its 30 days' notice that it would no longer be able to care for him and his brother. Nana agreed to become their caregiver. She had visited with them off and on over the years and felt they had a good connection. In addition, she was 3 years into recovery from an alcohol addiction and felt that the counseling she had done would help her with her grandsons.

Liam was initially calmer when he went to live at Nana's house. However, by the time he was nine, the extreme anger returned, and he would hit Nana, her husband, and Toby, his younger brother. Recently, Liam had thrown a heavy glass paperweight through their sliding glass door and punched a number of holes in the walls of their house. One day Liam scared Nana by choking Toby, and she was terrified to think what might have happened if she hadn't been there to stop him. Nana called her counselor, who recommended that Nana call Darryl, a white DDP therapist who was skilled in working with rageful, aggressive children. On the phone, Nana told Darryl about Liam's violent temper, but also said she felt he had a good heart. Liam and Nana were sitting in Darryl's office.

After some preliminary conversation, Liam told Darryl, "I get mad to the point that I hit people and yell," then hung his head. Darryl asked more questions about his anger, but Liam was silent, finally saying, "I don't want to talk about it." In the past, when kids had refused to talk about their feelings, it was upsetting to Darryl. He might have tried several strategies to get them to talk, like bribing them with candy, telling them that he could help them if they would just let him, or even threatening them with some vague form of punishment if they didn't comply. None of these things ever helped, and they just left him and the kid feeling frustrated and miserable.

Over the past 2 and a half years, Darryl had embedded both DDP and Polyvagal Theory in his work with the children in his practice. Citing Deb Dana, his supervisor taught him, "It is a ventral vagal state and a neuroception of safety that bring the possibility for connection, curiosity, and change" (2018, p. 7). He also learned that traumatized children often feel shame, the pressing sense that there is something profoundly wrong with them.

Darryl knew that Liam probably felt ashamed of his anger because it seemed out of proportion to what was happening around him. Furthermore, it upset Nana, and he knew she was trying hard to help him. Darryl was curious about Liam's experience. "What's that like for you, to get mad to the point that you hit people and yell?"

Liam looked at him, sizing him up, trying to see if this was a trick, thinking about what he might say and how Darryl might respond.

Darryl said, "No, really. I am just interested in what that's like for you. Some kids just space out after they get mad like that, because those feelings they were having were so big. Some kids really get down on themselves, thinking to themselves that they're a bad kid. Some kids just get really depressed and hopeless and feel like giving up, like dying would be better than what just happened."

Liam looked out from under his bangs, his head cocked to one side. "Yeah, all of that," he replied softly. Darryl said that it must be pretty rough, to get mad like that, then to have all those feelings.

Liam kept looking at Darryl without saying anything, but his shoulders dropped a little, and his breathing got a little deeper. Darryl's curiosity about Liam's experience was helping Liam to feel a little safer. At the neurobiological level, Darryl's safe connection has lifted Liam out of dorsal vagal shutdown. After a few minutes, Liam was better able to register what Darryl was saying. After making more guesses about Liam's experience, which helped him to relax further, Darryl felt Liam was ready for a bit of exploration.

Watching Liam's face to gauge if what he was saying was making Liam nervous, Darryl said, "It's such a yucky feeling to feel like you're a bad kid. That feeling can just make you want to curl up into a ball and disappear." No sign of tensing, no looking away. "If you ARE a bad kid, then you're just kind of stuck with it. You just have to get used to the fact that you're a bad kid, and there's nothing you can do about it. What a raw deal, to find out that you're a bad kid."

Darryl let out a long and heavy sigh. Liam softened even further. "Let me ask you a question, Liam. If one of my superpowers is dissolving a kid's feeling, and I can dissolve the feeling that you are a bad kid, just make it all break up into littler and littler pieces and make it float away, how would you feel then? What would that be like? Wouldn't that be nice?"

Liam nodded, and his shoulders relaxed even further, but he still didn't say anything.

Darryl held Liam's gaze. "What if you didn't feel like a bad kid anymore, and it was so long since you felt that way, that you kind of even forgot what that was like for you? Do you think you would still get mad like that? That you would get mad and hit and yell and feel all terrible inside?"

Liam shook his head, eyes widening in wonder instead of fear.

"Do you think that your anger would be so much of a problem?" Darryl asked, his eyes wide with wonder now, too.

So loudly that it shocked them both a little, Liam said, "I wouldn't. I wouldn't get angry anymore. If I wasn't feeling so terrible, I don't think I would get angry very much at all!"

With his excitement matching Liam's, Darryl said, "I bet people tell you that you have an anger problem, but they don't know about all this. They don't know that if your bad feelings about yourself all dissolved, you probably wouldn't get angry very much at all! They don't know that about you."

Darryl slapped both hands to his cheeks quickly enough that they made a little smacking sound. "Liam, you know what?! I don't think you have a problem with anger at all! I think you have a problem with feeling like a bad kid."

Now it was Liam's turn to let out a long, heavy sigh. Liam looked up at Nana's face to see tears streaming down.

A polyvagal-informed DDP therapist knows that the patient's neuroception of safety or danger is a continuous, out-of-awareness process that determines the patient's state of receptivity or defensiveness. The therapist himself engages in a monitoring process that parallels neuroception, observing nonverbal cues of the child's autonomic state and adjusting his own nonverbal behavior in response to what he observes. Because therapy requires conversations about difficult topics, especially with children who have experienced traumatic events, the therapist does more than send signals of safety. He must also know when to introduce a painful theme and when to retreat and allow the child to direct the flow.

In this example, Darryl creates an understanding with Liam that the goal of their therapy is to address his feelings that he is a bad kid. From talking with Nana, Darryl suspected that Liam responded to his rageful episodes by experiencing shame, a humiliating feeling that there is something fundamentally wrong with him. By understanding Liam's experience of shame and empathizing with how difficult that experience must be, Darryl joined Liam in that painful and lonely experience and helped make the experience bearable because it was shared.

REGULATING ONESELF TO REGULATE OTHERS

Helena, a Latina therapist trained in PVT, was doing an in-home session with Sam, a white 4-year-old she had worked with for several months. She was sitting on the floor, playing with Sam when Sam's mom came into the room with Beau, their puppy. Beau bounded through the door straight at the therapist and nipped her on the back of the head. Helena put her hand up to see that she was okay, then turned to the mother, who was saying, "I'm so sorry, I'm so sorry, I'm so sorry" in a frightened tone. Even though Helena was a little shaken by the charging puppy , she did her best to hold it together and let the family know she was okay. She said she wasn't seriously hurt, and she emphasized how scary that was for everyone. She turned to Sam and noticed that he was staring at her with a blank expression, so she said loudly and dramatically with a lot of musicality in her voice, "Wow! Beau must have thought I was hurting you! He was really protecting you. He was really keeping you safe." After a few minutes of talking like this, Sam started responding, and they made plans for their next session.

When Helena got in her car, she allowed herself to experience what had just happened. She realized she was trembling a little and allowed her body to shudder until that reaction subsided. She called her supervisor, told him what happened, explained she was still a little shaken up, and asked to be excused from the rest of her day's appointments so she could center herself.

This example shows how the Polyvagal Theory can guide a clinician to use her self-regulation and state of being as therapeutic instruments to help the family maintain their own self-regulation. *State begets state.* Self-regulation begets regulation of others. The dog's threat, as startling as it might be, is also an opportunity to demonstrate to the mother that self-control is possible and valuable. If this mother is just starting to learn about the Polyvagal Theory, this event may provide a vivid touchstone to which Helena and the mom can return as they explore the effect of the parent's autonomic state on the child's autonomic state.

BECOMING MORE PRESENT: CHILDREN MIGHT HAVE TO FIGHT BEFORE THEY CAN ENGAGE

The social engagement system is the optimal zone for doing psychological work. In social engagement, a person feels connected and safe enough to embody their experiences. Correspondingly, Dan Siegel (2012) says people have a "window of tolerance" (pp. 281–286), a range of emotional intensities that they can experience without becoming dysregulated (see Chapter 2). Within this range, they can reflect on their thoughts and feelings and can pay attention to urges without acting on them. Siegel says that when we leave the window of tolerance, we go into chaotic hyperarousal or a state of rigid thinking and shutdown. As depicted in Figure 2.2, these states correlate to fight-or-flight and freeze-shutdown respectively, and the optimal arousal zone within the window of tolerance corresponds to a state of ventral vagal social engagement.

Many psychiatric symptoms are rooted in intolerable experiences. A therapist needs to be alert to their client's state to help them stay near the edge of their comfort zone, the edge of their window of tolerance, without going into fight-or-flight or shutdown, so that they can stay present to more difficult experiences. The therapist supports the client to practice making the intolerable tolerable, thus widening the window of tolerance. A wider window of tolerance means more opportunity for ventral vagal social engagement.

Consider Waris, a 13-year-old son of Somali immigrants, admitted to a psychiatric residential treatment center because he hurt people and destroyed things at his house when he became emotionally dysregulated. Prior to moving to the US at age 3, Waris witnessed violence and death, and his family lived in fear. His father noted that even by that young age Waris tried to remain stoic in the face of distressing situations. At the residential facility, his team noted that he often dissociated when other children were dysregulated and screaming, and also when things got loud for happier reasons, such as when there was exuberant shouting in the gym. The team understood his dissociative shutdown as an attempt to cope with inescapable suffering, a dorsal vagal phenomenon. He checked out when things got too intense. In addition, they appreciated that Waris blew up when his anguish was too much for his dissociation to contain.

The team maintained a steady Playful, Accepting, Curious, and Empathic (PACE) attitude (Baylin & Hughes, 2016) to help Waris stay present to his surroundings and inner experiences, especially those at the edge of what he could tolerate. Their increased signals of safety co-regulated him while he navigated these turbulent boundary waters. The team's intention was to strengthen Waris's ability to observe and articulate distressing feelings safely and with support, so that he would not need to use dissociation as a retreat and sanctuary. Indeed, they noticed that, through these efforts, Waris became more connected with himself, his experiences, and things going on around him. In turn, his fits of emotional flooding diminished in their intensity as well. However, as the outbursts improved, he paradoxically became ill-humored and irritable almost all the time.

Waris's parents and insurance company were concerned that his irritability meant that he was regressing. The team, while understanding their concern, explained their clinical impression that Waris's ill-tempered dysphoria indicated that he was now in a continuous state of fight-or-flight, a sign that he was making progress up the autonomic ladder. The team had observed that children who used dissociation as a strategy to suppress their destabilizing emotions often go through a period of sustained irritability as they become more present.

At first, like Waris's parents and insurance company, the team worried that when these children's moods worsened, it meant that the treatment was no longer working. However, they also noted that these children were simultaneously more able to allow their caregivers to co-regulate their emotions, an encouraging sign that the children were becoming more trusting in spite of their deteriorating moods. Eventually they recognized that the irritability was a manifestation of sympathetic fight-or-flight. They concluded that children who had been in prolonged dorsal vagal shutdown may need to pass through an extended period of sympathetic activation as they climb the autonomic ladder on their way to developing self-regulation skills.

The team anticipated that Waris's emotional state would improve, as they had seen with other children, if they continued to support him with the PACE attitude. Over the next two months, as the team predicted, Waris's irritability decreased substantially. He felt more comfortable letting the staff and his parents co-regulate his upsets. Additionally, he could more easily participate in spontaneous fun activities with the staff and other children and with his family members as well. Having made it through sympathetic activation to more a stable, resourceful, and enjoyable social engagement, the intensity of Waris's blowups subsided to the point where his parents felt that they could safely manage them at home. On the day of his discharge, the staff and other children on the unit celebrated his hard work and success.

A few weeks after discharge, Waris's family called the residential therapist to report that Waris had been doing well at home. He still got angry at times, but now he could ask his parents for their help in getting settled down. Thanks to the team's crucial awareness that irritability was a paradoxical sign of improvement, Waris had the support he needed to climb through sympathetic activation as he traveled from dorsal to ventral vagal.

THE POLYVAGAL-INFORMED TEACHER

Redmond didn't know that Michael, then 9, was haunted by memories no one had shared with her. So, she did what any teacher would do: She sent him to the principal's office.
—ROCHELLE RILEY, 2020

If you spend more than a few minutes talking with teachers, you hear them describe the tension between meeting the academic needs of their students and meeting their social-emotional needs. *Do I teach them math, or do I help them discover that they are an okay kid?* many wonder. Helping children move into ventral vagal so that they can socially engage is a prerequisite for teaching cognitive skills and abilities. Polyvagal-informed teachers understand that, just as one can't meditate in a war zone, their students can't learn their school lessons while in fight-or-flight or freeze-shutdown.

Tavia Redmond, the 24-year veteran teacher in the quote above, is repeatedly asked to teach children who have experienced horrific things. Unfortunately, teachers in her state receive no systematic training in how to support these children. Another teacher from that state, after learning that one of her students tried to kill herself, said, "My circle of concern is huge. But my circle of resources and what I can do . . . is minuscule" (Riley, 2020). Where will the resources come from to help teachers in this situation help children? The Polyvagal Theory identifies a resource that has not yet been widely utilized: accessing support to bring the social engagement system online.

Ms. Redmond sent Michael to the principal's office because he screamed that he hated her, screamed at the other students, and then ran away. He was fighting, then fleeing. If someone had taught the teacher the Polyvagal Theory, she would have recognized that Michael was dysregulated and become curious about why he felt so unsafe. She would have known that a nervous system that's focused on danger can't focus on learning. Given Ms. Redmond's dedication to Michael's success (Riley, 2020), it is certain that she would have embraced Polyvagal Theory and used its insights to soothe Michael's nervous system. Without that kind of understanding, she has no recourse other than sending him out of the room. She didn't know that she needed to help him feel safe.

Helping kids feel safe serves two major educational goals: (1) Move them toward learning; and (2) move them toward emotional well-being. Understanding that humans learn best when they're in the social engagement system suggests that creating safe environments and a *felt sense* of safety needs to be a primary goal of education. Just as you prepare a kid to do multiplication by teaching them addition first, you prepare a child to learn anything by first communicating to their autonomic nervous system that it's safe to relax, let their guard down, and focus on learning something new.

In the fight-or-flight state, a child's mind is hypervigilant and alert for danger. In this state, survival functions are sharpened, and nonsurvival functions are suppressed. Pupils dilate to let in more light and better detect potential threats. Blood flow to skeletal muscles is increased. On the other hand, digestion, which isn't necessary for survival, is suppressed. Thinking and decision making are also suppressed because careful consideration of a situation may prevent survival when action needs to happen instantly.

A student in the classroom who arrives in fight-or-flight mode is looking to see what might hurt her next. The teacher's attempts to get her attention will be viewed by her nervous system as an interference with its ability to survive. Therefore, the nervous system will do its best to block out the lesson that the teacher is trying to teach. This can look like an attention deficit disorder. Instead, teachers may find it more helpful to think of it as a *safety deficit disorder*. This child may be able to pay attention if she has a felt sense of safety. This child needs someone, like Mrs. Dupree, below, who understands the neurobiology of safety and threat.

Creating Emotional Safety in the Service of Learning

Mrs. Dupree is a white teacher who has discovered the value of applying Polyvagal Theory in the classroom. She knows that a nervous system that's focused on danger can't focus on learning. The nervous system first needs to know that it's safe. Mrs. Dupree says, "My goal with my kids is to make sure they have 7 hours in which they feel safe. Maybe before school they got yelled at and after school they got beaten. But at least while they're here with me, they're safe" (personal communication, January 29, 2020). Mrs. Dupree explains:

Kids arrive in the morning in a heightened state. So I try to help them get calmed down first thing. If we can start the day off in a calmer state, the whole day goes better. Sometimes I use music; sometimes I turn the lights down; sometimes I walk through the classroom and just lightly touch each of the kids. I change the tone of my voice. If one thing doesn't work, I'll try another. Teachers are taught to do things a certain way, but we need to be flexible. We need to try something different if what we are trying isn't working.

Emotional well-being in the classroom looks like a child whose basic needs are met— she's fed, in clean clothes, has a place to live, and is not in danger. She has a sense of self-agency and self-efficacy, meaning that she has some idea about what she wants and how to get it. She has the ability to collaborate with other students in games, social interactions, and group learning activities, as well as to collaborate with the teacher in completing assignments. Her mood is generally positive, and when it does shift, it tends to be a smooth shift with a clear reason for the change. The child can put her experience into words and feel comfortable expressing her experiences to others.

Children who arrive in a dysregulated state can behave in numerous ways. They may be resistant to following instructions. They may not be paying attention to what the teacher is saying. They may be annoying or distracting the other children. They may be completely withdrawn and disconnected from what's happening around them. They may be okay until they get a cognitive challenge, which to their ANS can be a signal of danger that throws them into anger, aggression, or running out of the room. One difficult math worksheet can throw an easily dysregulated child completely off balance.

Like healthcare providers who have not traditionally seen

themselves as addressing emotional well-being, teachers may not have seen their job as sending safety signals. If a teacher has a classroom with kids who are in the fight-or-flight stage, what are her options? If she doesn't address their felt sense of safety, she won't be able to teach what she needs to teach. So for the individual teacher, the question that needs to be answered is, "How can I address safety to help the children learn?"

The State Is the Signal

Ms. Larson, who is white, is another teacher who incorporates Polyvagal Theory. She vividly remembers the first day a Black child we'll call Saretha came into her classroom (personal communication, May 19, 2020). At the end of the day, Saretha stopped doing what Ms. Larson asked and stared at the floor instead. No amount of playful cajoling could motivate her to reconnect with Ms. Larson. Because this was a therapeutic classroom, there were aides present and another teacher had just wandered in. They were discussing whether the child might just be asserting her will by refusing to answer, sending the message that she didn't have to comply if she didn't want to.

Since Ms. Larson was educated in PVT, she was confident she recognized the signs of a dorsal vagal shutdown. Looking back on the day, she could see how Saretha had gotten progressively overwhelmed until she was immobilized. Ms. Larson explained what she was seeing to the aides and the other teacher, and she noticed a shift in their state: from being irritated with the child to feeling empathy for the anxious misery the child was enduring. Reflecting on the experience, Ms. Larson acknowledged that she didn't feel completely confident in how to help a child transition up the autonomic ladder from shutdown. Still, she believed this child was suffering, which led her to treat Saretha with kindness. At least,

Ms. Larson said, she didn't make things worse by criticizing her for being uncooperative.

Ms. Larson structured her school day to start with a breathing exercise she learned at a conference sponsored by her district. A speaker described the Polyvagal Theory and how to strengthen a ventral vagal response by spending more time in exhalation. The speaker also described neuroception, and Ms. Larson explained her understanding: "The kids' [neuroceptive] systems are always going. I need to be always alert to them. The children aren't just able to turn off the neuroception and listen to my math lesson. I could fight that, or just understand what is happening and help them with it" (personal communication, May 19, 2020).

Like Mrs. Dupree and our fictional characters, Dr. Austin and Darryl, Ms. Larson also learned the importance of creating a feeling of safety. To help Saretha feel secure, Ms. Larson told her she could do what she needed to do to be comfortable. If she needed to sit quietly in the corner for a few days, that would be fine. If she needed to take breaks from the schoolwork, that would be fine, too. Ms. Larson knew pushing Saretha too hard would drive her back into shutdown, and she would never learn in that frame of mind.

Polyvagal Theory tells us autonomic state prepares us energetically to meet the needs of our current situation, but it serves a second function as well. Our autonomic state communicates our neuroception of the environment to others. My social engagement signals that I have detected safety. My sympathetic or dorsal vagal state signals that I sense danger. If someone faints in a crowd, others almost always gasp in unison.

Ms. Larson's main goal was to establish a safe connection with each child in her room. She knew that her autonomic state would signal Saretha's autonomic state, and she aimed to communicate a sense of curiosity, remembering that, as Levine noted

(2010), "playful curiosity [is] one of the prima facie 'antidotes' for trauma. Curious exploration, pleasure, and trauma cannot coexist in the nervous system; neurologically, they contradict one another" (p. 175). Thinking about how to safely connect with Saretha, Ms. Larson noticed Saretha digging for worms during recess and decided to join her. She made small comments and watched for Saretha's reaction. "Oh, man, I hope we find some worms!" Ms. Larson said. Saretha just stared at her with a puzzled look as if to say, "I thought being a girl who liked digging for worms was weird enough. Now there are two of us?!" Ms. Larson had become the object of Saretha's curiosity, and Saretha responded by continuing to dig for worms.

THE RESOURCES WERE WITHIN US ALL ALONG

Thinking again about the lack of resources available to assist educators brings us back to the benefits of incorporating Polyvagal Theory into the classroom. The behavioral hierarchy of the autonomic nervous system, when working well, matches the right resources for varying degrees of safety and danger. Dorsal vagal collapse maximally conserves resources under conditions of threat to life and also avoids predators. Sympathetic fight-or-flight states mobilize massive resources for survival when danger is imminent. The ventral vagal social engagement system provides resources for collaboration, cooperation, creativity, and play.

Because state begets state, social engagement begets social engagement, giving even a discouraged teacher additional resources, such as her curiosity and engagement with the children. Her safe engagement can awaken their social engagement as well, allowing the ventral vagal joys of childhood to pour forth. To find that buried treasure, the teacher must see the compelling camouflage of the dorsal vagal state for what it is, an attempt to avoid predators by appearing dead. The teacher must see that it's the children's autonomic state that is discouraging her, not the children themselves.

To restore her students' vitality, the teacher must also recognize that dorsal vagal states are mostly temporary, that her students are not permanently locked into a hollow emptiness. She must remember that, just as animals in a state of freeze-shutdown will return to life once the danger has passed, her students can do the same. It may, however, be a slower process. Her regulated state can help her kindle her students into a ventral vagal state of vibrant connection, if only she can sustain her social engagement. Baylin and Hughes (2016) observe that when two people are together their brain states tend to resonate and synchronize with each other. In general, when two people engage with each other from two different autonomic states, whoever can hold their state longest will bring the other to that state.

Over time, the children in Ms. Larson's class relaxed, learned, and enjoyed themselves. They saw what Ms. Larson hoped they would see. Instead of projecting their fears and mistrust, they saw she was an actual person just like each of them , and she enjoyed spending time with them. They became *socially engaged*, embedded in a delicious connection that delights, satisfies, excites and soothes, all at the same time. Because this all makes sense at a deep level of our being, it also makes sense that Ms. Larson would wear her tennis shoes on Fridays, because that was "tag day," the day she joined the children in a rowdy and hilarious game of tag.

WHEN PROFESSIONALS EMBRACE BRAIN AND SOUL

When we aim for universal and generalized social engagement, we treat people with dignity and reverence. We are aware that beneath most any kind of surliness is a softer, more human center. In contrast, focusing on others' intimidating demeanor makes us defensive, and we won't want to look beneath the surface. Furthermore, our defensiveness kindles the embers of the other's defensiveness. Porges says a compassionate perspective sees the contextual root of a person's irritability (personal communication, 2019, October 31), enabling us to discover the wound that is being protected. If we treat that wound with care, the disquieting defenses often drop, revealing a kindhearted receptivity and reciprocity.

The professional who is authentically interested in a child and their parent demonstrates how much the child and parent matter. When the child and parent feel that, their trust awakens. They can then relax and place their trust in the professional's hands, because they know, no matter what, they will find safety there. Even if the professional makes a mistake that sets their progress back a bit, the child and parent will rest easy because they know that the professional wants the best for them. They will come to understand that they are involved in a human endeavor, and human endeavors are sometimes messy, but also succulent and consequential. The professional who connects with soul enlivens and quickens the soul of the other, whether it is their patient, client, student, or the parent of a child. They enter that domain where two souls are revealed to each other in their blemishes and glory.

When a technical endeavor, for instance, to save a life, heal a psyche, or create a path to learn, is introduced into a soulful relationship, there may be tension at first. For now there is not only heart and soul but also a second thing: brain and skill. When the tension is held for sufficient time, a third thing arises that lives in a tender, profound, and mysterious space. To operate, literally as a surgeon, or figuratively by practicing one's profession, in that space is to be in a state of flow and of grace. To live from one's heart and soul and brain and skill is to be fully and gratefully human.

CHAPTER 8

The Polyvagal-Informed Organization: Building a Safe Environment to Nurture Optimal Human Functioning

I'd like to give you all an invisible gift. A gift of a silent minute to think about those who have helped you become who you are today . . . Whomever you've been thinking about, imagine how grateful they must be, that during your silent times, you remember how important they are to you. It's not the honors and the prizes and the fancy outsides of life which ultimately nourish our souls. It's the knowing that we can be trusted. That we never have to fear the truth. That the bedrock of our lives, from which we make our choices, is very good stuff.
—FRED ROGERS, 2002

An organization's culture has a profound impact on the functioning of its members and the people with whom they work. The Polyvagal Theory says that people need safety and connection to function at optimal levels. Therefore, a polyvagal-informed organization will actively and systemically present the people it touches with features of safety to optimize social behavior and to shift people's neurophysiological state to one geared to be creative and generative (Porges, 2015a). This chapter shows organization leaders what it means to be a polyvagal-informed organization and why that is important. We explore the key actions that move organizations toward greater awareness of autonomic state and more time spent in ventral vagal. We examine how a polyvagal-informed organization approaches training, supervision, and structure and how it supports the repair of relationships when trust is difficult.

WHAT IS A POLYVAGAL-INFORMED ORGANIZATION?

An organization is polyvagal-informed when it operates on two premises: (1) a person's autonomic state has a profound effect on their functioning; and (2) state can be influenced by the relationships, environment, and culture in which the person is embedded (Porges, 2001). In this paradigm, leaders of polyvagal-informed organizations no longer consider the autonomic state to be solely an out-of-awareness phenomenon beyond their influence. Autonomic state determines what people pay attention to, perceive, or understand. Autonomic state controls whether thinking is rigid or flexible. Autonomic state governs the degree to which people are able to communicate, collaborate, cooperate, and coordinate. This knowledge motivates the polyvagal-informed organization to move as many people as possible into the ventral vagal state, to maximize their ability to work well together and support the children and families they serve.

To illustrate these principles, let's imagine a psychiatric residential treatment facility for children and adolescents called the Good Hands Residential Center. Their motto is, "When you are at Good Hands, *you are in good hands.*" Although the staff know it's a little corny, they like their motto because they work hard to create this feeling. Their CEO, Lanelle Williams, a Black woman, is tracing the steps a family would take as they drop off their child. She knows how important it is to take a walk and observe how safe she feels along the path patients take as they arrive. On her way to the parking lot where she begins to trace this path, she reflects on what families experience even before they get to the facility. When families call Good Hands, the referral coordinator fields their calls. Families tell Lanelle that the referral coordinator goes out of her way to answer their questions and make sure they understand the program. Now Lanelle is looking at the sign they recently put up in the Good Hands driveway, "You made it! You are now in Good Hands." Even though she was intimately involved in the process to create a welcoming sign that makes people feel safe, she notices herself smiling and relaxing. She hopes seeing the sign also helps Good Hands's families. A white woman and boy get out of their car and look around nervously. The CEO says, "Hey, friends. Can I help you find something?" The woman says, "I am bringing my foster son Peyton to stay here for a while. Do you know where we should go?"

"Great," the CEO thinks to herself. "I can follow them and see how they respond to our program." Aloud, she says, "Sure thing. I am just heading to the intake office myself. I will walk you there. My name is Lanelle, and I am the CEO here." Bending down to look the boy in the eye, she says, "I just heard a boy named Peyton was coming today. We've been expecting you." Then she stands to face the woman. "What is your name, ma'am?" Peyton's foster mom introduces herself as Marsha and thanks Lanelle for helping them. Lanelle asks how far they have come and how their trip was. Marsha says that they came from a rural community 2 and a half hours away, and they don't get into the city much. Lanelle asks Marsha how she does with city driving, and Marsha says it stresses her out. Lanelle confides that even though she has lived here for 25 years, she still hasn't gotten used to the traffic.

Lanelle enjoys meeting people and getting to know them, and this quality has made her a respected leader at Good Hands. As she learned about the Polyvagal Theory, she realized she has always enjoyed putting people at ease. Putting people at ease is another way of saying that she is helping Marsha feel that Good Hands is a safe place for her and her foster son. Lanelle continues her casual chat with Peyton on the way to the intake building and learns that he is 11 years old and a big fan of Star Wars.

Inside the building, decorated with large photos of children and adults laughing and playing together, they meet Victoria, who is responsible for the intake process. Victoria, a Latina woman, asks how they are doing and whether they are thirsty or hungry. She shows them the restroom, knowing that nervous families often don't pay much attention to bodily needs as they travel. When they come out, she gives Peyton the peanut butter and jelly sandwich and a bottle of water he had requested. She hands Marsha the cup of coffee she wanted. Then Victoria sits down with them to explain how the program works— including the names of the people on their treatment team. When she asks Marsha if she has questions, Marsha wants to know when she can call and talk with Peyton. Soon, the nurse shows up to give Peyton a physical exam in the room next door. Because he's a little anxious about separating from his foster mother, the nurse suggests that Marsha let him hold her car keys so he will know that she won't leave him when he's not looking. The nurse takes Peyton, and Victoria walks Marsha through the various forms and notices required to admit a child to a residential program.

When the forms are signed and the nurse has brought Peyton back, Victoria meets with Marsha and Peyton together again. This time she focuses on learning some things about Peyton. She asks what foods he likes and doesn't like, what he likes to do for fun, and what his favorite color is. She wants to know who lives in the house, if he has any pets, and what other animal he would get if he could. She asks what he likes about school and what he doesn't like. Then she asks him to describe himself in three words. He says, "fast, friend, and 'the Force.'" Later, Victoria will email Peyton's responses to his treatment team so they will have a picture of Peyton that's much broader than the problems that brought him to Good Hands for treatment.

Lanelle, the CEO, decided to keep looking at Good Hands through the eyes of Marsha and Peyton, so she hung around the intake office. In the meantime, she got to see and hear some of Victoria's conversations with the mom and boy and to see how the nurse helped Peyton feel more secure by holding his mom's car keys. She overheard several of the receptionist's phone calls. A dad called to ask for help reaching his child's therapist after he missed their scheduled phone call. A staff member's partner called to leave a message about picking up their child. The UPS driver dropped off a package. With each of these interactions, the receptionist was warm and friendly. She made empathic comments ("Everyone misses an appointment sometimes"), supported the staff member by helping him solve his childcare problem, and continued her friendship with the UPS driver by asking about his son who was graduating from high school after having a hard time. Lanelle tells herself that the receptionist's congeniality sends just the right message to people entering the front door of Good Hands: we are approachable and neighborly.

Nadeem, the unit manager and son of Syrian immigrants, comes to show Peyton and Marsha where he will be living. Lanelle walks with them to continue her exploration of the progress Good Hands was making in moving people into a ventral vagal state. Nadeem shows them Peyton's room, which is fairly small and spare. Nadeem asks how Peyton usually sleeps, what's helpful, and what, if any, the challenges are. Then Nadeem says it's about time for Peyton to say goodbye to his mother. Giving Peyton a heads-up about this transition gives him time to prepare himself for what's coming and maintain a sense of control. Before they separate, Nadeem takes a picture of Peyton and Marsha, prints it out, and tapes it to the wall of Peyton's new room. Then Nadeem introduces them to Kanesha, an 11-year-old Black girl who's been at Good Hands for 5 months. Because she is developing her capacity to regulate herself, the community of staff and patients on the unit gave her the job of showing new kids around. Of course, she remembers the moment when her caseworker dropped her off at Good Hands, and she went through the same ritual Peyton was going through now. So she connects with Peyton and Marsha as she had practiced, looks them in the eye, tells them she's glad they're here, and says she will make sure that Peyton knows everything that he needs to know.

Marsha is startled at her reaction to this child. Kanesha, who is a patient in a psychiatric residential treatment facility, made her feel more welcomed than she almost ever felt before. She knows Peyton is feeling something similar because, in a rare show of affection, he kisses Marsha on the cheek, hands her back her car keys, says goodbye, and then starts his unit tour with Kanesha. With a tear welling up in her eye, Marsha turns to face Lanelle, whose eyes are moist as well. Marsha says, "I have never been to a place like this before. I heard it was special, but we've just had such different experiences at the other places we've been. At those places, and we've been to two other residential centers and five acute psychiatric hospitals, I always felt like there was something . . . I don't know . . . something wrong with me and Peyton. No one ever said that, of course, but the feeling was there. Because of that feeling, I lost hope of ever finding Peyton the help he needs. Here . . . I don't know . . . You seem to see the Peyton that I have been trying to get back, the Peyton I can see sometimes when he lets his guard down, and we are just having fun. And you all have seen it so fast. Why is this place so different from the other places we've been?"

Lanelle turns to look Marsha in the face. She says she's sorry that Marsha hasn't felt like this at other places, and comments on how hard that must have been for them. Then Lanelle confesses that Marsha might not have felt this way at Good Hands just a few years ago. Lanelle explains that they are learning about the science of safety and connection and realized that feeling seen and received with care is crucial to being able to relax and connect. She says:

> Unless this sort of relaxing happens, at least a little, then it's hard to do much learning or healing or psychological work. So now, creating an atmosphere of safety is our highest priority. I am glad that you feel that, but I should also say that we have our fair share of upsets. Relationships are messy, and feelings get hurt. We just want to help people move out of the upset when the time feels right for them. So, when things have gone sideways, we focus a lot on patching them up. Actually," she says, leaning in, "showing kids that *nothing gets so broken that we can't fix it* is another way that we give them a sense that they are safe. Perfection doesn't get much oxygen here.

As Marsha collects herself to say goodbye, Lanelle promises to check in with her over the next few days. Marsha sits in her car, gripping the steering wheel, thinking about the last thing Lanelle told her before they parted. Many parents who bring their children to Good Hands felt an enormous burden in caring for their special needs child, but they have also been more than a bit terrified to leave them there, too. Recognizing that she has felt both burdened and terrified, Marsha nods to herself, tightens her grasp on the wheel, inhales deeply, then exhales. With each inhale and exhalation, she acknowledges, then releases, the weight of what she has been carrying. Feeling lighter than she has in a very long time, Marsha decides to take herself to a nearby hotel and spend the night there, rather than making the long drive back home. Suddenly none of the things on her to-do list seem as urgent as they did on the way there. She thinks to herself, "It is true. My son is in good hands here."

Polyvagal Theory can produce epiphanies about how and why our deeply held convictions emerge from fundamental human neurophysiological processes, and Lanelle has had her share of epiphanies. Before learning about the Polyvagal Theory, she knew that understanding a child and family's experience reveals crucial insights into their struggles. She knew that many of these struggles are natural reactions to difficult circumstances. She knew that reactions such as fighting, fleeing, and shutting down obscure the innate strengths and solutions these children and families might discover. She knew that creating safe spaces in which they can explore with curiosity allows them access to greater awareness, power, and ability. Now with Polyvagal Theory, she can integrate her clinical experience with what she has learned about neurobiology and physiology. The new knowledge gives her a sense that she is including more of what she knows in an increasingly holistic understanding of who and what we are as humans.

Let's now look at how Lanelle created a polyvagal-informed organization at Good Hands.

THE FOUNDATIONS OF A POLYVAGAL-INFORMED ORGANIZATION

Good Hands was started by a group of therapists who had come from a psychodynamic tradition. They recognized that there were a number of children in their community whose severe emotional and behavioral issues caused them to require intensive residential programs beyond those available locally. These therapists wanted to create a program right in their community so that the children could stay near their families, even though they were not living at home. They understood that maintaining and improving important relationships would be a key element of these children's and families' healing. Shandra, the biracial board chair of Good Hands, was one of these therapists. She had learned of the Polyvagal Theory 3 years earlier, right as Good Hands was going through a search process to hire its second CEO. Their first CEO spent 8 and a half years with them, guiding the organization through their 18-month start-up phase and the first 7 years of operation. He was someone who enjoyed the process of creating, but when Good Hands reached a level of stability, he was ready to seek new challenges.

During its first 7 years, Good Hands was successful in taking care of most of the children in their program. Four out of five got better with the structures put in place to keep them safe and with the kindness and interest showed them. They became calmer, less violent, more able to collaborate with adults or with other children. But there were 10–20% of the children who rejected care from parents, teachers, and therapists. They were skilled in their ability to push adults away, even the highly motivated and skilled people trying to help them.

Shandra was inspired by a presentation on the Polyvagal Theory at a conference and saw how understanding the autonomic state of the children Good Hands hadn't been able to reach might open new doors to helping them. She was ready to make an understanding and practice of Polyvagal Theory central to Good Hands's next phase of development. To do so, she needed to find the right person to lead the effort, a leader who could embody the kind of safety and connection she had felt in the presenter at the conference. Lanelle, a licensed clinical social worker who was program director at the Boys and Girls Club, came highly recommended. Colleagues commended her boundless energy and understanding of the power of personal connection. Lanelle liked to say that her success was based on the radical idea that nothing much of value can be accomplished if you don't have trustworthy relationships with the people with whom you work. Good Hands's Board of Directors also received some training in the Polyvagal Theory. They agreed with the chair's proposal to hire Lanelle to lead an organizational change process to embed the principles and values of Polyvagal Theory in their work and culture.

When Lanelle started to learn about Polyvagal Theory, she quickly understood staff needed to prioritize learning to trust. In one of their early meetings, Lanelle told Shandra, "These kids need to know in their bones that we are interested in them, that we see them as worthy of care, and that we won't hurt them. They have to know in their hearts that we care about them." She was excited to think they could demonstrate safety through vocal prosody, open faces, open postures and valuing the children's experiences. She recognized that Polyvagal Theory described a neurobiology of trustworthiness, the same trustworthiness she had made the center of her personal philosophy. Lanelle and Shandra spent more than an hour excitedly talking about this quote from Porges' paper: "Safe states are a prerequisite not only for optimal social behaviour, but also for accessing the higher brain structures that enable humans to be creative and generative" (Porges, 2015a). They were inspired by the idea that, if they could move the children into a ventral vagal state, they would better position them to learn and grow and heal.

ACTION STEPS FOR BUILDING A POLYVAGAL-INFORMED ORGANIZATION

Lanelle and Shandra discussed a plan for integrating Polyvagal Theory as the Good Hands philosophy of care. They decided to base their program on understanding two fundamental principles: (1) A person's autonomic state has a profound effect on their functioning; and (2) a person's autonomic state can be regulated by the relationships, environment, and culture in which they work.

Their staff would need good training in these two principles, so they could and would recognize people's states and learn to manage them. The structure of the organization needed to convey safety and belonging, as it had for Marsha's arrival with Peyton. They also knew that the organization needed to convey safety for their staff as well. It takes well-regulated adults to regulate dysregulated children, and a sense of safety is crucial to the ability to stay regulated. The staff also needed a theory of leadership. Though Lanelle and Shandra had experiences with good supervisors who created a sense of psychological safety, they didn't know of any organizations that explicitly made creating safety the core of their culture in the way that they were envisioning. They planned to meet these needs and build their polyvagal-informed organization through five action steps: training employees, supporting the children they work with to spend more time in ventral vagal states, supporting staff to work from ventral vagal themselves, scaffolding the organization's safety with ventral vagal teams, and creating a polyvagal-informed culture and leadership.

ACTION STEP ONE: Educate Staff on the Polyvagal Theory

Children come to Good Hands because they are emotionally and behaviorally dysregulated. They have problems with anger and aggression. Sometimes they take their anger out on themselves in self-destructive acts. For many, as was the case with Peyton, these issues stem from early traumatic experiences, from neglect, abuse, and loss. They have not had the kinds of good enough parenting described in Chapters 2 and 3 that produce emotional regulation, impulse control, and a capacity for collaboration. From their mistreatment, they conclude that adults will hurt them and should not be trusted. It is important for the clinical team and direct care staff to understand their outbursts, upsets, meltdowns, and storms are seeded by reminders of past dangers and traumas. Gestures, facial expressions, movements, and words that, at first appearance, seem harmless to the staff can easily trigger sympathetic fight-or-flight and dorsal shutdown states. Without this understanding, staff will misinterpret what is going on with the children.

Lanelle and Shandra experimented with ways to teach staff three main points of Polyvagal Theory: hierarchy of response, co-regulation, and neuroception. They found a video that uses a metaphor of a traffic light to present the three states in the hierarchy of response (Nerd Nite, 2017). A red light represents a dorsal vagal shutdown in response to life threat. The yellow light is sympathetic fight-or-flight in response to danger, and green is ventral vagal safety and social engagement. They liked this metaphor because it allowed them to discuss the difference between how a traffic light switches colors and how the autonomic system switches states. They would say to the staff, "A traffic light will turn green if you wait a bit. But to help a child switch states, you can't just sit there and wait. You have to do something. To 'turn a child's light green,' you need to speak with an animated face and voice, use friendly gestures, or mirror their emotional energy. If the child is not yet in a ventral vagal state," they were instructed, "you need to keep sending these signals of safety until they are." By using the traffic light metaphor, Good Hands explains why and how the staff are responsible for managing the child's state through co-regulation. The child is not able to shift their state on their own. If the child could, the child would not need Good Hands.

Good Hands taught their staff ways to co-regulate the children's states and turn lights green, including by adopting the playful, accepting, curious, and empathic attitude championed by Dan Hughes, creator of Dyadic Developmental Psychotherapy or DDP. Lanelle and Shandra learned of Hughes's work as they researched the Polyvagal Theory, and they discovered that DDP was a polyvagal-informed therapy that helped children who have experienced developmental trauma learn to create bonds of attachment with their parents. Hughes and his collaborator Jon Baylin taught that a Playful, Accepting, Curious, and Empathic (PACE) attitude helps children feel safe, even when they have evolved a pervasively mistrustful stance in response to trauma (Baylin & Hughes, 2016). Good Hands wanted their staff members to treat children's experiences with care, so that their mistrustful predispositions can eventually relax. They knew that a trusting relationship provides a foundation for a child to heal from trauma.

Of course, Good Hands wanted their staff to understand that people see themselves and the world differently when they are in each of the three autonomic states. So they asked staff members to complete the personal profile map created by Deb Dana (2018) by embodying each of the three autonomic states, and then noticing what they themselves are thinking and feeling in each. While staff members didn't have exactly the same experiences in each state, they found that each of the three states had a profound effect on everyone's sensations, mindsets, and motivations. By comparing notes with their coworkers, staff members concluded they needed to be in a ventral vagal state themselves to work effectively with the children. If the children were in states of fight-or-flight or shutdown, the first thing the staff needed to do was to help them move toward a ventral vagal state. They developed slogans to capture their insights: "State begets state," and "We need a green light before we can go."

This training also showed staff members that children's frame of mind depends upon their present moment's neuroception of their environment. Because of this exercise, the staff members themselves could now explain why a dysregulated adult can't regulate a dysregulated child. The dysregulated child is neurocepting danger. A dysregulated adult is simply one more signal of danger pushing the child further into defensiveness. In defensiveness, a child cannot hear what the staff member is saying. So the dysregulated adult is not able to have a positive impact on the child's frame of mind. They also understood why telling a dysregulated child, "Use your coping skills" or "Use your words" is often not helpful. Coping, when in sympathetic activation, means to fight harder or run away faster. To help the child move to a ventral vagal green light state requires co-regulation, which was a good way to introduce the topic of Polyvagal Theory and child development.

Infants and toddlers can't resolve their own disrupted states; they can't turn their own lights green. Because their brains do not yet have the ability, they need co-regulation for many months before they can start regulating themselves (Porges, 2011). You can't just tell an upset 1-year-old to use their coping skills and expect them to regain their composure. As described in Chapter 3, young children can increasingly participate in the serve-and-return interactions so vital to building brain architecture. After brain maturation and much practice with co-regulating caregivers, young children can start to settle themselves down.

Many children at Good Hands needed the same kind of support that much younger children need. It helped the staff to consider that the children's brains had not yet been given the chance to mature. The staff liked to think that they were helping the children build new brain circuits and that they were instructors at a brain academy.

ACTION STEP TWO: Support Children Toward Ventral Vagal

The second action step Lanelle and Shandra took to build a polyvagal-informed organization was to look for ways to support children's movement toward the ventral vagal state. In addition to training the staff in both nonverbal and verbal ways of showing the children that they were safe and valued, they knew that a structured, predictable environment also enhances a sense of security. So they defined the rhythms, routines, and rituals that created a structure that the children could usually count on.

Each of the units at Good Hands has eight children who live together as a family. A clinical team consisting of a therapist, case coordinator, nurse, unit manager, and psychiatric provider come together to develop a multidisciplinary clinical understanding of each child's issues. The providers then design a treatment plan based on their collaborative understanding. The direct care staff members spend each day with the children, guiding them through the program.

Each unit has their own schedule for the day, based on the age of the children and the needs of that particular group. In general, there are morning routines to get ready for the day and evening routines to get ready for bed. The rhythms of the day recognize the children's need for a variety of activities, for learning in school, for play and exercise, and for a balance of loud and quiet activities.

The units all have rituals that define what the staff and children do in various situations. We have already seen a bit of the welcoming ritual performed when a new child is admitted to the unit. A child who has made progress in mastering their emotions and impulses greets the new child, shows them around, introduces them to the other members of the community, and answers any questions that they might have. There are welcoming rituals for visitors to the unit as well that involve a greeting, introductions, and answering questions. Lanelle learned that when your efforts enabled another person to feel that they belong, it increases your own sense of belonging too. Consequently, these welcoming rituals enhance everyone's sense of belonging.

Upsets are common at Good Hands, and they developed a standardized approach for handling them, especially when they occur in a group of children. At the first sign of emotional dysregulation, staff take notice of what is happening and gently bring the group to a full stop, saying, "We need to take a time out here since things aren't going so well." The staff member acknowledges the feelings they observe, then asks what is happening to cause an upset, getting perspectives from all of the children. Once they know what is happening, they make a correction based on what they learned. When it seems that things have settled down, the staff member says "Remember, we need a green light before we can go. Is everyone feeling like they can move forward now?" If someone still doesn't feel ready, the staff member asks, "What else needs to happen?" and continues the process until everyone is ready to go.

Good Hands also knows the importance of balancing limit-setting and empathy, which are sometimes seen as being in opposition to each other. In learning about Dyadic Developmental Psychotherapy, Lanelle and Shandra came across the concept of "the two hands of parenting: Hand one provides connection with warmth and nurture. It gives the child appropriate autonomy matched to his developmental and emotional age. Hand two provides structure, supervision and boundaries. A child needs both of these; connection and correction" (Golding, 2015, p. 158). When there is a warm connection, such as occurs in the ventral vagal state, the child feels valued and known. The hand of connection and relationship affirms that children are much more than their behavior alone. The child's uniqueness is seen and celebrated as they relax and open to the world around them and to the inner world within. Caregivers use the hand of structure and correction to address behaviors that need to be reined in and to communicate that there are limits to what will be tolerated. Setting limits conveys safety by showing that the adult will not allow things to get out of control. However, if the adult doesn't also provide care, the hand of discipline is simply a manipulation of the child's behavior without acknowledgement of who the child is as a person.

ACTION STEP THREE: Support Employees' Ventral Vagal States

Lanelle and Shandra knew that if they wanted the staff to support the children to move toward ventral vagal, then they had to support the staff to move toward ventral vagal themselves. In order for staff members to feel secure, they too needed a structured, predictable environment with rhythms, routines, and rituals. Lanelle and Shandra knew things would not always go well, and they would need to attend to upsets when they occurred. They wanted their staff to have permission to make mistakes and learn from them. To see what that looks like, let's return to Peyton, to see how he is doing.

For his first three weeks at Good Hands, Peyton held himself together by staying on high alert, wary of what would happen if he blew up here like he did at home. He still had vague memories of his biological father breaking lamps when he was upset with Peyton, so he was afraid of what the staff would do if he did things they didn't like. It got harder for him to stay so wary, and this honeymoon period slowly ended. Also, as he saw the staff were generally calm, he started to let his guard down for a few moments here and there. On this particular morning, he no longer had the strength or motivation to suppress his emotions, and he blew up at Peggy, the staff member assigned to supervise him. Peggy, a white 22-year-old recent college graduate, had worked on the overnight shift at Good Hands for just 6 weeks. She usually finished her shift at 7 a.m., but she had agreed to stay an extra 3 hours to cover for a staff member who needed to come in late. More than a bit exhausted from her overnight shift, Peggy was frustrated and worried about how she would get all the kids to school. In response to her repeated requests to pick up his room and get ready for breakfast, Peyton got suddenly angry and told Peggy he wasn't going to do what she said, "because that's stupid and so are you!" Peggy found herself reflexively snapping back at him, saying, "You better watch your mouth."

Jonathan, a white staff member, came over and said, "Peggy, why don't you let me take over?" But Peggy said, "I've got this," and waved Jonathan's help away.

Peyton's refusal to get ready made them later and later for breakfast, and Peggy finally said in an intense whisper, "I've had it with you. You're never going to discharge from here. I can see why your foster mother doesn't want you back."

Peyton turned red, ran into the bathroom, and refused to come out.

Peggy slumped against the wall, put her forehand in her hands, and felt she was a failure. With a sinking, ashamed feeling, she told herself she would never learn to do it right.

She and Peyton were both in defensive states. As she got louder, he felt more like retreating. They were in a race to the bottom of Dana's autonomic ladder (2018), and it is hard to tell who got there first. Peggy had received polyvagal training, and she knew she had messed up badly.

Just then, Nadeem, the unit manager, came around the corner with Jonathan and said to Peggy, "Hey, kid, let's you and I take a break. Jonathan can repair things with Peyton." Jonathan knew what just happened likely had a particular meaning for the boy because of the violence in his birth family. Jonathan knew that Peyton's father would break things, and his mother would hit his father. Jonathan wanted to hear how Peggy's dysregulation had affected Peyton, and to let him know that staff at Good Hands help each other if they get upset.

Nadeem guided Peggy to his office and offered to make her some tea. He said, "Rough morning, huh?" as the kettle started to whistle. Peggy, whose dream was to earn a graduate degree in counseling so she could help kids like Peyton, said, "Yeah, very rough." She watched Nadeem closely to see how he responded. He said, "It's so frustrating. We want to help them so much. But the little rascals just push our buttons and push us away. I think this is the hardest part of the job—learning to manage how bad the kids can make us feel sometimes."

Peggy was astonished. She was bracing herself to get yelled at and then maybe fired. Instead, her manager made her feel better. Unexpectedly, she found herself starting to cry a little, and confessed, "I do want to help them so much. I didn't realize how much I wanted that. Do you think there's any hope for me?" Nadeem smiled, leaned forward and took in Peggy's earnest face. "I'd say there's more than a little hope for you. You care. You want to make a difference, and you are ready to learn how to do it. As they told you in training, it is going to be hard work. But you will have days when you feel better about yourself than you ever imagined possible. If you can stay open to what you are feeling, like you are now, and keep working with us to get better, there's no chance you won't succeed. Welcome to the team. Today you passed a big test."

Nadeem saw Peggy's ability to remain open to his efforts to connect with her, even in the midst of a shame-filled experience, as a sign that she would become a good staff member. His goal was to help Peggy get regulated again and then to learn from the experience. He wanted Peggy to have the same goal with the children, to help them get regulated when they lose it, and to learn from what happened. In a polyvagal-informed organization, returning everyone to ventral vagal regulation is one of the highest priorities. Reviewing this point, Nadeem talked with Peggy about the need to first help Peyton get regulated before she tries to get him ready for school. The manager reminded Peggy, "We need a green light before we can go."

Peggy told Nadeem, "I sounded just like my dad when I said those things to Peyton. He could be a real drill sergeant when I was growing up. I used to hate it when he would bark orders at us. Sometimes we would tell him 'no' to piss him off." Nadeem told Peggy that it made sense that she responded to Peyton's defiance like that, given her experience with her father. He looked her in the eye and said, "Even though it makes sense to me how this happened, you can't do it again. We have to create a safe space for the kids above all else." That stung for Peggy, but she knew it was right. She said to Nadeem. "It won't happen again. I have learned a lot today. In the future, I will get help when I start to go down the ladder." Nadeem told her that he would help her repair this serious relationship rupture with Peyton, then saw her shoulders relax. Nadeem nodded and smiled. To himself, he was thinking that the two hands approach applies to staff as well as children. Along with empathic nurturing, staff too need limits to feel safe.

Supervision is just one way the polyvagal-informed organization supports staff members' movement toward ventral vagal.

There are scheduled meetings where staff members can check in with their supervisors and managers and discuss how they have been doing. Have they been able to stay regulated? If not, what triggered their movement down the autonomic ladder? How was it handled? Did they ask for and receive support? What can be done to prepare for similar challenges in the future? Daily transition meetings occur at shift change and allow unit managers and shift supervisors to see how both the children and the staff have fared that day. One staff group debriefs before they go home; then the next crew makes plans for their shift. If the staff members feel a little frazzled, the manager or supervisor listens patiently to help them move back up their autonomic ladders. In weekly team meetings, team members review the children's progress, making sure they understand what is happening with them and that they are making predicted gains. Then there are unit meetings every 2 weeks to discuss and improve overall unit function. Staff also know in meetings they can talk about difficult issues, like disagreements about how to manage the children or unit. Unit leaders work to make it safe for perspectives to be shared and upsets to be aired. The structure of these meetings and the openness to discussion creates a sense of psychological safety that will allow staff members like Peggy to stay open and engaged as they work with children like Peyton.

Nadeem knew that relationship repair was a specific skill that Peggy needed to learn in her work. Breaks in relationships, such as the one that Peggy and Peyton experienced, are bound to occur. Repairing this rupture is crucial to Peyton's psychological healing (Baylin & Hughes, 2016; Dana, 2018). Peggy's own experience with Nadeem had solidified her understanding that conflict, upset, and disappointment are not the end of a relationship. She now had a grounded understanding that repairing breaks in relationships leads to deeper and more secure connections. Empowered by her own sense of security with Nadeem and mindful that at Good Hands nothing gets so broken that it can't be fixed, Peggy set out to repair her relationship with Peyton.

Peggy and Nadeem led Peyton into the unit living room, and first explained that he wasn't in trouble, as children often fear when brought in to talk with adults. Peggy explained that she felt awful about what she had said to Peyton and apologized for losing her temper and saying such mean things to him. When Peyton said, "Oh that's okay," Peggy used the approach she practiced with Nadeem: "Well, Peyton, that's nice of you to say," she responded, "but I bet that was really hard to hear. What was it like for you when I said those horrible things?"

Peyton was quiet for a moment, then looked at Nadeem. Nadeem gave a little nod, indicating that it was okay for Peyton to say what he was thinking. Then Nadeem said, "It's hard to talk about these kinds of things. But we really want to have good relationships with each other here, so we talk about these kinds of feelings a lot." Peyton said, "I'm, I'm not sure what to say." Peggy took a deep breath and let it out, then said, "I bet it really hurt your feelings when I said those things." Peyton nodded, and after a bit, Peggy continued, "We were starting to get to know each other and things had been going good. Then I said those things. That was probably kind of shocking and pretty confusing." "Yeah," Peyton answered. "And I didn't want to even see you again." "Yeah, you probably wanted me to be as far away as possible," Peggy replied. The conversation continued like this for some time, with Peggy accepting Peyton's feelings without a need to change them, curious about how he would describe them, and empathizing with the pain she had caused.

As things were winding down, Peyton looked at Peggy and asked, "Why are you talking with me like this?" Peggy looked at Nadeem who answered, "You haven't had someone apologize like this to you before," and watched as Peyton nodded. Then Peggy continued, "Our relationship is important to me, and I don't want to let anything come between us. I want you to know that you can tell me anything without having to worry if it might hurt my feelings. I know that when I said the mean things, I was making it so hard for you to ever talk with me again. But I wanted to try to see if you would give me another chance." Peyton nodded and said, "Okay. I'll give you a chance." Then Peggy and Nadeem asked Peyton if he wanted to go shoot some baskets, because they knew that basketball was his favorite sport. They walked to the playground, Peyton in the middle, and began a new chapter.

ACTION STEP FOUR: Scaffold the Organization's Safety With Ventral Vagal Teams

As powerful as the interactions between Nadeem, Peggy, and Peyton were, Lanelle and Shandra's vision of a polyvagal-informed organization goes beyond two or three individuals' abilities to have deeply meaningful connections. They wanted their staff to become team members who support each other to stay regulated, an interdependent network of people who ask each other, "How are we doing?" and reply to each other, "We've got this." To make their vision explicit, Lanelle and Shandra created diagrams of what this ventral vagal scaffolding looks like, so their teams can share in their vision as well. They want the staff to increasingly understand the concept that *state begets state*, and if they feel a connection with their regulated teammates, the connection will help them stay regulated, too. Furthermore, state begets state between the staff teams and groups of children as well, with teams of well-regulated staff members conveying that the children are connected, protected, and cared for. See Figure 8.1 for an illustration of a well-functioning team. Once Lanelle and Shandra depicted reciprocal sharing of smiles, warm tones of voice, and encourag-

210 POLYVAGAL THEORY AND THE DEVELOPING CHILD

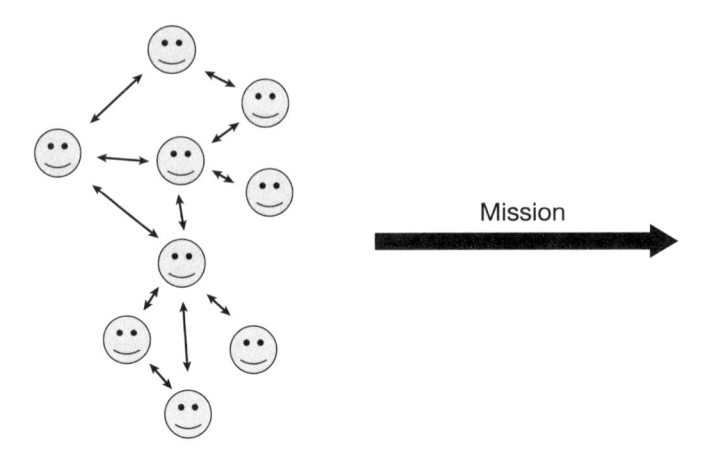

FIGURE 8.1

When the team works together in the Social Engagement System, each sending the other signals of safety through face-to-face connection, their attention is free to focus on accomplishing their mission.

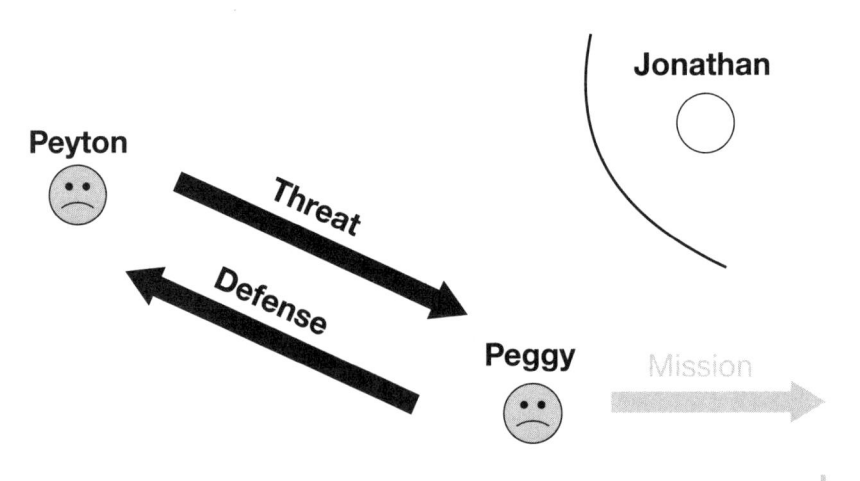

FIGURE 8.2

Peggy is not able to stay regulated on her own when Peyton repeatedly refuses to do what she says. She reactively defends herself from Peyton by verbally assaulting him, rather than focusing on her mission to help Peyton with his need to push caring adults away. In a parallel fashion, she pushes her coworker Jonathan away. He is not simply a bystander. As a witness to her shameful dysregulation, Jonathan may go into a dorsal vagal state himself, frozen while watching what is happening without being able to help.

ing gestures creating a widening network of ventral vagal connections, they also showed what it looked like when things went awry. For example, they drew the disastrous interaction that occurred between Peggy and Peyton like Figure 8.2.

Lanelle and Shandra knew a threat that sends an isolated individual into fight-or-flight is less likely to have the same impact on a group of people. Connecting to trusted teammates helps us neurocept less danger, even when presented with the same threat (see Figure 8.3).

The social engagement system makes teamwork possible by inhibiting our defensive instincts so that we can come together in the service of nurture, collaboration, and play. Belonging to a group gives us a felt sense of safety. As Peggy increasingly feels that she is part of her team and knows support is available to her at a moment's notice, she feels safer, and it is easier for her to stay emotionally regulated. Good teamwork is related to team members' resiliency, retention, engagement, and job satisfaction. Good teamwork is also correlated with better, safer clinical outcomes as

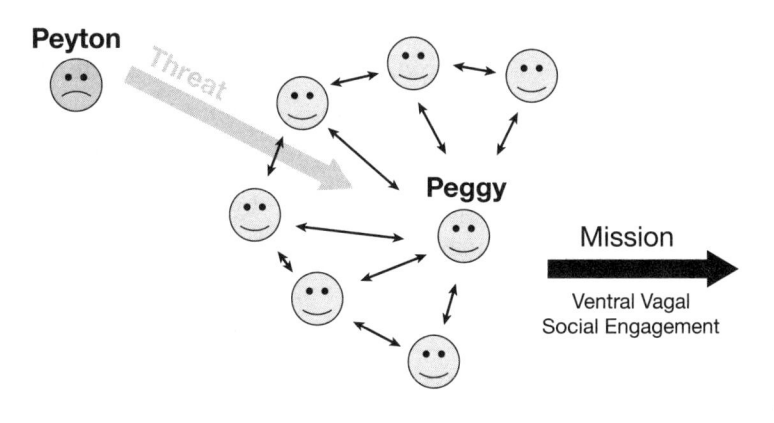

FIGURE 8.3

In a polyvagal-informed organization, the team supports each member to stay emotionally regulated and in ventral vagal social engagement. Then, from that autonomic state, they work together to accomplish their mission.

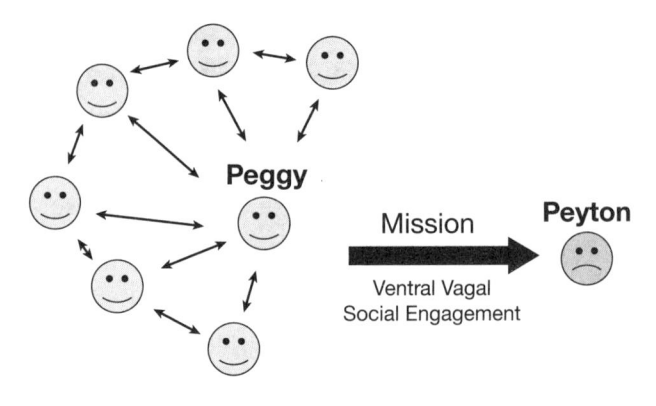

FIGURE 8.4

When a team member is embedded and supported within an emotionally regulated team, she is empowered to stay in a ventral vagal state supporting social engagement, even when working with highly dysregulated children.

well (Rosen, DiazGranados, Dietz et al., 2018). Good teamwork frees Peggy to focus on helping Peyton, rather than on keeping herself safe (see Figure 8.4).

Professionals who work with children are often faced with situations and stimuli that their own neuroception could consider dangerous. At Good Hands, a child could abruptly and unexpectedly go into a rage. In emergency rooms, there is danger that a patient could die. Even the chaotic noise of a middle school cafeteria or gymnasium can feel hostile and unwelcoming. No matter what the state is, there is a risk that flight-or-flight or shutdown can spread to a whole team facing danger. In a dangerous situation, they are no longer able to engage in productive action toward their goal. It's everyone for themselves, and some of the team members even fight each other (see Figure 8.5).

Lanelle and Shandra worked to create an explicit understanding that teams have the power to keep each other regulated in the most challenging of situations. Even when a team member gets dysregulated, the rest of the team can have their

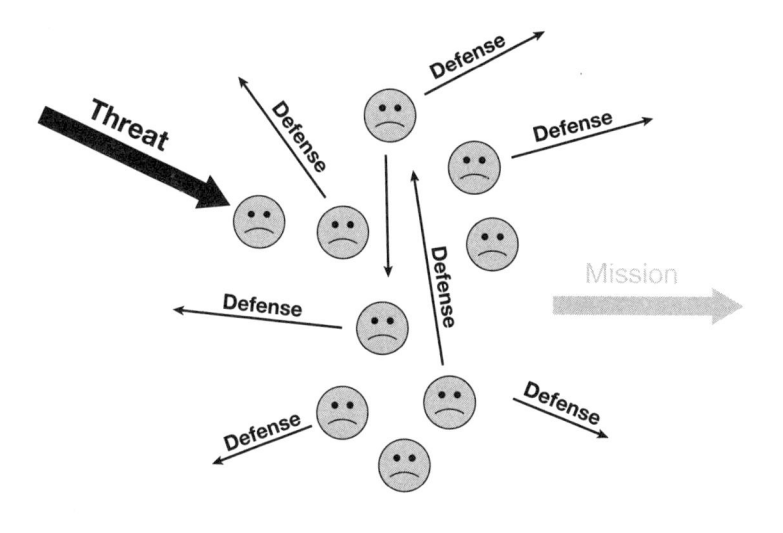

FIGURE 8.5

Team members amplify external signals of danger when they shift into defensive states. Defensive autonomic states change a team's focus of attention from mission to defense. Individuals are prepared to protect themselves, but they are not able to mount a coordinated response to the threat when they are in fight-or-flight.

back. Supporting each other means supporting each other to stay regulated.

The situation with Peggy and Peyton demonstrated that state also begets state in disturbing and challenging ways. As a part of the healing from the event, and in order to learn from it and continue to improve their program, Lanelle got a group of people together to take a serious look at the dynamics of the situation. They included Peggy, Jonathan, and the unit manager, and they even had Peyton participate for a portion of the discussion. The group asked themselves, "What happened that *that* happened?" a question they asked in many situations, with staff, children, families, or whomever. They wanted to explore what context made the situation possible and how they could change the context to give rise to a different situation next time.

One idea that came out of this exploration was for teams to

use a code message to signal to a triggered staff member that their teammate was going to take over for them. The message they decided on was, "You have an important phone call in the office, and you need to go there right away." The plan was for the staff member to go to the office to cool down before rejoining their team. Recognizing that a staff member who is dysregulated might not immediately respond to the signal, they agreed on how to escalate their request by saying, "Peggy, this is urgent. Listen to me. You need to go to the office. There is a crisis on the phone, and you need to handle it." From a polyvagal perspective, they realized that for Peggy to let go of the situation with Peyton, she may need to neurocept the same level of danger from the code message that she is experiencing from the situation with the boy. In this way, a team can help a dysregulated member to take the space needed to pull herself together, while the team continues to function (see Figure 8.6).

That afternoon, Lanelle made sure to call Peyton's foster mom, Marsha, with whom she kept in touch. She had already alerted Marsha to what Peggy had said to Peyton, and Peggy had apologized to Marsha directly. Lanelle wanted Marsha to know that, not only were they sorry for what happened, they were changing their structure to make sure it didn't happen again. Lanelle could see in her mind's eye the scaffolding of safety her teams were creating. Each rupture in relationship brought an opportunity to learn from their mistakes and to strengthen their structure. She felt proud of their efforts and renewed her commitment to herself to keep learning how to lead her teams toward greater safety, connection, collaboration, and harmony.

FIGURE 8.6

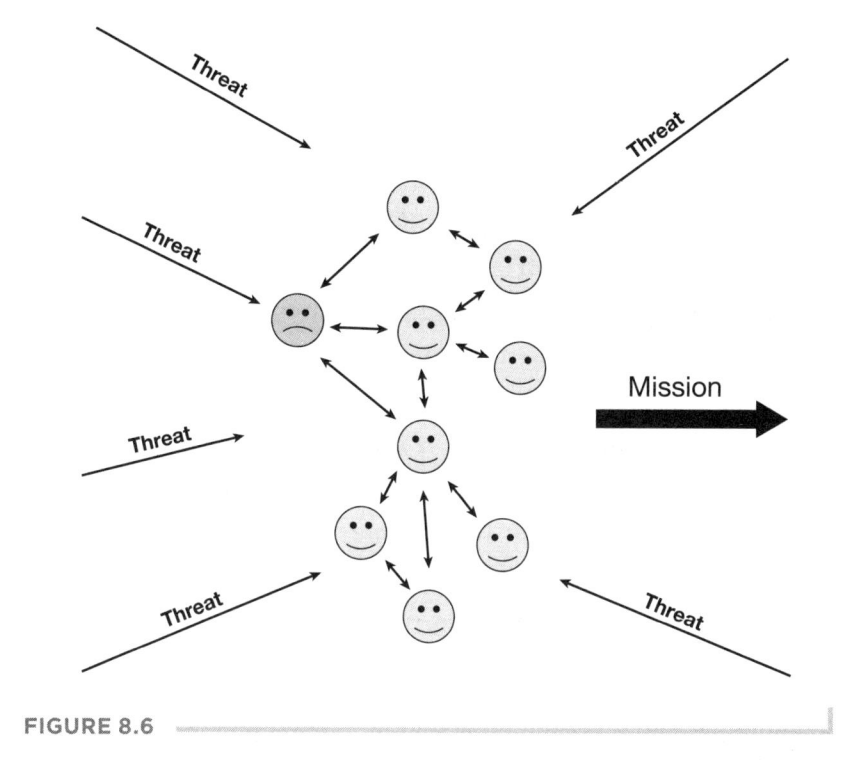

A well-functioning team under intense stress can stay regulated, even when one of its members gets dysregulated, as represented by the frowning face. In this situation, these smiling faces indicate the vagal brake has lifted, and the other team members are using a boost in sympathetic energy to accomplish their mission. On some days, multiple threats appear simultaneously and can dysregulate a member of the team, such as Peggy.

ACTION STEP FIVE: Culture and Leadership in a Polyvagal-Informed Organization

As Lanelle and Shandra contemplated ways to embed Polyvagal Theory more deeply and broadly at Good Hands, they naturally started studying how organizations create their cultures. Reading Coyle's *The Culture Code* (2018), they resonated with the statement, "Culture is a set of living relationships working toward a shared goal" (p. xx). Coyle proposes that successful group culture arises from three skills, and Lanelle and Shandra observed that all three fit with Polyvagal Theory: building safety, sharing vulnerability, and establishing purpose. They learned that teams succeed when they feel psychologically safe with each other, no matter if they are investment bankers, orthopedic nurses, Google employees, or the cast and writers at *Saturday Night Live*. "Of course!" they thought. Polyvagal Theory doesn't just apply to psychiatric facilities. As Duhigg (2016) points out, all humans work better together and are more productive when they feel safe with each other.

That principle was fleshed out in a playful interview with Stephen Porges, called *How to know if you're working with mammals or reptiles (and why it matters to your creativity)* (Baer, 2013). Because mammals have to care for their young, their survival depends on connection and collaboration. In contrast, baby reptiles usually start life alone, slicing their way out of their eggshells themselves and venturing into the world without nurturance or support. To illustrate his concept, Porges imagines how reptilian and mammalian work cultures differ. Reptilian work cultures, based in fear and defense, will focus on preservation of resources and maximization of productivity and profit, while a mammalian approach will see corporate work as an interdependent activity that requires empathy and trust to support boldness and creativity.

Finally, Lanelle and Shandra studied leadership from a polyvagal perspective. They saw that visionary leaders create organizations to make a difference in people's lives. Those organizations have a meaningful mission. Safety and social engagement create the cultural context for successful collaboration, but collaboration is empty until it is focused on a worthwhile goal. A polyvagal-informed leader, they concluded, will direct her employees' attention to the meaning of the work they do together. They taught the staff to look for small signs of change in the children and clarified the significance of those changes in light of their mission. For example, when a girl who usually refused help asked

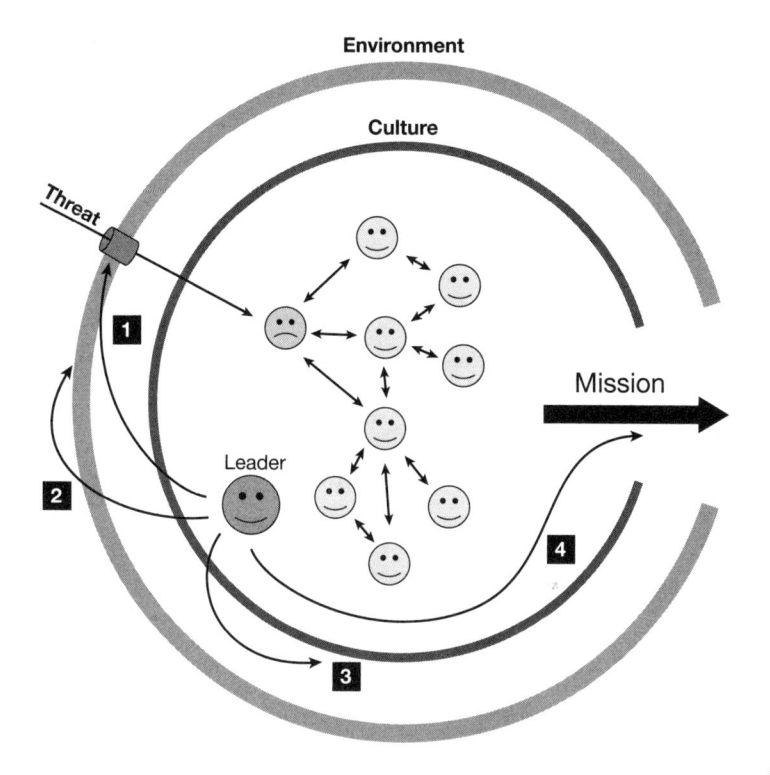

FIGURE 8.7

The polyvagal-informed leader can take four actions to move people to ventral vagal. (1) Detect and filter threats from the environment. (2) Modify the environment itself. (3) Create, maintain, enhance a ventral vagal–promoting organizational culture and climate. (4) Align employees to work together to accomplish the mission.

a staff member to assist her in putting on her shoes, Nadeem held a small staff celebration, explaining how that one change was the first step in the girl learning to let her parents love and care for her. When a boy who was being discharged was asked what he had learned at Good Hands, and he said, "I learned how to be sad," Nadeem held another staff celebration and talked about the importance of the boy's ability to tolerate and claim his experiences as his own.

Lanelle and Shandra felt they now had a grasp of the elements of polyvagal-informed leadership. They outlined four actions the leader could take to build a polyvagal-informed organization:

1. Detect and filter threats.
2. Modify the environment.
3. Enhance the culture and climate.
4. Align employees toward the mission.

These actions are in addition to the usual responsibilities that organizations ask leaders to assume (see Figure 8.7).

When the leader detects threats from the work environment, she can serve as a buffer between the environment and her people. By detecting threats early, assessing their impact, and creating solutions to those threats, the leader filters and metabolizes the danger before it can impact the organization as a whole. Porges points out that when a threat evokes enough fear, it is immobilizing (personal communication, October 31, 2019). He further suggests that a better approach is for leaders to reframe threats as problems, "because a problem evokes solutions rather than paralysis." For example: The superintendent of a juvenile detention facility learned that one of her officers had been giving drugs to the youth there. She met with her leadership team and framed the situation as a series of problems to be solved and then created an action plan in which each member of her team was assigned a specific problem and took responsibility for creating a solution for it.

The nurse on Nadeem's unit learned that a child would be admitted who had a history of extreme self-harm behaviors. Knowing how nervous this would make the staff, the nurse, the therapist, and Nadeem created a plan for how they would keep the child safe, step by step, from the moment she arrived. Then they met with their staff, explained the girl's behaviors and history, and presented the plan to them. The staff gave their feedback and the plan was modified in several important ways to include their insights.

The leader can also make changes to the environment itself, both the environment in which the organization is embedded and the internal environment where they work. As one example, the program director for an autism day treatment center realized that their periodic fire drills caused the kids who had auditory sensory sensitivities substantial distress. She got clearance from the fire marshal to give the children an alert 5 minutes before the fire alarm would ring, so that they could get mentally prepared for the loud noise. The fire marshal also gave her permission to have the children who were most disturbed by the shrill alarm to go outside to the playground before and during the fire drill to avoid the situation altogether.

A polyvagal-informed leader can take actions to create, maintain, and enhance a mammalian organizational culture and climate that nurtures neuroception of safety, warm connection, and shared values. When the chief clinical officer at KidsTLC, another psychiatric residential treatment facility, instructed his team to "write your credo," he required them to codify their basic assumptions about how change occurs (M. Siegmund, personal communication, 2015). The credo became their constitution, which is taught to all incoming employees and reviewed regularly as a touchstone for their work. This constitution creates and affirms a culture that cares about "children—their connections, experiences and development" (KidsTLC, 2018, p. 1) and provides a lived experience of the social engagement system. It is prominently displayed on buildings across the campus, and team leaders use the constitution as a guide when addressing difficult situations (see Appendix).

Given that the first three actions support a safe environment, the leader is now free to focus staff attention on the mission of the organization. In addition to understanding the "Why?" of the overall mission, Lanelle and Shandra trained their managers to point out the "Why?" of each task they asked the staff to do. They wanted the staff members to link their duties to the reasons they came to work at Good Hands in the first place. As Lanelle and Shandra had read in Duhigg's book (2016), "Once we start asking why, those small tasks become pieces of a larger constellation of meaningful projects, goals, and values. We start to recognize how small chores have outsized emotional rewards, because they prove to ourselves that we are making meaningful choices, that we are genuinely in control of our own lives" (p. 36).

CONCLUSION

Lanelle reflected once more on the question that Marsha had asked her, "Why is this place so different from the other places we've been?" Lanelle took a deep breath and held it for a moment before letting it go. How would she answer that question now? It is a place that gives people the safety and support to take on the challenges that are most important to them, and to do so with the support of people who care for them and about whom they care. Lanelle knew that a child who overcomes trauma must discover that he is bigger than what happened to him. She now realized that everyone Good Hands touched had a similar opportunity to discover an expanded sense of self that was bigger than the challenges they had faced. That included Peyton and Peggy, Victoria and Marsha, all the children and their families, and the staff and their managers. Lanelle and Shandra felt bigger as a result of the work they had done in creating Good Hands, but they also felt humbled by the way this had all unfolded. And they felt grateful. Lanelle thought, "Feeling gratitude is probably an experience that arises from ventral vagal too."

SECTION IV

EMBODYING POLYVAGAL THEORY IN LIFE AND IN THE WORLD

CHAPTER 9

Social Connectedness in the Time of COVID-19

Trust is the only legal performance-enhancing drug. Whenever there is more trust in a company, country, or community, good things happen.
—DOV SEIDMAN IN FRIEDMAN, 2020

RECALIBRATING THE AUTONOMIC NERVOUS SYSTEM

In December 2019, we first heard of a novel virus taking hold in Wuhan, China. The virus was identified as a coronavirus and was named COVID-19. Its genetic sequence was quickly described. By January 2020, China had experienced an exponential rise in new viral infections, and deaths rose quickly. We have prior experience with coronaviruses. The SARS and MERS epidemics took heavy tolls, but the dimensions of COVID-19 are exponentially worse. This virus, unlike others, infects and kills both the young and apparently healthy as well as the elderly or infirm. U.S. healthcare providers, public health officials, and some government officials expressed concerns.

In January 2020, the first U.S. coronavirus cases were reported. U.S. residents began dying. Our individual and collective autonomic nervous systems reacted. Feelings of danger or terror quickly overwhelmed any momentary neuroceptions of safety and security. Increasingly, healthcare authorities and the media sounded the alarm. If we do nothing, they said, there will be millions of deaths. The World Health Organization labeled COVID-19 a pandemic. In the meantime, European countries took seemingly drastic steps. They shut down all business and travel. Their governments confined people to their homes. European borders of the European Union, formerly free and open, shut down. The terms *social distancing* and *sheltering in place* first appeared.

We all developed new survival strategies. We used our social engagement systems to connect with family and friends. We reassured each other with presence and compassion. However, just below the surface was fear for our own lives, the lives of our families and friends, financial insecurity, and the loss of what we called *life as we know it*.

In March 2020, governors issued executive orders to shut down nonessential businesses. They requested people to shelter in place or to socially distance at work if they were essential employees. Massive layoffs and furloughs threatened the viability of the economy. A handful of governors never formally shut down their states. Restaurants closed except for takeout. Gyms, theaters, sports activities, and even the Olympics were shuttered. Colleges, universities, and local public and private schools closed. Students were sent home, often on little notice, and told they would have online education beginning in a few days. College students were released for spring vacation and told not to return. Overnight, teachers and professors adapted their educational strategies to online coursework. Parents became teachers.

The authors are healthcare providers. We experience COVID-19 as physicians as well as spouses and parents. We watched as healthcare providers, first responders, grocery workers, truck drivers, and other essential workers struggled to adapt to the needs of the pandemic. Often, they lacked appropriate personal protective equipment (PPE). Our hearts filled with pride as young nurses and physicians graduated early to work in overwhelmed emergency rooms. Our hearts ached as we heard story after story of healthcare providers who were infected with COVID-19, some of whom died. We cringed when we heard that young healthcare providers with children were writing wills to ensure their children would be cared for if they succumbed to COVID-19.

Every day, we assess our own neuroceptions of danger and try to recalibrate our autonomic nervous systems so we can help regulate our patients, their families, and our staff. Our work lives are now all COVID, all the time. Countless time is spent developing COVID-19 protocols based upon the best available information, tempered by realities of PPE availability. We reuse PPE knowing that a mere 6 months prior the thought of reusing a mask was considered completely inappropriate and unsafe. We do the best we can to regulate our staff as they worry that each new patient is now a danger, and PPE supplies are limited. Staff members wonder whether they will become vectors of the virus that infect their families. They are all worried. Many healthcare providers are living separately from their loved ones to minimize their feelings of responsibility. To make matters worse, because of the dangers of COVID-19, some healthcare provider parents are in legal custody battles brought by former spouses who are not in health care (Twohey, 2020).

We now meet patients and parents through a mask. We interact through a mask. We try to build trust through a mask. We give bad news through a mask. We have our eyes, other nonverbal signals, and our voices available to build and sustain trust. Due to dramatic changes in visitation policies, at one time there were either no face-to-face visitations or limited interactions with only one parent at a time. The parents also wear masks.

We worry that we will get COVID-19. We worry more about the impact of being seen and experienced through a mask. After all, bad guys wear masks—not good guys. How do we build trust leading to neuroceptions of enough safety and security to sustain patients and families, many of whom are experiencing the trauma of having a sick child on top of their baseline allostatic load?

ESTABLISHING EPISTEMIC TRUST WHILE SOCIAL DISTANCING

> *Epistemic trust is there to ensure that the individual can safely change his/her position; it triggers the opening of what we can think of as an epistemic superhighway—an evolutionarily protected mechanism that signals readiness to acquire knowledge.*
> —PETER FONAGY AND ELIZABETH ALLISON, 2014

Our biological imperative is to socially engage with other humans. Our evolutionarily determined ecological niche is finding safety and security in the presence of others (Porges, 2011). Yet sheltering in place and social distancing now define the boundaries of our world. Minute by minute, healthcare providers, trusted public health officers, responsible government officials, and the media message us to avoid physical proximity to others. Physical proximity puts you at risk—avoid touching and exchanging secretions. Every countertop is potentially a vector for acquiring the virus. Wear masks outside the house, maintain social distance at all times, wear gloves, and do not open packages for at least 24 hours.

Print, digital, and television media all bombard us with data. We are all now self-declared experts in epidemiology. Many people can recount exactly how many new COVID-19 cases, hospital admissions, and deaths occurred in their town or state in the past day, week, or month. How do we manage this tsunami of information? Whom do we trust to provide accurate and timely information?

Epistemology is simply the study of knowledge. Epistemic trust is "the ability to appraise incoming information from the social world as accurate, reliable, and personally relevant, allowing the information to be incorporated into existing knowledge domains" (Orme, Bowersox, Vanwoerden, Fonagy, & Sharp, 2019, p. 14). Our openness and appraisal of new information is biologically embedded through our earliest exposures to caregiving relationships. Epistemic trust builds through caregiving relationships (see Figure 9.1). The attuned and sensitive caregiver interacts with the newborn and then with the infant or toddler with contingent responsiveness, turn-taking, and delight recognizing the growing intentionality of the child. The child who feels known by the adult caregiver develops an internal working model of self-worth and value and thus, feeling known and valued, can trust the caregiver to provide reliable information. For the youngest infants and children, the information conveyed is the reliable physical and emotional proximity of the

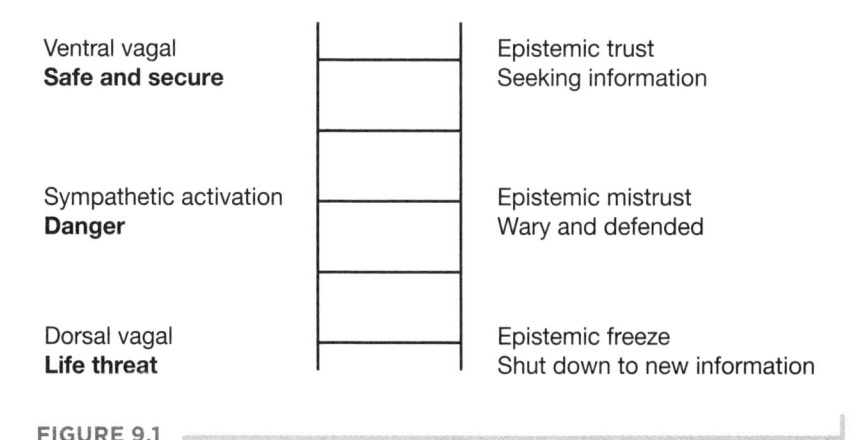

Ventral vagal **Safe and secure**		Epistemic trust Seeking information
Sympathetic activation **Danger**		Epistemic mistrust Wary and defended
Dorsal vagal **Life threat**		Epistemic freeze Shut down to new information

FIGURE 9.1

Polyvagal Theory and epistemic trust. Created with data from Dana, D. (2018) and Fonagy, P., & Allison, A. (2014).

caregiver. The infant becomes the child who experiences the sensitive and attuned caregiver. The child develops epistemic trust in his caregivers to provide reliable information. Now on the epistemic superhighway, the child is open to acquiring knowledge.

Development of epistemic trust, however, is far from a foregone conclusion. Even very young infants are able to assess the reliability of information; they are vigilant to disruptions of social connectedness. Some vigilance is protective and reinforces safety and security. When the parent leaves the room, the 8-month-old may whimper or cry. Developmentally, he fears being alone and does not feel his parent is available once they are outside the room. As they turn, return to the bedside, and comfort and touch the child, they reinforce to him that they will be there when needed. Sadly, for some infants, their caregivers are rarely in emotional or physical proximity. They feel epistemic hyperviligance and mistrust, experienced as danger to their well-being. Finally, those infants and young children who are chronically abandoned sit at the bottom of the epistemic ladder, in freeze or life threat (Fonagy & Allison, 2014).

An epidemic of epistemic mistrust and freeze now afflicts us individually, in our communities, and in our larger society. Socially distanced, sheltered in place, and isolated from our larger families, friends, and communities, we yearn to trust an authority figure who will provide accurate and timely information amidst the continuing uncertainty. We seek to identify what we know and to narrow the range of what we do not know. For all of us, the uncertainty is potentially dysregulating. For some, it is intolerable, and epistemic freeze substitutes strong belief systems for more solid scientific information and recommendations deriving from them.

Anthony Fauci, the director of the National Institute of Allergy and Infectious Diseases, stands apart from others in his just-the-facts approach to reporting the state of COVID-19. Bottle-openers, coffee mugs, and bumper stickers display his face with the tagline, "In Fauci we trust." Yet, at the same time, there are countless Twitter accounts pushing the hashtag "#FauciFraud" and enough death threats to lead to the appointment of a personal security detail (Specter, 2020).

The scientific gold standard is hypothesis-driven research generating data that is analyzed and leads to evidence-based conclusions. In the COVID-19 pandemic, the public is seeing science unfold in real time. Physicians and other scientists are sharing their experiences and their evolving evidence and research on social media, blogs, and podcasts to avoid the delays inherent in publishing in peer-reviewed journals. In the absence of scientific training, the public might not understand the difference between belief systems and evidence-based science.

We need to empathize with the distress caused by uncertainty, have compassion for the dysregulation uncertainty causes, and emphasize the necessity of using accurate and timely data to drive our behaviors. At home and in the workplace (for some), we try to engender trust, allay fears, and reach down the ladder to assist those whose autonomic nervous systems are overwhelmed. How can we as parents, spouses, friends, and professional caregivers reach across the gulf of social distance to engender good enough safety and security? As polyvagal-informed clinicians, we offer the general recommendations below for mitigating some COVID-19 related distress Although the pandemic may have waned as you read this book, lessons from this crisis can be applied to future periods of adversity.

1. **REEVALUATE OUR SOURCES AND TIMING OF RECEIVING INFORMATION.** There are vast differences in the sensory signals we receive from live television, digital media, and

print. Some news sources, trusted in calmer times, are now dysregulating. We have come to appreciate others who previously may not have seemed as crisp in their assessments. Now their straightforward approach is easier to hear and assimilate. Print lacks the immediacy and multi-sensory impact of the digital or live television experience. It may be more tolerable right now. Consider silencing your notifications. Does your autonomic nervous system really benefit from knowing the latest death tolls or numbers of new cases in the moment?

2. **DISCUSS HOW, WHEN, AND WHAT INFORMATION WE SHARE WITH FAMILY, FRIENDS, AND COWORKERS.** Use of social media enables us to send and receive information. The nature and quality of the information varies widely. The degree of activation news reports cause among people varies dramatically. For example, a recent headline in a local paper, "Newborn baby among 16 additional COVID-19 deaths in Connecticut" caused alarm and fear among pregnant and newly delivered young mothers and families. The baby was 6 weeks old and was positive for COVID-19. The final cause of death was not known when this unfortunate headline was published (Putterman, 2020).

3. **ENRICH OUR CONVERSATIONS WITH EXPLICIT DISCUSSIONS OF EMOTIONS AND EMOTIONAL STATES.** When we are not in the room, we may well miss the subtle verbal and nonverbal signals of a person's neuroceptive state. Their muscle tension, hand signals, posture, and facial expressions are impossible to discern over the phone or in text and may be difficult to interpret when using online visual platforms. When we consider the ordinary challenges in communicating in text or online, the additional allostatic

load of COVID-19 challenges even those of us who are typically trusting and near the top of the ladder.

Talk about emotions and feeling states. We often hesitate to ask people about their feelings, citing concerns for privacy. This is the time to ask and to be forthcoming when asked. "Are you worried about your child, your partner, your job, your mental health, your physical health, your relationship with your partner, your financial security? Do you feel anxious, depressed, or isolated? How do you address your anxiety, depression, or isolation?"

If you hear hesitation, ask more questions. "Are you safe with your partner, do you have enough to eat, do you have money for rent, food, and medications? Are you engaging in risky or self-injurious behaviors?" If you sense they feel in danger and are moving down the autonomic ladder, ask if they have thoughts of hurting themselves or anyone else. Do they have someone they can depend upon if they feel desperate or likely to harm themselves, a child, a partner, or anyone else? Pay particular attention to conversations with people who are at higher risk for taking their own lives, including physicians, nurses, and elderly persons (National Academy of Medicine, 2020). This is not the time to hide behind privacy concerns. The principle of respect for privacy may unwittingly contribute to someone falling in harm's way. Your question may well save a life.

RACIAL DISPARITIES IN COVID-19 INFECTION AND OUTCOMES

COVID-19 is a magnifying glass that has highlighted the larger pandemic of racial/ethnic disparities in health.
—DAVID WILLIAMS AND LISA COOPER, 2020

As we saw in Chapter 5, people of color in the U.S. often receive substandard healthcare, and these racial disparities in healthcare are associated with a prevalence of white decision-makers. African American, Latino, and other persons of color are at increased risk for COVID-19 infection and deaths. For example in Chicago, African Americans had rates of infection and mortality more than twice the rate of white residents (Colvin & Murphy, 2020). Furthermore, age adjusted COVID-19 associated-mortality of Latino and African Americans in New York is more than twice white residents (Latino persons 187/100,000; African American persons 184/100,000, and white persons 93/100,000) (NYC Health COVID-19 data, 2020).

Kim and Bostwick (2020) link the higher death rates by neighborhoods among African Americans in Chicago to increased social vulnerability and health risk factors. Social vulnerability is a construct that combines sociodemographic characteristics including percentages of poverty, less than high school education, female headed households with children, median household income, and employment ratio. Deaths from COVID-19 were highly correlated with neighborhoods of increased social vulnerability and health risk factors. Areas with higher death rates mapped onto neighborhoods with increased percentages of African American residents. Likewise, areas with lower death rates mapped onto neighborhoods that had low social vulnerability, low health risk factors, and a higher percentage of white residents.

Kim and Bostwick (2020) indicate these racial disparities in outcomes are not unique to COVID-19. They are documented in a long history of natural disasters including infectious disease pandemics. Given the autonomic impact of structural stigmatization and systemic racism (Neblett & Roberts, 2013), COVID-19 challenges us individually and systemically to deconstruct the pathways to poor outcomes and design ways of being with others and structural interventions that begin to level the playing field. Williams and Cooper (2020) recognize health equity begins with equitable health care, both in terms of access and quality. But, as they point out, good health depends upon access to the social determinants of health, often insufficient in racially segregated, non-white neighborhoods. Even with equitable access to high-quality medical care, the health of marginalized communities will not improve until housing, income, education, employment, and neighborhood environment are equalized as well.

REACHING OUT TO YOU THROUGH MY EYES

Those eyes so wise, so warm, so real
How I love the world your eyes reveal
—LESLIE BRICUSSE, 1967

Porges (2011) explicitly discusses the power of social engagement through the face-heart connection to regulate our own autonomic nervous systems and neuroceptive states. Throughout evolutionary biology, the more highly evolved ventral, smart, or social vagal nerve body moved forward in the brainstem. In this new location, the ventral vagus linked the control of the heart with regulation of the muscles of the face, neck, and head. Because of this co-location, the muscles of the eyes, middle ear, face, mouth, throat, and neck send and receive signals both of our own neuroceptions of safety or danger, and the neuroceptions of others. What others see in our eyes and our facial expressions, hear in our voices, and notice in the positions of our heads signals either approach or avoidant behaviors.

When we put on masks, the muscles of the face and mouth are not visible; signals from our voices may be muffled as we inhale our masks with each breath. If the situation requires full personal protective equipment (PPE), we add goggles or a full face mask with shield. In full PPE, we may resemble the avenging forces from a science fiction movie. We project only our eyes, our head position, the rhythm and music of our voices, and our gestures.

What strategies and skills can we use to signal approach rather than avoidant behaviors? How can we build neuroceptions of safety and security in an environment that broadcasts danger in the presence of others? How can we reassure and gain trust of those whose prior traumas and disruptions of connectedness without repair make them particularly vulnerable to both short- and long-term dysregulation and suffering?

According to Wong (2020), Robertino Rodriguez, a respiratory therapist in San Diego, sparked a viral movement among healthcare workers to wear a large photo of themselves smiling on the front of their PPE. "A smile goes a long way in comforting a scared patient—bringing some brightness in these dark times," Rodriguez said. We intuitively recognize the value of a smile, and one's person's actions can remind us all of what we already know. The HuffPost interviewed one physician from Los Angeles, and she said, "she hopes the photos take some of the strangeness out of the experience for patients with COVID symptoms." According to Wong, the physician went on to say:

> These patients come in with a cough, shortness of breath, or fever and the question on their minds and everyone's mind is, 'Do I have COVID?' she said. I can only imagine how intimidating it is seeing a team of nurses, respiratory therapists and doctors entering their room in full PPE gear, on top of everything else. A photo, she said, helps patients connect a human and a smile to the walking spacesuit and masks in front of them.

ACKNOWLEDGE THE IMPACT OF COVID-19 ON DAILY ROUTINES AND RELATIONSHIPS

As we now greet new patients, clients, customers, and students, we can be explicit that these are unusual times. Invite others to discuss how COVID-19 has altered their routines, their immediate family, and their local and remote relationships. Pay close attention to both their narrative and their nonverbal expressions.

Some may find it easier to use images to describe their feelings or challenges. As mentioned other places in this book, it may be helpful to use the autonomic, automatic ladder developed by Deb Dana (2018, 2020). Dana says "The automatic autonomic ladder is a way to create a shared language and shorthand" (personal communication, 2020) (See Figure 9.2). Once you have a shared language,

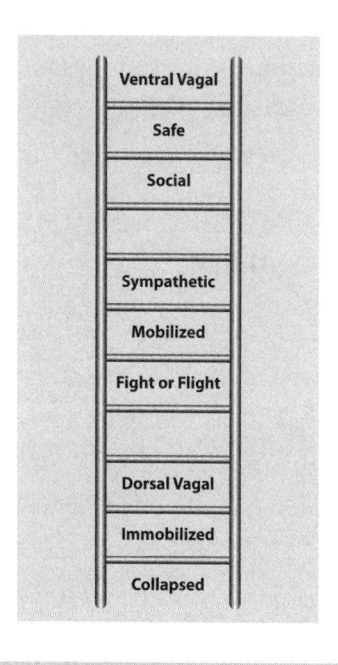

FIGURE 9.2

The automatic, autonomic ladder. From THE POLYVAGAL THEORY IN THERAPY: ENGAGING THE RHYTHM OF REGULATION by Deb Dana. Copyright © 2018 by Deb Dana. Used by permission of W. W. Norton & Company, Inc.

you can begin to explore the signals of danger in the present environment and assist others to define and make explicit what they need to feel safer.

REDUCE UNCERTAINTY BY PROVIDING INFORMATION PROACTIVELY ON THE CHANGING ENVIRONMENT

As of this writing, we are deep into the COVID-19 pandemic. Many lives are lost. Many more will still die. Personal protective equipment may be a signal of danger to some (e.g., patients) and safety to others (e.g., healthcare staff, delivery drivers, first responders). For patients, the hospital emergency room is a signal of both relief and terror as they are separated from their loved ones who will go back to the car or home while the patients are triaged and seen. Taking the time to explain how they will see people dressed and why, reassuring them you are there to assist, and asking families for information on their loved ones' likes and dislikes will all signal your humanity and commitment to seeing their relatives are cared for well.

CAN YOU HEAR MY SMILE?

Let your eyes speak to the wisdom, warmth, and care you feel. From the time we are infants, we are drawn to the direct gaze of another person. Infants as young as 4 weeks old look for their mother's eye gaze during nursing. By 3 months, infants smile in response to eye contact and stop smiling when another's eyes are averted. Older children and adults use the frequency of eye contact to judge a social relationship (Jarrett, 2016).

Illness is associated with enhanced vulnerability that often broadcasts danger. When you know and trust your healthcare providers, that danger may be mitigated by your earlier experiences, allowing you to feel safe enough as long as you are progressing well. COVID-19 upends our typical paradigm of seeking health care from our usual providers. Primary care providers may be on limited schedules, often using telehealth for patient visits. When you are seriously ill, you are directed to the emergency department, where you know no one, the staff is dressed in full PPE, your family is asked to wait elsewhere, and you are aware many who enter the hospital do not leave. If patients are already sliding down the autonomic ladder, they have little distance to fall before collapse, immobilization, and terror rule.

We can try to pull our patients up the autonomic ladder by clear introductions of ourselves and our role. Perhaps, like Robertino Rodriguez, you might wear a full-face picture on your PPE. Let your eyes convey your warmth and caring and smile as you welcome them to your care. They will see the smile in your eyes and notice the rearrangement of your mask as your facial muscles conform to a smile. You may wish to explain that your mask muffles your voice and ask them if they can hear you. Your unconscious head tilt to the right allows you to speak right brain to right brain as you explore the reasons the patient sits before you and how you can help. When you bring a ventral vagal presence to the room, the healing process begins as the patient feels welcomed into your world. The seeds of trust may be sown early in the interaction. Even in the brief time you are with the patient, you can ease their distress no matter what their eventual health outcome by your presence and being with them.

HEALTHCARE PROVIDERS ARE DYING

The authors are graduates of U.S. medical school training. Together, we have over 70 years of medical school education, postgraduate training, and practice. We trained prior to implementation of work duty hours. We routinely worked and continued to work long shifts. Families and childbearing were delayed. We often ask ourselves, how did we make it through the long sleepless nights? How did we develop permanent relationships that sustain us? How did we have the time (or the courage) to start our own families and parent the children who taught us about perseverance, commitment, and unconditional love?

The social engagement and connectedness we experienced with fellow trainees, the support we received from our friends and families, and the gratitude we received and cherished from patients, families, and staff sustained us through exhausting and dark times. COVID-19 is a disruption of layers of connectedness both inside and outside the hospital system. It is challenging for all of us. It is killing some of us.

Deep and enduring relationships are the constant that buoyed us as individuals and preserved our mental health and emotional well-being. When the wards were overwhelming, we worked among fellow trainees, shared loads, traded responsibilities, and looked out for those who might be floundering. We ate together, savoring a few minutes between admissions or crises. We stepped up to take the late admission because we knew someone else needed to get to daycare to pick up a kid or was exhausted from a long call night. We laughed at the ironies, were outraged by the ridiculous, and sobbed in each other's arms when tragedies struck. Trusting and supportive friendships often evolved with our nursing colleagues as we soldiered on side by side through challenging situations. We were only rarely afraid of each other or our patients.

Prior to COVID-19, Southwick and Southwick (2020) called attention to decreasing social support among physicians associated with increased burnout, loneliness, and social isolation. They cited excessive time devoted to the electronic health record, shift work, greater workloads, a more corporate-driven environment, and increased time on social media platforms. None of these factors remitted during COVID-19. With cruel irony, there are even fewer face-to-face interactions, as all meetings, professional learning, and conversations are online. During virus surges, many outpatient visits use telehealth. Meeting online is a critical containment strategy. Using telehealth is essential, especially given the number of medically fragile patients for whom we care. Unfortunately, the cumulative effect of this distancing from colleagues and patients robs us of the good stuff—the camaraderie, the sense of collegiality, and the joy of team successes. Unremitting social distancing creates an increased allostatic load that leaves us with the bad stuff—endless exhaustion; despair due to high mortality and limited resources; isolation from family, friends, and natural support systems; and fear and terror as personal protective equipment may be locked up and distributed like precious metals. Watching isolated patients suffer and die carries its own allostatic load for healthcare providers. As physician Dhruv Khullar (2020) commented, "There are no families whispering well wishes or holding patients' hands. Watching someone suffer alone is its own form of punishment." For some, the ghosts of the dead, the refrigerator trucks outside the hospitals, and the sense they just couldn't do enough and were responsible for deaths have tragic consequences as healthcare providers themselves die of COVID-19 or physicians, nurses, and other healthcare providers take their own lives (Dean, 2020).

POLYVAGAL LEADERSHIP IN THE TIME OF COVID-19

At this moment, states are lifting lockdown and reopening personal services and businesses. The healthcare community knows too robust a retreat from social distancing will have a dire cost in suffering and loss of life. Our grave concern, however, competes with the sense of danger and life threat coming from others waving the flag of individual freedom and potentially irreparable economic loss. In this time of uncertainty and not knowing, we found professionals across employment sectors who embody polyvagal-inspired leadership.

Physician Ken Gross (2020) is chief of staff at Bryan Medical Center in Lincoln, Nebraska. In a recent newsletter, he reminded his staff, "If we don't take care of ourselves, we might not be able to help others. We need each one of us as we move forward. It's like the days of old and the bucket brigade. Each person on that line was crucial to putting out the fire. They counted on each other to keep the water flowing consistently and without delay. And we are counting on each other now." He goes on to encourage staff to build connections, monitor themselves for burnout and stress, identify ways to reduce burnout and stress, stay socially connected, try something new, and to make an action plan. Dr. Gross's imagery of the collective effort of the bucket brigade invites virtual social connectedness as he works to ensure his troops are as safe and secure as possible under the circumstances.

A particularly striking example of a public official who demonstrates polyvagal leadership is Tom Tait, the former mayor of Anaheim, California (2010–2018), a city of 350,000 (Tait, personal communication, 2020). In his 8 years as mayor of Anaheim, Tait established Anaheim as a City of Kindness with initiatives including A Million Acts of Kindness in the Anaheim elementary schools. As mayor, Tait asked himself, "What would a kind city do?" as he approached the myriad of challenges in his medium-sized, diverse community.

Tait, who is also the CEO of TAIT and Associates, talked about what needs to be done right now to assist people. "We've adopted a company of kindness core value. I put out a weekly video of me at home just talking, and I talk about kindness every time. I ask them to lean in and be kind. We put out a kindness newsletter every week. We talk about stories of kindness and try to get people to write. It becomes contagious. I had to jump out of my comfort zone to do this. The feedback is really great."

Tait uses vivid images to build social engagement and social connectedness, such as a story about his wife Julie's childhood on a ranch in Wyoming as one of eight kids. "Her dad took an old wooden matchstick and he'd break it. Then he'd take 10 matchsticks and say, you can't break these. I used this to say, we are all in this together. We are strong and resilient."

Tait said Anaheim's City of Kindness campaign during his mayoral terms also made it easier to stand up to special interests groups. "This kindness campaign is like looking out for your family. You represent the people. Kindness creates a special bond and makes doing the right thing much, much easier."

"What's so great about this is that everyone is a leader in something, be it family, a small group of friends, a teacher, a student in a classroom, a principal. If you just start talking about it, it just happens." For example, Tait worked with the chief of police and the police union to establish a program in which police officers brought persons with substance use concerns into treatment rather than arresting them. With pride, Tait reported that gang and juvenile crime decreased dramatically after the City of Kindness initiative began. The local school system reported that both bullying incidents and suspensions were cut in half (Tait, personal communication, 2020).

Professor Paula Sanders teaches at Rice University and directs the Boniuk Institute for Religious Tolerance (personal communication, 2020). Like educators throughout the country, she transitioned from face-to-face to virtual instruction in 2 weeks. Rice sent students home throughout the United States and to countries as far as the Asian continent. Sanders asked herself, "How am I going to create a sense of engagement and community if I have to teach entirely online? This is not about technology. This is about social and intellectual issues." With ongoing feedback from her students, Sanders developed a curriculum for the rest of the school year. Drawing upon her sense of humor, she included use of emoticons and rubber duckies suitable to the weekly content to convey tone. The school year ended, and Sanders noted that feedback from her students was overwhelmingly positive. "Knowing that someone cared about them was critically important. Students repeatedly said, 'Thank you for your flexibility, and thank you for your kindness.'" Looking at the implications for education moving forward, she commented, "COVID-19 exposes all the educational gaps secondary to deep structural inequities. Foremost is a deep structural deficit in infrastructure that promotes nurturing and connection" (personal communication, 2020).

In a message to her youngest constituents and their families, New Zealand Prime Minister Jacinda Ardern commented, "You'll be pleased to know that we do consider both the Tooth Fairy and the Easter Bunny to be essential workers. But as you can imagine at this time, of course they're going to be potentially quite busy at home with their family as well and their own bunnies. And so I say to the children of New Zealand: if the Easter Bunny doesn't make it to your household, then we have to understand that it's a bit difficult at the moment for the bunny to perhaps get everywhere" (Garcia, 2020). With whimsy and gentle reassurance, Ardern used her self-regulatory capacity and her platform as prime minister to disseminate a message of calm and resilience. Even at a time of uncertainty and calamity, Ardern assured her young stakeholders that she recognized the importance of their neuroceptions of safety, danger, or life threat by acknowledging the Tooth Fairy and Easter Bunny as essential workers. The prime minister even foresaw and forestalled a potential downward slide on the autonomic ladder by asking for empathy for the beleaguered bunny who may find his own allostatic load increased.

The distance in time between writing this chapter and its publication will reveal a future not yet imaginable. During even this seemingly impossible epoch in our collective experience, leaders arise who keep their own neuroceptions of the safety, danger, or life threat of others in mind. While all of these professionals are experts in their own fields, few have extensive education or training in Polyvagal Theory. By listening to their own autonomic nervous systems, they are beacons and regulators for others in distress. We are all learning about ourselves, our relationships to those closest to us, to those we serve, and to our larger global community. We are persisting, adapting, and succeeding in ways we would previously have thought impossible. As we learn to find safety and connection in new ways with others, we ask ourselves, "What next?" The final chapter of this book addresses both challenges in the unimaginable world ahead and polyvagal-informed ways of being that show promise in leveraging our collective strengths.

CHAPTER 10

Safe to Do What? The Vitalizing Power of the Social Engagement System

In working with trauma for over three decades, I have come to the conclusion that human beings are born with an innate capacity to triumph over trauma. I believe not only that trauma is curable, but that the healing process can be a catalyst for profound awakening—a portal opening to emotional and genuine spiritual transformation. I have little doubt that as individuals, families, communities, and even nations, we have the capacity to learn how to heal and prevent much of the damage done by trauma. In so doing, we will significantly increase our ability to achieve both our individual and collective dreams.
—PETER A. LEVINE, 2008

In 2021, the world continues to fight the COVID-19 pandemic. The Johns Hopkins University & Medicine Coronavirus Resource Center reports hundreds of millions of documented cases of COVID-19 globally with millions of deaths. In the United States, we've had millions of cases and more than 500,000 deaths (Coronavirus Resource Center, 2021). There is no end in sight. Effective vaccines are now available that will both limit the spread of the virus and prevent severe infection or death in those who subsequently become infected. The Coronavirus Resource Center still reports tens of thousands of new cases and hundreds of deaths daily.

We believe that embodying Polyvagal Theory is an essential part of healing from our individual and collective traumas and creating what we have only dreamed is possible. What are the opportunities to embed Polyvagal Theory in our lives as we fear both for ourselves and the lives of those we love? Many of us enjoy lives of privilege by virtue of socioeconomic status, skin color, gender identity, and education. We were born lucky, even though we struggle with our neuroceptions of danger and life threat for ourselves and those we love. How do we understand the neuroceptions of danger and life threat experienced by the sick and infirm, those disadvantaged by poor access to health care, and immigrants whose status as residents is at risk? Even more difficult, how do we understand the neuroceptions of danger and life threat of those with whom we most vigorously disagree on effective ways to diminish COVID-19 risks? Finally, what actions are indicated for less fortunate and oppressed peoples to increase access to care, education, and economic reparations for prior harms?

Our neuroceptions are driven by the deeply embedded experiences of prior generations and are the template upon which our own emotions and behaviors are generated. The English language has many familiar idioms that refer to the visceral and bodily expressions of the ANS. "I feel it in my gut," "I follow my heart," "I know it in my bones," "I seized up," and "I feel uncomfortable" are all expressions whose meaning we intuitively know even if we have no familiarity with Polyvagal Theory or neuroception. In a well-modulated ANS, the sensory input of "I feel uncomfortable" is processed and modulated in the prefrontal cortex, finally reaching the frontal cortex. In the well-exercised frontal cortex, our prior knowledge, experience, and clues from the external environment are brought to bear, signaling the lower centers that we are safe or in danger.

However, in a dysregulated ANS that experienced prior adversity or recurring trauma, the sense of "I feel uncomfortable" may not reach the prefrontal cortex as fear or terror causes a recurrent cycling through the limbic system. The amygdala sounds an alarm; the hippocampus reiterates the distress call as it retrieves old memories; the HPA axis and the SNS are activated, eventually resulting in cortisol and adrenaline release that pulls a person down the autonomic ladder with ongoing sympathetic activation or immobilization or collapse.

DEVELOP AN IMPLICIT AND EXPLICIT LANGUAGE OF POLYVAGAL-INFORMED COMMUNICATION

Polyvagal-informed persons provide cues of safety using their facial expressions, gestures, and the intonation of their voices. When there is more ventral vagal influence to the muscles of the larynx, sounds are more variable and calming. Likewise, vagal influence on the middle ear muscles produces higher frequency soft sounds that communicate safety to the mammalian brain. This musical way of speaking that the child development literature calls *motherese* (e.g., Fonagy & Allison, 2014) is what adults intuitively use when speaking to infants and is found in many lullabies; it broadcasts signals of safety and security.

In healthy relationships, adults learn to listen for the soundtrack the children with whom they live or work are hearing. Adults know the musical score influences the child more powerfully than any particular word. Polyvagal-informed adults engage in emotional serve and return with infants and young children who feel increasingly seen, heard, and known. As caregivers and their young children develop this communication, they use their ability to speak in words of safety. The musicality of the voice scores the scenes that they are enacting.

Scenarios in Chapters 6, 7, and 8 are examples of polyvagal-informed interactions that implicitly convey safety and calm to children both through nonverbal and verbal communication. Assisting children in identifying where they are on the autonomic ladder in the moment helps them explicitly notice their sensations and the accompanying feeling states. Having recognized their feelings, they can then identify signals and triggers to which their autonomic nervous system (ANS) responds and with a trusted adult explore the fit to their emotions and behaviors.

USE UNDERSTANDING OF OUR AUTONOMIC NERVOUS SYSTEM TO BUILD A SAFETY CIRCUIT

Whether it is with our own children, our life partners, our families of origin, friends, coworkers, or larger communities, becoming polyvagal-informed starts with an understanding of, acceptance of, and respect for our own autonomic nervous systems. Trauma expert Bruce Perry's (2013) neurosequential model demonstrates the bottom up organization of the brain from the brainstem to the limbic system midbrain, to the prefrontal cortex, and finally to the top or neocortex. As the mammalian brain develops from bottom to top, both plasticity and complexity increase. Perry emphasizes the critical importance of addressing the brainstem, midbrain, and limbic system components of trauma before we can expect ourselves to significantly change our behaviors.

As we become more polyvagal-informed, we are aware of the bodily sensations that precede our affects, emotions, and subsequent behaviors. When we bring curiosity to this process, we link sensation and affect to form an increasingly coherent narrative life story. The coherence of our narrative builds, and we modify our behaviors to maintain calm and minimize sympathetic activation or immobilization or freeze. Each of us has a neuroceptive thumbprint (an autonomic profile) that is unique to us. However, unlike the thumbprint we are born with and will die with, our neuroceptions are often modifiable. Bringing self-compassion and deliberate attention to bodily sensations, we understand that our neuroceptions of danger and life threat often represent our past, not our present or our desired future. Increasing our bodily awareness and coherent narrative builds safety circuits to guide us in our daily lives.

In the idealized circuit, we feel safety and security in our earliest relationships that foster ventral vagal social engagement leading to social connectedness (see Figure 10.1). Since social connectedness enhances safety, we become attached to one or more early attachment figures. The circuit becomes iterative as these early attachments foster a positive working model of self that then reinforces safety, opening the door to an increasingly robust circle of persons with whom we socially engage, connect, and attach.

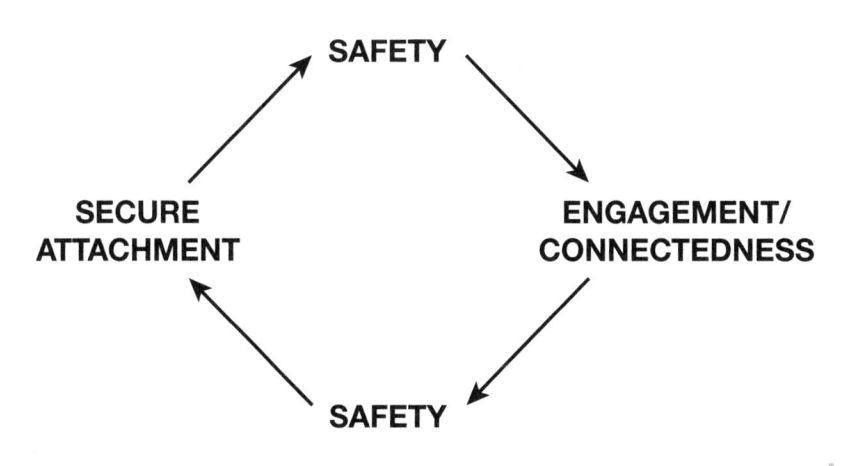

```
            SAFETY
           ↗      ↘
   SECURE          ENGAGEMENT/
 ATTACHMENT        CONNECTEDNESS
           ↖      ↙
            SAFETY
```

FIGURE 10.1

The safety circuit.

When a momentary misattunement ruptures the connection, caregivers can repair the relationship by acknowledging the disharmony, providing empathy and an apology for the upset caused, and explicitly stating how much the relationship means to them.

However, early disruptions without repair disrupt this circuit of safety and security. Developmental traumas, including child abuse, neglect, or indifference are early and severe disruptions. The cost of feeling unloved is high. These children often grow up without a positive working model of self, feeling unworthy, unloved, and shamed. They may ask questions such as, "Do I even deserve to exist?" Their neuroceptions are of danger and life threat because of their aloneness in formative years. Moreover, they wear the scars and scabs of their early disruptions and losses that may present as chronic depression, suicidality, substance use, or workalcoholism.

Turning to the future, if we continue to integrate polyvagal insights into relationships, education, and programs and make them explicit, professionals will assist parents to manage and redirect distressing physiological states of mind and body, rather than being at their mercy. These programs will be an elite brain and heart academy, where both staff and clients learn to operate their nervous systems deliberately. They can shape and exercise their ANS and choose their own neuroceptive diet. They will work together to be in the most empowering and enjoyable mind/body states, and from there, learn to overcome any obstacle, to build and maintain resilient relationships, and to work and play together.

Becoming polyvagal-informed is an opportunity to begin transforming ourselves and others from victims of our neuroceptions to resilient and active agents of change. We see implications for parenting education, professional education and training systems, provision of early childhood services, and policies that provide protections, safeguards, and support to the most vulnerable among us.

TEACHING PARENTS POLYVAGAL THEORY INITIATES AN INTERGENERATIONAL TRANSMISSION OF AUTONOMIC WISDOM AND EXPERTISE

I hope that instead of falling into a guilt pit of "I'm a bad parent/ teacher," you will choose the battle cry of wisdom: "I can see more clearly now—and I use my power to choose where I go from here."
—CLAIRE WILSON, 2018

It is never too early to start educating parents-to-be, new parents, and experienced parents about neuroception and the autonomic nervous system. Each of us meets with new parents in the hospital and the healthcare provider's office as well as the many neighborhood and community settings that ordinarily host infants, young children, and their families. All new parents want to know that you cherish their child. Lose no opportunity to "ooh" and "ahh" over the baby, paying particular attention to the baby's attempts to locate the parents with eye gaze and vocalizations. Notice the beauty of the sensitive and attuned parent's return of this gift of recognition. Take a moment out from your business with the baby to comment on what you see: "Look how he gazes at you . . . what gorgeous eyes he has . . . his smile when he sees you makes me melt." No one was born knowing how to be a parent, and the affirmation parents receive from you builds competence and confidence in their caregiving. Make no assumptions that any professional training or other expertise confers the skills necessary to be a good enough parent.

As you talk with parents about their parenting and their children, notice how readily a parent is able to mentalize their child's experience. Mentalizing, defined by Fonagy and Target (1997) as the "capacity to envision mental states in self and others" (p. 679), depends on the adult caregivers' abilities to reflect upon their own sensory inputs processed by the autonomic nervous system and given life as neuroceptions. In other words, if you cannot respect your own ANS, you cannot appreciate your own neuroceptions and thus you cannot reflect upon your own mental state. Recognizing your own neuroceptions of safety, danger, or life threat is a precondition for the capacity to mentalize the experience of others. As providers, we can help parents notice their own automatic reactions and relaxations, then use their self-awareness to look for changes in their children's states.

The Center for the Study of Social Policy's (CSSP) Strengthening Families framework (Doyle et al., 2019) highlights the importance of building parental resilience and social connections as the first two key steps in promoting healthy development and mitigating risk. Furthermore, they advise providers to use positive affirming feedback to guide well-child visits and interactions with families. The CSSP website (2020) is replete with excellent information for both providers and families. However, absent from these materials is education on the evolutionarily determined neurobiologic explanations for their recommendations. The website includes updated materials for families and providers to assist them in weathering the COVID-19 pandemic.

Incorporating Polyvagal Theory into parenting education will enrich the materials by providing the neurophysiologic and biologic "Why?" in addition to the "What to do?" And knowing the "Why?" helps give meaning to "What to do?" Particularly when public divisiveness over the balance of risk and freedom abounds, redirecting and supporting families to our evolutionarily determined biological imperative to socially engage helps us both understand the "What to do?" and reinforces safer and less risky ways of connecting with those we love.

An example of a polyvagal-informed framework for parenting is the Circle of Security (2020) developed by Cooper, Hoffman, and Powell. Using an attachment-based framework, Circle of Security assists parents and other caregivers to function as the necessary secure base from which young children learn to explore their environment. It offers a safe haven when young children neurocept danger and life threat in their lives. In its curriculum, Circle of Security emphasizes caregivers developing relationship capacities rather than learning techniques. The Circle of Security also addresses disruptions in connectedness using a mutual repair routine that includes a neutral "Time-in spot" where the parent guides the child to express their feelings, talks about the adults' own feelings, and remains a physical presence until the child calms. As Cooper and colleagues (2018) say, "Bottom line: It's the relationship (and only the relationship) that will build the child's capacity to organize her/his feelings. My child's problem may look like something is being done on purpose. But at its root, it's an issue of needing to reconnect and learning how to handle difficult feelings in a safe and secure way."

Teaching parents Polyvagal Theory builds a momentum that counters some of the ways that trauma can travel generationally. As we saw in Chapters 4 and 5, when trauma is not addressed, its effects will be passed from generation to generation in caravans of risk, each successive generation bearing a neuroceptive imprint from the preceding generation. When caregivers embody and embrace polyvagal-informed child rearing, they prepare their children to meet the challenges of the world with more ventral vagal composure. When the children become adults, they will have more capacity to move through difficult times successfully because they will know what to do when neurocepted dangers start pushing them down the autonomic ladder. When challenged, they can notice their state and take self-correcting steps to return to ventral vagal, working to regulate their own nervous systems and asking for support when needed.

Caregivers who embrace polyvagal-informed child rearing make an impact beyond their own families because each person who embodies polyvagal knowledge sends ripples of safety into the world. These ripples extend across time as well, as these children become parents themselves. Adults whose parents understood their infants' early need for co-regulation will spontaneously co-regulate their own children when they are distressed. They will understand that they first need to guide their children back to social engagement before moving on to anything else. Imagine if each generation is a little more regulated, a little more autonomically aware, a little more connected. Polyvagal-informed child rearing can set in motion the intergenerational transmission of autonomic wisdom and expertise.

PROVIDE CUES OF SAFETY AND ATTEND TO AND REPAIR DISRUPTIONS IN PROFESSIONAL EDUCATION AND TRAINING

We need to access the neuroceptions of medical students and help them feel safe so they can access their best selves.
—ISABELLA KNOX, 2020

Professional education and training programs, whether in health or mental health care, education, social services, or other professions that touch people's lives, need both content and assurance of profession-based skills and competencies. Professional competence is typically demonstrated by graduating from an accredited professional school, passing standardized examinations, completing postgraduate training, and acquiring certifications and licensure. Beyond the content, technical skills, and competencies, however, there is another implicit curriculum, that of building and sustaining relationships. To build and sustain relationships, professional educators and students across the professional disciplines benefit from creating safe learning culture environments.

In the language of Polyvagal Theory, educators provide cues of safety and security and attend to or repair disruptions. Like the adult caregiver in Circle of Security interactions, educators provide a secure base from which learners can safely explore, consider, create, and learn. Educators also are a safe haven to which a learner can retreat for reassurance when cues of danger lurk. In effect, the educator may become an attachment figure for the learner. As John Bowlby (1988) reminded, "All of us, from the cradle to the grave, are happiest when life is organized as a series of excursions, long or short, from the secure base provided by our attachment figure(s)" (p. 61).

For example, consider the following vignette and how instilling Polyvagal Theory modifies the experience for the learner.

- Jack, an Asian man, is a recent medical school graduate who earned a surgical residency position in a distinguished program. Jack is eager, diligent, and hardworking. He also has a warm, gentle, giving personality. Many were surprised to hear Jack chose surgery and worried that he would get chewed up during surgery training.
-     On his first rotation, he is assigned to work with a technically excellent surgeon who is known for his unpredictable episodes of rage. During Jack's first two operations with Dr. Notorious, a white man, the surgery was straight forward, and Dr. Notorious was pleased with Jack's

- performance. The third time, the surgery was prolonged due to bleeding. Jack felt dizzy and nauseated, and he had to be relieved. As he stepped away, Dr. Notorious glared and said through his teeth, "Well, there goes your evaluation for the rotation. If you can't even stay in the game, how do you expect to be a surgeon?" For the rest of the rotation, Dr. Notorious deliberately avoided choosing Jack to scrub in and assist. Jack was anxious even when he passed Dr. Notorious in the halls. Jack tried to make eye contact and say a pleasant hello, but Dr. Notorious ignored him and walked on. Jack felt he was branded a loser, struggled through the next rotations feeling he had not given his best performance, and now is seriously reconsidering his choice of specialty.

What if, instead, the following occurred:

- As Jack stepped away, the chief surgeon, Dr. Generous, asked with curiosity in his voice, "Are you okay, Jack? Let's chat a little later." After he was done with the surgery, Dr. Generous, a Black surgeon, found Jack, sat down with him, and asked with a warm curiosity in his voice, "What do you think just happened in there?" Jack tried to look Dr. Generous in the eyes but found it difficult. Jack said, "I don't really know. The patient reminded me of my mom. I just suddenly felt nauseated and dizzy and like I was going to faint." With a soft smile, Dr. Generous said, "Oh, I get it. That used to happen to me early in my career. Any time I had a patient who reminded me of someone in my family, I got really anxious. One time I did actually faint. I was embarrassed and humiliated, and I questioned if I would ever make it as a surgeon. Then, I was talking to one of the nurses and shared what was happening. The nurse said she thought it meant that I considered my obligation to all my patients as if they were a family member and gave them the same care I would want my family to get. She told me my sensitivity would make me a really good surgeon, one people would want for themselves and their family." Jack felt himself begin to relax as his heart rate and breathing slowed. Dr. Generous went on to say, "You are really talented, Jack, and I think with time, you can be a terrific surgeon. Don't ever let go of your humanity."

In the first scenario, Jack had bodily sensations that triggered a neuroception of danger, moving toward immobilization (fainting). Dr. Notorious's annoyed voice amplified Jack's neuroception of danger, and Dr. Notorious's comment that Jack had ruined his evaluation pushed Jack even farther down the autonomic ladder. Without someone to pull him up the ladder, Jack questioned his skills and even his choice of a surgical specialty. If Jack's dorsal vagal state continues, he will tell himself even more stories about his incompetence, his failure, and the futility of trying to turn things around. Dorsal vagal collapse has cost the world considerable human and social capital. On the other hand, in the second scenario, Dr. Generous caught Jack on the autonomic ladder by showing curiosity and extended a hand by saying they would talk later. Dr. Generous befriended and attended to Jack (and Jack's ANS) when he asked Jack if he was okay and requested to chat. As Dr. Generous shared his own experience, he established resonance with Jack's autonomic nervous system, and Jack began to ascend the autonomic ladder (Dana, 2018). In a 5–10 minute conversation, Dr. Generous restored Jack to ventral vagal safety, allowing him to continue exploring and learning as a physician-in-training.

Needless to say, Dr. Generous utilizes a polyvagal-informed approach to mentoring, while Dr. Notorious does not. If we ask ourselves how we can understand Dr. Notorious's irritation, we may think of what we have learned about "disruptive" physicians or about abuse in the supervisor-supervisee relationship. Though those perspectives might contain elements of truth, viewing the situation through those lenses alone may cause us to miss some opportunities to assist Dr. Notorious to approach Jack's fainting from a different angle. What if Dr. Notorious himself had a supervisor who heard what happened and looked at it from a polyvagal perspective? The supervisor might consider the discussion from Chapter 6 about providers whose vagal brakes disengage too soon. She may remember the conversation in Chapter 7 about the difference between saying someone is a dysregulated rather than a disruptive physician. Whether Jack and Dr. Notorious are dealt with from a polyvagal perspective or not could make all the difference between having a successful career in medicine and leaving the field altogether.

Both teachers and learners often limit their definition of success in medicine as proficiency in technical skills (e.g., placing the tough intravenous line) and cognitive skills (e.g., developing an exhaustive differential diagnosis). The science of human relationships is not often explicitly discussed; the expectations are nebulous, and the learners or trainees are without expert guidance. If anything, they may be taught in their neuroscience, behavioral health, or mental health experiences that the sympathetic and parasympathetic systems are antagonistic and mutually exclusive. There is little attention paid to evolutionary biology and the biological imperative of caregiving relationships. Many behaviors are framed pathologically, rather than seen as adaptive stress responses. The critical importance of attachment relationships as the foundation for future health and development is understated and underrated. Instead, attachments may even be viewed as pathological dependencies.

As physicians trained in allopathic medical schools, the authors of this book are most familiar with curricula and training expectations in medical training. However, our commentary and recommendations are often generalizable to other caregiving learning experiences and training programs. We invite the reader to consider how Polyvagal Theory might be infused into their own disciplines' training programs.

We propose there are universal aspects of relationship building that are relevant to and can be taught to health and mental health professionals, social workers, early childhood professionals, teachers, lawyers, and other helping professions. For example, Bailey (2020) and Brenner (2018), both attorneys, advocate for the value of applying Polyvagal Theory in high-conflict custody disputes and in mediations.

Problem-based learning is a concept that offers a unique opportunity to incorporate an understanding of Polyvagal Theory and the autonomic nervous system into professional programs. As conceived by Barrows and Tamblyn (1980),

> Problem-based learning is the learning that results from the process of working toward the understanding or resolution of a problem. The problem is encountered first in the learning process . . . Problem-based learning provides a potent format for interprofessional learning in the health sciences. Since the patient and his problem are the focus for health-care delivery, around which all members of the team perform, a problem can serve as an organizing structure for students from various professions to develop an understanding of each other's concerns and skills and to develop a team approach. (p. 1)

Imagine the power of creating collaborative educational forums that include seasoned providers as well as trainees from health and mental health care, social service, education, and law, who can focus on the impact of the autonomic nervous system on behavior. Consider how they might approach an 8-year-old child who presents to the emergency department repeatedly with asthma exacerbations? Each of these professionals brings the content and knowledge of their disciplines. As they socially engage with each other, they will be exposed and open to all of the perspectives represented there. Ventral vagal cross-pollination will produce novel understandings and approaches to medical symptoms, stress management, and preventable suffering. Such an all-encompassing and global curriculum may be a key to the transformation and triumph over trauma Peter Levine foretells.

PROVIDE ACCESSIBLE POLYVAGAL-INFORMED EARLY CHILDHOOD SERVICES

We want to build a robust system of care for children and families in which professionals from multiple disciplines use their appreciation of the power of social engagement and connectedness to educate family and other caregivers, foster sustaining relationships, and provide programs and services that promote health and well-being across the lifespan. Given how many young children and their families experience toxic stress and early adversity, early childhood professionals are bound to encounter them frequently in their offices, clinics, and classrooms. Patient care benefits when these professionals develop and sustain trauma-informed services. Trauma-informed services focus upon avoiding retraumatization. The services diligently work to decrease or eliminate neuroceptions of danger. Polyvagal-informed services, however, broaden the perspective. Those involved proactively design programs that provide cues of safety and security, keeping children and families at the top of the autonomic ladder. Of course, we need to anticipate and avoid potholes that disrupt relationships and hamper healthy growth and development. However, in addition to repairing disruptions of connectedness, we also need to head toward generative and creative collaborations that emerge from individual and collective ventral vagal states.

Childhood services are currently siloed in a patchwork across significant distances. Children see a health provider in one location, the dentist in another, and childcare or early education in yet a third location. If social work or mental health consultants are recommended, they are often in yet another location. Services may be difficult if not impossible to access based upon transportation, parents' work schedules, lack of adequate insurance, language barriers, or systemic discrimination. Furthermore, the individual providers rarely if ever speak to each other, citing HIPAA, busy schedules, and competing demands as impediments.

Imagine, however, a different system in which services that address children's and families' needs to promote health and well-being are co-located, i.e., housed in the same location, and the providers speak about and with children and families both individually and collectively. Think about the group of professionals in training we envisioned in a collective, problem-based learning session, now working side-by-side in a polyvagal-informed organization. They are meeting in their regularly scheduled twice weekly GIST (Group Interactive Structured Treatment) session among all the professionals who get to the heart of the matter to optimize patient and family well-being. The GIST group, chaired by a social worker, also includes the office manager, triage nurse, care coordinator, visiting nurse, general pediatrician, dentist, psychologist, attorney, and representative from the city health department. If all are not present in the building, they connect remotely. Let's consider how Matthew, the the 8-year-old Black child whom we met in Chapter 6, might benefit from such a group of professionals speaking with each other.

- Barb, a Black social worker and chair: *Let's start the meeting. Who has a GIST concern to discuss?*
- Louise, a white triage nurse: *I got a report from Children's Hospital that Matthew was in the emergency department for his asthma last night. This is his third ED visit in the past month. I worry something has changed. I know his mom is really stressed—she mentioned concerns for her job last time they were here.*
- Poonam, a female pediatrician whose parents were from India: *I'm concerned, too. Matthew recently missed his annual visit with me. He is one of my favorite patients because he is such a funny, outgoing kid. He makes me laugh. We tried to reach his mother to reschedule, but the phone number we have isn't correct.*
- Rina, a Filipina visiting nurse: *I saw Matthew and his mom last month. Mom didn't seem like her usual self. She is usually really friendly and invites me in to chat. This time, she just stood at the door and was distracted.*
- Anthony, a Latino attorney: *I am working with Mom on her housing. She has noticed some mold recently which she worries is making Matthew's asthma worse. Her landlord won't return her calls. We filed a complaint with the housing authority, but you know how long those things take to get through the system.*
- Rebecca, a white woman from the city health department: *Anthony, I'm glad you told us. I am one floor from the housing authority. I have a friend there who is helpful*

> moving things along, especially when she knows a kid's health is suffering.
>
> Anne, a biracial psychologist: *I'm concerned, too. Matthew has a lot of anxiety about his asthma. He feels that he never knows when he is going to have an attack. He's especially worried because basketball season has just started, and he loves to play. If his asthma isn't controlled, and he can't play, it will have a huge impact on him. He gets a lot of good feedback from his basketball coach. I'm working with Matthew on some approaches like breathing to enhance his calm states.*
>
> Barb, social worker: *Okay, in summary I'm hearing that everyone has significant concerns for Matthew and his mom. It sounds like his asthma flare is rooted in the home environment. As far as an action plan, Anthony and Rebecca will work to address mold. Rina, are you willing to go see Mom again and check things out? I see in his chart, we have his grandmother's phone number. Perhaps you can use that to reach his mom. Let her know we are working on the mold and that Poonam and Anne are really hoping to see Matthew soon. After all, he's just started basketball this year, and we want to make sure he's able to play the whole season.*
>
> *Let's touch base at our meeting next Monday to chart our progress.*

Could Matthew's pediatrician or psychologist alone have developed this plan? While they may have had questions or thoughts about the bigger picture, their ability to gather the information and formulate the plan would clearly not have been as comprehensive. What makes this interaction polyvagal-informed? In the polyvagal-informed organization, the typical hierarchy of professionals is minimized. Everyone's concerns, ANS responses, and neuroceptions are equally valued. The credential to participate is the willingness to examine your own ANS and to appreciate the ANS and neuroceptions of others. The pediatrician recognizes Matthew's typical ventral vagal states, notes her connectedness to Matthew and their typical mutual co-regulation, saying he makes her feel good, too. The psychologist sees that Matthew's asthma sympathetically activates him and spells danger as he worries he will lose his connectedness with his team and coach. The attorney and health department representative, appreciating the neuroceptions of danger from other team members, join in the collective effort to prevent Matthew and his mom from falling down the autonomic ladder, and the visiting nurse will be the point person to let Mom and Matthew know help is on the way. Finally, the social worker ensures there will be a timely check-in to note progress and reevaluate the plan as needed. Remembering the motto, *it's not what's wrong with you; it's what happened to you*, the team of professionals works diligently to understand and address the conditions experienced by this mom and child with whom they are connected.

Head Start, the federally funded program for children from birth to 5 years old and pregnant women, incorporates many of the components of the model described above. Head Start began in 1965 as part of Lyndon B. Johnson's War on Poverty. Both Head Start and Early Head Start receive strong bipartisan support for their annual funding. Together the programs serve more than 1 million children each year. As originally conceived and implemented, there are four program components: education, parent involvement, social services, and health. The initial health objectives for Head Start (Zigler, Piotrkowski, & Collins, 1994) were to "provide a comprehensive health services program that encompasses a broad range of medical, dental, nutrition, and mental health services, including handicapped children; to promote health services and early intervention, and to attempt to link the child's family to an ongoing health care system to insure that the child continues to receive comprehensive health care even after leaving the Head Start program" (p. 519). At the program's inception, hundreds of health and mental health professionals volunteered their time to support this new and innovative program. As Head Start demonstrates, there is professional, public, and governmental support for such collaborative care models. Policy makers often cite cost-benefit ratios as barriers to creative programming. The outcomes potentially speak for themselves: 10 minutes of interdisciplinary time versus multiple visits to the emergency department.

IN GOOD HANDS: PROMOTING THE INTENTIONAL "WE" THROUGH SOCIAL ENGAGEMENT AND CONNECTEDNESS

> *COVID-19 attacks our physical bodies, but also the cultural foundations of our lives, the toolbox of community and connectivity that is for the human what claws and teeth represent to the tiger.*
> —WADE DAVIS, 2020

The Polyvagal Theory explains why and how community and connectivity power human survival. For a theory to increase the chances of civilization's survival, that theory must be tested, then embraced, embodied, and enacted. Here we offer discrete opportunities to intentionally integrate Polyvagal Theory into daily life to increase our individual and collective survival odds.

The transformative improvements in health and well-being that began as public health measures—such as sanitation, clean water, and routine vaccinations—emphasize collective behavior and well-being over individual autonomy. At the end of 2020, many months into the COVID-19 epidemic, we eagerly awaited an accessible and effective vaccination that would shield us from the illness, loss of life, economic losses, and loneliness and isolation associated with the pandemic. Most poignantly, we hoped for a return to the illusion of predictability and order. All of us, whether we experienced personal or family illness from COVID-19 or not, yearned for the social engagements that would nurture and sustain us—the connectedness that Porges (2015a) notes is a biological imperative for mammals to survive. Current disruptions to our connectedness were pervasive and persistent; the opportunities for repair challenged our creativity and resourcefulness. Any way we wanted to splice it or dice it, *virtual was just not the same as being there* to our distressed autonomic nervous systems.

As we formulated repair strategies during the uncertainty of the pandemic, and as we face challenges right now and into the future, Polyvagal Theory can serve as a template upon which we build policies and programs supporting the collective feeling that we are in good hands. When our autonomic nervous systems sense we are in good hands, we feel safe and secure. A prerequisite for developing a polyvagal-informed society requires an understanding that state begets state and ongoing ventral vagal states build safe environments that care for persons individually and collectively.

However, a polyvagal-informed culture pits some stakeholders in a head-on collision with others over their individual values of agency and autonomy. As we consider our next steps, Rogers' *Diffusion of Innovation Theory* (1995) reminds us that there is a usual order of innovators and leaders who help societies incorporate novel concepts and navigate cultural transitions. He identified five groups of people by the sequence in which they respond to and accept new products, ideas, or ways of doing things: innovators, early adopters, early majority, late majority, and laggards. *Innovators*, such as John Bowlby, Stephen Porges, Deb Dana, Dan Hughes, and Heidelise Als, are the first to embrace groundbreaking departures from the familiar. These adventurous risk-takers promote ideas that may initially have little support from peers, colleagues, or the larger world. They have the ability to understand and apply complex technical knowledge and tolerate high degrees of uncertainty.

Rogers goes on to explain that the next group to endorse innovations are the *early adopters*, opinion leaders that others look to for cutting edge trends and ideas. Then comes the largest group, the *early majority*, who take their time in deciding to adopt the innovation. They are neither the first kid on the block to try something new, nor the last. The *late majority* are doubters and questioners who sometimes don't adopt the innovation until they have no choice. And finally, *laggards* are tethered to the past, and their decisions are based upon what was previously done. They are suspicious of innovators and change agents.

Moving forward to a polyvagal-informed society challenges all of us to notice our own neuroceptions and attend to the neuroceptions of others, irrespective of their openness to innovation or willingness to embrace change. In the full spirit of inviting social engagement and encouraging social connectedness to enhance our collective vagal tone, we must recognize all neuroceptions as valid expressions of lived experiences of previous and current generations. This does not, however, translate to acceptance of all behaviors. As we understand the neuroceptions of danger and life threat of those with whom we disagree, we begin to build a platform for new communications that brings us up the autonomic ladder together.

PERFORMANCE FOR THE POLYVAGAL-INFORMED

Safety is critical, but it is not the final goal of being human. Even more important are the achievements and experiences that neurocepted safety makes possible. From a foundation of ventral vagal social engagement, teams accomplish remarkable feats no solo human could ever match. The bigger the achievement, the more personally rewarding they are. Any leader who knows this will push the envelope of her group's performance. President Kennedy pointed us to the moon, and Martin Luther King, Jr. pointed us to the promised land, presenting us with seemingly impossible challenges because they knew that audacious goals inspire heroic actions. Functioning at this altitude is frightening, invigorating, and deeply satisfying.

There is no work plan or prescription for a polyvagal-informed life or community. It is built moment by moment in interactions and relationships between people who each have their own unique neuroceptive thumbprint. The authors' polyvagal journeys began with an introduction to Stephen Porges and his work and continued when Deb Dana welcomed us into the family of polyvagal practitioners. Our polyvagal journey has deepened through our collaboration with each other. We know the power of polyvagal awareness and mastery and want to share it with you.

We invite you to examine your key relationships, your workplace, your community, and the larger world to ask how you can apply Polyvagal Theory in your life. We invite you to consider, given your neuroceptive thumbprint, this question: how do you choose to nourish yourself and your family, colleagues, and community? We invite you to choose and create relationships and environments that bring cues of safety to all involved. We invite you to become a center of ventral vagal regulation sending ripples of safety into your world. You are an integral part of a larger family accelerating the momentum of autonomic wisdom and expertise. We challenge you to use your foundations of safety to create your own awesome innovations.

Become an early adopter of Polyvagal Theory, infuse it into your lives, and enjoy the benefits of ventral vagal social engagement. With gratitude for our mentors and learning, we welcome you to the polyvagal family.

APPENDIX

KidsTLC Constitution

We CARE about CHILDREN – their CONNECTIONS, EXPERIENCES and DEVELOPMENT – through our treatment and all other actions.

Because we value CHILDREN'S CONNECTIONS – meaning kinship, bonds, social interactions and relationships –

1. We care for children and the people in their lives
   a. We treat all people with kindness, respect, and compassion, no matter their behavior, background or beliefs
   b. We lower their shame and enhance their dignity
   c. We provide what people need and cannot provide for themselves
   d. We repair relationships when trust becomes difficult and offer alternative ways in which to achieve healthy communication
2. We work together with children and the people in their lives
   a. We support each other's success in therapeutic communities, families and as a larger community, including support in overcoming barriers that prevent success
   b. We learn and teach how to ask for and accept care, guidance and support
   c. We help parts of the brain work together as designed
   d. We seek to influence while allowing ourselves to be influenced as well

Because we value CHILDREN'S EXPERIENCES – meaning what they have lived through, are living through and will live through –

3. We keep children safe physically and emotionally
   a. We don't hurt children
   b. We don't let them hurt others
   c. We don't let them hurt themselves
   d. We don't let them get hurt
4. We seek meaning in behavior and action
   a. We make sense of our own behavior and the behavior of others
   b. We understand what motivates behavior based on contexts before correcting and shaping it (unless unsafe)
   c. We act with the purpose and passion of our goals and aspirations
   d. We empower others to act on their goals and aspirations

Because we value CHILDREN'S DEVELOPMENT – meaning learning, healing and growth –

5. We help children and the people in their lives
   a. We stay emotionally regulated and co-regulate the emotions of others
   b. We help them to approach their own and others' experiences with connectivity, acceptance, curiosity and empathy
   c. We help them develop the knowledge, skills and attitudes they need to succeed
   d. We help them to develop awareness of the impact of their actions on others
6. We keep going and don't give up
   a. We take care of ourselves
   b. We manage discouragement
   c. We rely on each other for support
   d. We encourage and empower others to keep going, too

© 2018 KidsTLC, Inc.

Reprinted by permission from KidsTLC, Inc., 2021: KidsTLC Constitution, copyright 2018.

REFERENCES

Adler, H. M. (2002). The sociophysiology of caring in the doctor-patient relationship. *Journal of General Internal Medicine, 17*(11), 883–890. https://doi.org/10.1046/j.1525-1497.2002.10640.x

Agorastos, A., Pervanidou, P., Chrousos, G. P., & Baker, D. G. (2019). Developmental trajectories of early life stress and trauma: A narrative review on neurobiological aspects beyond stress system dysregulation. *Frontiers in Psychiatry, 10.* https://doi.org/10.3389/fpsyt.2019.00118

Ailes, E. C., Dawson, A. L., Lind, J. N., Gilboa, S. M., Frey, M. T., Broussard, C. S., & Honein, M. A. (2015). Opioid prescription claims among women of reproductive age — United States, 2008–2012. *Morbidity and Mortality Weekly Report (MWR), 64*(2), 37–41.

Ainsworth, M. D. S., Blehar, M. C., Waters, E., & Wall, S. (1978). *Patterns of attachment: A psychological study of the strange situation.* Lawrence Erlbaum.

Aktar, E., Qu, J., Lawrence, P. J., Tollenaar, M. S., Elzinga, B. M., & Bögels, S. M. (2019). Fetal and infant outcomes in the offspring of parents with perinatal mental disorders: Earliest influences. *Frontiers in Psychiatry, 10.* https://doi.org/10.3389/fpsyt.2019.00391

Als, H. (1982). Toward a synactive theory of development: Promise for the assessment and support of infant individuality. *Infant Mental Health Journal, 3*(4), 229–243.

Als, H., & Gilkerson, L. (1997). The role of relationship-based developmentally supportive newborn intensive care in strengthening outcome of preterm infants. *Seminars in Perinatology, 21*(3), 178–189. https://doi.org/10.1016/s0146-0005(97)80062-6

American Academy of Pediatrics. (2021). www.aap.org

American Association of Medical Colleges. (2019) Diversity in medicine: Facts and figures 2019. https://www.aamc.org/data-reports/workforce/interactive-data/figure-18-percentage-all-active-physicians-race/ethnicity-2018

Ammaniti, M., & Gallese, V. (2014). *The birth of intersubjectivity: Psychodynamics, neurobiology, and the self.* Norton Series on Interpersonal Neurobiology. New York: Norton.

Anda, R. F., Felitti, V. J., Bremner, J. D., Walker, J. D., Whitfield, Ch., Perry, B. D., Dube, S. R., & Giles, W. H. (2006). The enduring effects of abuse and related adverse experiences in childhood: A convergence of evidence from neurobiology and epidemiology. *European Archives of Psychiatry and Clinical Neuroscience, 256*(3), 174–186. https://doi.org/10.1007/s00406-005-0624-4

Arnold, L., & Thompson, G. (2010). Defining and nurturing professionalism. In J. Spandorfer, C. A. Pohl, S. L. Rattner, & T. J. Nasca (Eds.), *Professionalism in medicine: The case-based guide for medical students* (pp. 7–21). Cambridge University Press.

Ayanian, J. Z., Cleary, P. D., Weissman, J. S. & Epstein A. M. (1999). The effect of patients' preferences on racial differences in access to renal transplantation. *New England Journal of Medicine, 341*(22), 1661–1668.

Bach, P. B., Cramer L. D., Warren J. L., & Begg, C. B. (1999). Racial differences in the treatment of early-stage lung cancer. *New England Journal of Medicine. 341*(16), 1198–1205.

Baer, D. (2013, February 3). How to know if you're working with mammals or reptiles (and why it matters to your creativity). *Fast Company*. https://www.fastcompany.com/1682363/how-to-know-if-youre-working-with-mammals-or-reptiles-and-why-it-matters-to-your-creativity

Bailey, B., Dana, D., Bailey, E., & Davis, F. (2020) The application of the polyvagal theory to high-conflict co-parenting cases. *Family Court Review, 58*(2), 535–543.

Barcelona de Mendoza, V., Huang, Y., Crusto, C. A., Sun, Y. V., & Taylor, J. Y. (2018). Perceived racial discrimination and methylation among African American women in the InterGEN study. *Biological Research for Nursing, 20*(2), p. 145–152.

Barker, D. J., Winter, P. D., Osmond, C., Margetts, B., & Simmonds, S. J. (1989). Weight in infancy and death from ischaemic heart disease. *Lancet, 2,* 577–580. https://doi.org/10.1016/S0140-6736(89)90710-1

Barker, D. J. P. (2007). The origins of the developmental origins theory. *Journal of Internal Medicine, 261*(5), 412–417. https://doi.org/10.1111/j.1365-2796.2007.01809

Barnett, E. S., & Chung, P. J. (2018). Responding to parental incarceration as a priority pediatric health issue. *Pediatrics, 142*(3), e20181923. https://doi.org/10.1542/peds.2018-1923

Barrows, H. S., & Tamblyn, R. M. (1980). *Problem-based learning: An approach to medical education.* Springer.

Bartholomew, K., & Horowitz, L. M. (1991). Attachment styles among young adults: A test of a four-category model. *Journal of Personality and Social Psychology, 61*(2), 226–244.

Baylin, J., & Hughes, D. A. (2016). *The neurobiology of attachment-focused therapy: Enhancing connection & trust in the treatment of children & adolescents.* Norton Series on Interpersonal Neurobiology. New York: Norton.

Beebe, B., & Lachman, F. (2002). Organizing principles of interaction from infant research and the lifespan prediction of attachment: Application to adult treatment. *Journal of Infant, Child, and Adolescent Psychotherapy, 2*(4), 61–89. https://doi.org/10.1080/15289168.2002.10486420

Beebe, B., Jaffe, J., Markese, S., Buck, K., Chen, H., Cohen, P., Bahrick, L., Andrews, H., & Feldstein, S. (2010). The origins of 12-month attachment: A microanalysis of 4-month mother–infant interaction. *Attachment & Human Development, 12*(1–2), 3–141. https://doi.org/10.1080/14616730903338985

Beeney, J. E., Wright, A. G. C., Stepp, S. D., Hallquist, M. N., Lazarus, S. A., Beeney, J. R. S., Scott, L. N., & Pilkonis, P. A. (2017). Disorganized attachment and personality functioning in adults: A latent class analysis. *Personality Disorders: Theory, Research, and Treatment, 8*(3), 206–216. https://doi.org/10.1037/per0000184

Behnke, M., Smith, V. C., Committee on Substance Abuse, & Committee on Fetus and Newborn. (2013). Prenatal substance abuse: Short- and long-term effects on the exposed fetus. *Pediatrics, 131*(3), e1009–e1024. https://doi.org/10.1542/peds.2012-3931

Bennett, J. K., Fuertes, J. N., Keitel, M., & Phillips, R. (2011). The role of patient attachment and working alliance on patient adherence, satisfaction, and health-related quality of life in lupus treatment. *Patient Education and Counseling, 85*(1), 53–59. https://doi.org/10.1016/j.pec.2010.08.005

Berridge, K. C., & Kringelbach, M. L. (2013). Neuroscience of affect: Brain mechanisms of pleasure and displeasure. *Current Opinion in Neurobiology, 23*(3), 294–303. https://doi.org/10.1016/j.conb.2013.01.017

Black, L. L., Johnson, R., & VanHoose, L. (2015). The relationship between perceived racism/discrimination and health among Black American women: A review of the literature from 2003 to 2013. *Journal of Racial and Ethnic Health Disparities, 2*(1), 11–20.

Bowlby, J. (1982). *Attachment and loss series: Volume 1: Attachment.* Basic Books.

Bowlby, J. (1982). *Attachment and loss series: Volume 2: Separation: Anxiety and anger.* Basic Books.

Bowlby, J. (1982). *Attachment and loss series: Volume 3: Loss: Sadness and depression.* Basic Books.

Bowlby, J. (1988). *A secure base.* New York: Routledge.

Bradford, K., Shih, W., Videlock, E., Presson, A. P., Naliboff, B. D., Mayer, E. A., & Chang, L. (2012). Association between early adverse life events and irritable bowel syndrome. *Clinical Gastroenterology & Hepatology, 10*(4), 385–390. e1-3. https://doi.org/10.1016/j.cgh.2011.12.018

Braun, K., & Champagne, F. (2014). Paternal influences on offspring development: Behavioural and epigenetic pathways. *Journal of Neuroendocrinology, 26,* 697–706.

Braveman, P., & Gottleib, L. (2014). The social determinants of health: It's time to consider the causes of the causes. *Public Health Reports, 129*(2), 19–31.

Brenner, M. (2018). Mediation—Engaging the rhythm of polyvagal regulation. https://www.mediate.com/articles/brenner-polyvagal.cfm

Brindley, P. G., & Reynolds, S. F. (2011). Improving verbal communication in critical care medicine. *Journal of Critical Care, 26*(2), 155–159. https://doi.org/10.15766/mep_2374-8265.9934

Bronfenbrenner, U. (1991). What do families do? *Institute for American Values. Winter/Spring,* 2.

Bunn, H. F. (1997). Pathogenesis and treatment of sickle cell disease. *The New England Journal of Medicine, 337*(11), 762–769. https://doi.org/10.1056/NEJM199709113371107

Bureau of Labor Statistics, U.S. Department of Labor, The Economics Daily. (2017). Employment in families with children in 2016. https://www.bls.gov/opub/ted/2017/employment-in-families-with-children-in-2016.htm

Bystrova, K., Ivanova, V., Edhborg, M., Matthiesen, A.-S., Ransjö-Arvidson, A.-B., Mukhamedrakhimov, R., Uvnäs-Moberg, K., & Widström, A.-M. (2009). Early contact versus separation: Effects on mother-infant interaction one year later. *Birth, 36*(2), 97–109. https://doi.org/10.1111/j.1523-536X.2009.00307.x

Callaghan, T., Crimmins, J., & Schweitzer, R. D. (2011). Children of substance-using mothers: Child health engagement and child protection outcomes. *Journal of Paediatrics and Child Health, 47*(4), 223–227. https://doi.org/10.1111/j.1440-1754.2010.01930.x

Campbell, L., Pillai Riddell, R., Cribbie, R., Garfield, H., & Greenberg, S. (2018). Preschool children's coping responses and outcomes in the vaccination context: Child and caregiver transactional and longitudinal relationships. *Pain, 159*(2), 314–330. https://doi.org/10.1097/j.pain.0000000000001092

Carson, E. A., & Sabol, W. J. (2012). Prisoners in 2011. https://www.bjs.gov/content/pub/pdf/p11.pdf.

Carter, C. S. (2017). The oxytocin–vasopressin pathway in the context of love and fear. *Frontiers in Endocrinology, 8*. https://doi.org/10.3389/fendo.2017.00356

Cataldo, I., Azhari, A., Coppola, A., Bornstein, M. H., & Esposito, G. (2019). The influences of drug abuse on mother-infant interaction through the lens of the biopsychosocial model of health and illness: A review. *Frontiers in Public Health, 7*, 45. https://doi.org/10.3389/fpubh.2019.00045

Center for the Study of Social Policy. (2020). Building resilience in troubled times: A guide for parents. https://cssp.org/building-resilience-in-troubled-times-a-guide-for-parents/

Center for the Study of Social Policy. (n.d.). Strengthening families. https://cssp.org/our-work/project/strengthening-families/

Center on the Developing Child, Harvard University (2009). Maternal Depression Can Undermine the Development of Young Children: Working Paper No. 8. www.developingchild.harvard.edu.

Center on the Developing Child, Harvard University, Serve and Return. (n.d.). https://developingchild.harvard.edu/science/key-concepts/serve-and-return/.

Center on the Developing Child, Harvard University, Toxic Stress. (n.d.) https://developingchild.harvard.edu/science/key-concepts/toxic-stress

Chamberland, C., Fallon, B., Black, T., & Trocmé, N. (2011). Emotional maltreatment in Canada: Prevalence, reporting and child welfare responses (CIS2). *Child Abuse & Neglect, 35*(10), 841–854. https://doi.org/10.1016/j.chiabu.2011.03.010

Champagne, F. A. (2013). Early environments, glucocorticoid receptors, and behavioral epigenetics. *Behavioral Neuroscience, 127*(5), 628–636. https://doi.org/10.1037/a0034018

Ciechanowski, P. S., Katon, W. J., Russo, J. E., & Walker, E. A. (2001). The patient-provider relationship: Attachment theory and adherence to treatment in diabetes. *American Journal of Psychiatry, 158*(1), 29–35. https://doi.org/10.1176/appi.ajp.158.1.29

Circle of Security. (n.d.). Early intervention programs for parents & children. https://www.circleofsecurityinternational.com/circle-of-security-model

Cohn, J. F., & Tronick, E. Z. (1987). Mother-infant face-to-face interaction: The sequence of dyadic states at 3, 6, and 9 Months. *Developmental Psychology, 23*(1), 68–77.

Colvin, R., & Murphy, Z. (June 25, 2020). We've been failed. *The Washington Post*. https://www.washingtonpost.com/graphics/2020/national/black-chicagoans-covid-19-high-death-rate-system-of-neglect/

Cooklin, A. (2006). Being seen and heard: The needs of children of parents with mental illness (DVD). Royal College of Psychiatrists.

Cooper, G., Hoffman, K., & Powell, B. (2018). Repairing relationships with a time-in. https://www.circleofsecurityinternational.com/wp-content/uploads/COS_Time-In-1.pdf

Costello, P. C. (2013). *Attachment-based psychotherapy: Helping patients develop adaptive capacities*. American Psychological Association.

Council on Community Pediatrics, American Academy of Pediatrics. (2013). Providing care for immigrant, migrant, and border children. https://doi.org/10.1542/peds.2013-1099

Coyle, D. (2018). *The culture code: The secrets of highly successful groups*. Bantam.

Curley, J. P., Mashoodh M., & Champagne F. A. (2011). Epigenetics and the origins of paternal effects. *Hormones and Behavior. 59*(3), 306–314.

Dalia, C., Abbas, K., Colville, G., & Brierley, J. (2013). G49 Resilience, post-traumatic stress, burnout and coping in medical staff on the paediatric and neonatal intensive care unit (P/NICU)—A survey. *Archives of Disease in Childhood, 98*(Suppl 1), A26–A27. https://doi.org/10.1136/archdischild-2013-304107.061

Dana, D. A. (2018). *The polyvagal theory in therapy: Engaging the rhythm of regulation.* Norton Series on Interpersonal Neurobiology. New York: Norton.

Dana, D. A. (2020). *Polyvagal exercises for safety and connection: 50 client-centered practices.* Norton Series on Interpersonal Neurobiology. New York: Norton.

Dartmouth College Office of Communications. (2018, March 27). Revisiting Fred Rogers' 2002 Commencement Address. Dartmouth News. https://news.dartmouth.edu/news/2018/03/revisiting-fred-rogers-2002-commencement-address

Davis, W. (2020). The unravelling of America. *Rolling Stone.* https://www.rollingstone.com/politics/political-commentary/covid-19-end-of-american-era-wade-davis-1038206/

Deans, C., & Maggert, K. A. (2015). What do you mean,"epigenetic"?. *Genetics, 199*(4), 887–896.

Dean, W. (2020). Health care worker suicides hint at Covid-19 mental health crisis to come. *STAT.* https://www.statnews.com/2020/04/30/suicides-two-health-care-workers-hint-at-covid-19-mental-health-crisis-to-come/

DeCasper, A. J., Lecanuet, J. P., Busnel, M. C., Granier-Deferre, C., & Maugeais, R. (1994). Fetal reactions to recurrent maternal speech. *Infant Behavior and Development, 17*(2), 159–164. https://doi.org/10.1016/0163-6383(94)90051-5

Deci, E. L., Koestner, R., & Ryan, R. M. (1999). A meta-analytic review of experiments examining the effects of extrinsic rewards on intrinsic motivation. *Psychological Bulletin, 125*(6), 627–668. https://doi.org/10.1037/0033-2909.125.6.627

DeFede, J. (2003). *The day the world came to town: 9/11 in Gander, Newfoundland.* Regan Books.

Delahooke, M. (2019). *Beyond behaviours: Using brain science and compassion to understand and solve children's behavioural challenges.* John Murray.

Devine, P. G., Forscher, P. S., Austin, A. J., & Cox, W. T. (2012). Long-term reduction in implicit race bias: A prejudice habit-breaking intervention. *Journal of Experimental Social Psychology, 48*(6), 1267–1278. https://doi.org/10.1016/j.jesp.2012.06.003

Dickerson, C., & Fernandez, M. (2018, June 20). What's behind the tender age facilities opening for young migrants. *The New York Times.* www.nytimes.com/2019/01/17/us/family-separation-trump-administration-migrants.html

Dobbing, J., & Sands, J. (1973). Quantitative growth and development of human brain. *Archives of Disease in Childhood, 48,* 757–767.

Doyle S., Chavez S., Cohen S., & Morrison S. (2019). Fostering social and emotional health through pediatric primary care: Common threads to transform practice and systems. Center for the Study of Social Policy, September 2019.

Drury, S. S., Gleason, M. M., Theall, K. P., Smyke, A. T., Nelson, C. A., Fox, N. A., & Zeanah, C. H. (2012). Genetic sensitivity to the caregiving context: The influence of 5httlpr and BDNF Val66met on indiscriminate social behavior. *Physiology & Behavior, 106*(5), 728–735. https://doi.org/10.1016/j.physbeh.2011.11.014

Duhigg, C. (2016). *Smarter faster better: The secrets of being productive.* Random House.

Edmondson, A. (1999). Psychological safety and learning behavior in work teams. *Administrative Science Quarterly, 44*(2), 350–383.

Engel, G. L. (1992). How much longer must medicine's science be bound by a seventeenth century world view? *Psychotherapy and Psychosomatics, 57,* 3–16.

Feagin, J., & Bennefield, Z. (2014). Systemic racism and U.S. health care. *Social Science & Medicine, 103,* 7–14.

Felger, J. C., & Lotrich, F. E. (2013). Inflammatory cytokines in depression: Neurobiological mechanisms and therapeutic implications. *Neuroscience, 246,* 199–229. https://doi.org/10.1016/j.neuroscience.2013.04.060

Felitti, V. J., Anda, R. F., Nordenberg, D., Williamson, D. F., Spitz, A. M., Edwards, V., Koss, M. P., & Marks, J. S. (1998). Relationship of childhood abuse and household dysfunction to many of the leading causes of death in adults. *American Journal of Preventative Medicine*, *14*(4), 245–258.

Fenwick, J., Barclay, L., & Schmied, V. (2001). "Chatting": An important clinical tool in facilitating mothering in neonatal nurseries. *Journal of Advanced Nursing*, *33*(5), 583–593. https://doi.org/10.1046/j.1365-2648.2001.01694

Field, T. (1998). Maternal depression effects on infants and early interventions. *Preventive Medicine*, *27*(2), 200–203.

Field, T., & Diego, M. (2008). Vagal activity, early growth and emotional development. *Infant Behavior and Development*, *31*(3), 361–373. https://doi.org/10.1016/j.infbeh.2007.12.008

Finnegan, L. P., Connaughton, J. F., Jr, Kron, R. E., & Emich, J. P. (1975). Neonatal abstinence syndrome: Assessment and management. *Addictive Diseases*, *2*(1–2), 141–158.

Fonagy, P., & Allison, E. (2014). The role of mentalizing and epistemic trust in the therapeutic relationship. *Psychotherapy*, *51*(3), 372–380. https://doi.org/10.1037/a0036505

Fonagy, P., & Target, M. (1997) Attachment and reflective function: Their role in self-organization. *Development and Psychopathology*, *9*, 679–700.

Friedman, T. L. (2020, April 21). We need great leadership now, and here's what it looks like. *The New York Times*. https://www.nytimes.com/2020/04/21/opinion/covid-dov-seidman.html

Fries, A. B. W., Ziegler, T. E., Kurian, J. R., Jacoris, S., & Pollak, S. D. (2005). Early experience in humans is associated with changes in neuropeptides critical for regulating social behavior. *PNAS USA*, *102*(47), 17237–17240. https://doi.org/10.1073/pnas.0504767102

Garber, J., Ciesla, J. A., McCauley, E., Diamond, G., & Schloredt, K. A. (2011). Remission of depression in parents: Links to healthy functioning in their children. *Child Development*, *82*(1), 226–243.

Garcia, S. E. (2020, April 6). Easter bunny and tooth fairy deemed essential workers in New Zealand. *The New York Times*. https://www.nytimes.com/2020/04/06/world/australia/jacinda-ardern-easter-bunny-essential-worker-tooth-fairy.html

Gerretsen, P., & Myers, J. (2008). The physician: A secure base. *Journal of Clinical Oncology*, *26*(32), 5294–5296. https://doi.org/10.1200/JCO.2008.17.5588

Gilchrist, V. (2005). Physician activities during time out of the examination room. *The Annals of Family Medicine*, *3*(6), 494–499. https://doi.org/10.1370/afm.391

Gladstone, B. M., Boydell, K. M., Seeman, M. V., & McKeever, P. D. (2011). Children's experiences of parental mental illness: A literature review. *Early Intervention in Psychiatry*, *5*(4), 271–289. https://doi.org/10.1111/j.1751-7893.2011.00287.x

Glaze, L., & Maruschak, L. (2010). Parents in prison and their minor children. https://www.bjs.gov/content/pub/pdf/pptmc.pdf.

Golding, K. S. (2015). Connection before correction: Supporting parents to meet the challenges of parenting children who have been traumatised within their early parenting environments. *Children Australia*, *40*(2), 152–159.

Gomez-Pomar, E. & Finnegan, L. P. (2018). The epidemic of neonatal abstinence syndrome, historical references of its origins, assessment, and management. *Frontiers in Pediatrics*, *6*. https://doi.org/10.3389/fped.2018.00033

Gross, K. (2020, April 20). Covid-19 news. Bryan Medical Center.

Grossman, M. R., Berkwitt, A. K., Osborn, R. R., Xu, Y., Esserman, D. A., Shapiro, E. D., & Bizzarro, M. J. (2017). An initiative to improve the quality of care of infants with neonatal abstinence syndrome. *Pediatrics, 139*(6), e20163360. https://doi.org/10.1542/peds.2016-3360

Hagiwara, N., Kron, F. W., Scerbo, M. W., & Watson, G. S. (2020). A call for grounding implicit bias training in clinical and translational frameworks. *Lancet (London, England), 395*(10234), 1457–1460. https://doi.org/10.1016/S0140-6736(20)30846-1

Hall, S. L., Hynan, M. T., Phillips, R., Lassen, S., Craig, J. W., Goyer, E., Hatfield, R. F., & Cohen, H. (2017). The neonatal intensive parenting unit: An introduction. *Journal of Perinatology, 37*(12), 1259–1264. https://doi.org/10.1038/jp.2017.108

Harrell, C. J., Burford, T. I., Cage, B. N., Nelson, T. M., Shearon, S., Thompson, A., & Green, S. (2011). Multiple pathways linking racism to health outcomes. *Du Bois Review: Social Science Research on Race, 8*(1), 143–157. https://doi.org/10.1017/S1742058X11000178

Hatzenbuehler, M. L., & Link B. G. (2014). Introduction to the special issue on structural stigma and health. *Social Science and Medicine, 103*, 1–6.

Hebb, D. O. (1949). *The organization of behavior: A neuropsychological theory*. Wiley.

Herman, J. P., Ostrander, M. M., Mueller, N. K., & Figueiredo, H. (2005). Limbic system mechanisms of stress regulation: Hypothalamo-pituitary-adrenocortical axis. *Progress in Neuro-Psychopharmacology and Biological Psychiatry, 29*(8), 1201–1213. https://doi.org/10.1016/j.pnpbp.2005.08.006

Hobfoll, S. E., Stevens, N. R., & Zalta, A. K. (2015). Expanding the science of resilience: Conserving resources in the aid of adaptation. *Psychological Inquiry, 26*(2), 174–180. https://doi.org/10.1080/1047840X.2015.1002377

Hobfoll, S. E., Watson, P., Bell, C. C., Bryant, R. A., Brymer, M. J., Friedman, M. J., Friedman, M., Gersons, B. P. R., de Jong, T. V. M., Layne, C. M., Maguen, S., Yuval Neria, Y., Norwood, A. E., Pynoos, R. S., Reissman, D., Ruzek, J. I., Shalev, A. Y., Solomon, Z., Steinberg, A, M., & Ursano, R. J. (2007). Five essential elements of immediate and mid-term mass trauma intervention: Empirical evidence. *Psychiatry, 70*(4), 283–315. https://doi.org/10.1521/psyc.2007.70.4.283

Holt-Lunstad, J., Robles, T. F., & Sbarra, D. A. (2017). Advancing social connection as a public health priority in the United States. *American Psychologist, 72*(6), 517–530. https://doi.org/10.1037/amp0000103

Holt-Lunstad, J., Smith, T. B., Baker, M., Harris, T., & Stephenson, D. (2015). Loneliness and social isolation as risk factors for mortality: A meta-analytic review. *Perspectives on Psychological Science, 10*(2), 227–237. https://doi.org/10.1177/1745691614568352

Honein, M. A., Boyle, C., & Redfield, R. R. (2019). Public health surveillance of prenatal opioid exposure in mothers and infants. *Pediatrics, 143*(3). https://doi.org/10.1542/peds.2018-3801

Hughes, D. A., & Baylin, J. (2012). *Brain-based parenting: The neuroscience of caregiving for healthy attachment*. Norton Series on Interpersonal Neurobiology. New York: Norton.

Hughes, D. A. (2018). *Building the bonds of attachment: Awakening love in deeply traumatized children*. Rowman & Littlefield.

Hynan, M. T., & Hall, S. L. (2015). Psychosocial program standards for NICU parents. *Journal of Perinatology, 35*(S1), S1–S4. https://doi.org/10.1038/jp.2015.141

Institute of Medicine. Committee on Quality of Health Care in America, Kohn, L. T., Corrigan, J. M., & Donaldson, M. S. (Eds.). (2000). *To err is human: Building a safer health system*. National Academies Press.

Jansson, L. M., Dipietro, J. A., Elko, A., & Velez, M. (2007). Maternal vagal tone change in response to methadone is associated with neonatal abstinence syndrome severity in exposed neonates. *The Journal of Maternal-Fetal & Neonatal Medicine, 20*(9), 677–685.

Jarrett, C. (2016). The psychology of eye contact, digested. *Research Digest.* https://digest.bps.org.uk/2016/11/28/the-psychology-of-eye-contact-digested/https://doi.org/10.1080/14767050701490327

Jinpa, T. (2015). *A fearless heart: How the courage to be compassionate can transform our lives.* Penguin Random House.

Johns Hopkins University of Medicine Coronavirus Resource Center (2021). https://coronavirus.jhu.edu/

Kajstura, A. (2019). Women's mass incarcerations: The whole pie. https://www.prisonpolicy.org/reports/pie2019women.html

Keene, E. A., Hutton, N., Hall, B., & Rushton, C. (2010). Bereavement debriefing sessions: An intervention to support health care professionals in managing their grief after the death of a patient. *Pediatric Nursing, 36*(4), 185–189.

Khullar, D., & Chokshi, D. A. (2019). Challenges for immigrant health in the USA—The road to crisis. *Lancet, 393*(10186), 2168–2174. https://doi.org/10.1016/S0140-6736(19)30035-2

Khullar, D. (2020, April 8). (Medical dispatch). "A disembodied voice": The loneliness and solidarity of treating the coronavirus in New York. *The New Yorker.* https://www.newyorker.com/science/medical-dispatch/a-disembodied-voice-the-loneliness-and-solidarity-of-treating-the-coronavirus-in-new-york

KidsTLC Constitution. (2018). KidsTLC, Inc. https://www.kidstlc.org/wp-content/uploads/2020/11/KidsTLC-Constitution-2020-update-B.pdf

Kirby, M. L. (2007). *Cardiac development.* Oxford University Press.

Kok, B. E., & Fredrickson, B. L. (2010). Upward spirals of the heart: Autonomic flexibility, as indexed by vagal tone, reciprocally and prospectively predicts positive emotions and social connectedness. *Biological Psychology, 85*(3), 432–436. https://doi.org/10.1016/j.biopsycho.2010.09.005

Kim, S. J., & Bostwick, W. (2020). Social vulnerability and racial inequality in Covid-19 deaths in Chicago. *Health Education and Behavior, 47*(4), 509–513.

Korn, D. L. (2015). Treating complex trauma. Cape Cod Institute. Eastham, Massachusetts.

Kosfeld, M., Heinrichs, M., Zak, P. J., Fischbacher, U., & Fehr, E. (2005). Oxytocin increases trust in humans. *Nature, 435*(7042), 673–676. https://doi.org/10.1038/nature03701

Landi, N., Montoya, J., Kober, H., Rutherford, H. J. V., Mencl, W. E., Worhunsky, P. D., Potenza, M. N., & Mayes, L. C. (2011). Maternal neural responses to infant cries and faces: Relationships with substance use. *Frontiers in Psychiatry, 2.* https://doi.org/10.3389/fpsyt.2011.00032

Layne, C. M., Greeson, J. K. P., Ostrowski, S. A., Kim, S., Reading, S., Vivrette, R. L., Briggs, E. C., Fairbank, J. A., & Pynoos, R. S. (2014). Cumulative trauma exposure and high risk behavior in adolescence: Findings from the National Child Traumatic Stress Network Core Data Set. *Psychological Trauma: Theory, Research, Practice, and Policy, 6*(Suppl 1), S40–S49. https://doi.org/10.1037/a0037799

LeBaron, C. W., Rodewald, L., & Humiston, S. (1999). How much time is spent on well-child care and vaccinations? *Archives of Pediatrics & Adolescent Medicine, 153*(11), 1154. https://doi.org/10.1001/archpedi.153.11.1154

LeDoux, J. (2007). The amygdala. *Current Biology, 17*(20), R868-R874. https://doi.org/10.1016/j.cub.2007.08.005

Lepine, J. P., & Briley, M. (2011). The increasing burden of depression. *Neuropsychiatric Disease and Treatment*, 7(1), 3–7.
Lester, B. M., Conradt, E., LaGasse, L. L., Tronick, E. Z., Padbury, J. F., & Marsit, C. J. (2018). Epigenetic programming by maternal behavior in the human infant. *Pediatrics*, 142(4), e20171890. https://doi.org/10.1542/peds.2017-1890
Lester, B. M., Conradt, E., & Marsit, C. (2016). Introduction to the special section on epigenetics. *Child Development*, 87(1), 29–37. https://doi.org/10.1111/cdev.12489
Levine, P. A. (2010). *In an unspoken voice: How the body releases trauma and restores goodness*. North Atlantic Books.
Levine, P. A. (2008). *Healing trauma: A pioneering program for restoring the wisdom of your body*. Sounds True.
Lipari, R. N., & Van Horn, S. L. (2017). Children living with parents who have a substance use disorder. The CBHSQ Report. Substance Abuse and Mental Health Services Administration (U.S.). https://www.ncbi.nlm.nih.gov/books/NBK464590/
Liu, D., Diorio, J., Tannenbaum, B., Caldji, C., Francis, D., Freedman, A., Sharma, S., Pearson, D., Plotsky, P. M., & Meaney, M. J. (1997). Maternal care, hippocampal glucocorticoid receptors, and hypothalamic-pituitary-adrenal responses to stress. *Science, New Series*, 277(5332), 1659–1662.
Lyons, D. M., & Parker, K. J. (2007). Stress inoculation-induced indications of resilience in monkeys. *Journal of Traumatic Stress*, 20(4), 423–433. https://doi.org/10.1002/jts.20265
Main, M., & Solomon, J. (1990) Procedures for identifying infants as disorganised/disoriented during the Ainsworth Strange Situation. In M. T. Greenberg, D. Cicchetti, & E. M. Cummings (Eds.), *Attachment in the preschool years* (pp. 121–160). University of Chicago Press.
Malins, P. (2004). Machinic assemblages: Deleuze, Guattari and an ethico-aesthetics of drug use. *Janus Head*, 7(1), 84–104.
Manning, F. A., Morrison, I., Harman, C. R., Lange, I. R., & Menticoglou, S. (1987). Fetal assessment based on fetal biophysical profile scoring: In 19,221 referred high-risk pregnancies: II: An analysis of false-negative fetal deaths. *American Journal of Obstetrics & Gynecology*, 157(4), 880–884. https://doi.org/10.1016/S0002-9378(87)80077-7
Marlier, L., Schaal, B., & Soussignan, R. (1998). Neonatal responsiveness to the odor of amniotic and lacteal fluids: A test of perinatal chemosensory continuity. *Child Development*, 69(3), 611–623.
Maslach, C., & Leiter, M. P. (2016). Understanding the burnout experience: Recent research and its implications for psychiatry. *World Psychiatry*, 15(2), 103–111. https://doi.org/10.1002/wps.20311
Mason, O., Platts, H., & Tyson, M. (2005). Early maladaptive schemas and adult attachment in a UK clinical population. *Psychology and Psychotherapy: Theory, Research and Practice*, 78(4), 549–564. https://doi.org/10.1348/147608305X41371
Masten, A., & Barnes, A. (2018). Resilience in children: Developmental perspectives. *Children*, 5(7), 98. https://doi.org/10.3390/children5070098
Mattejat, F., & Remschmidt, H. (2008). The children of mentally ill parents. *Deutsches Aerzteblatt Online*, 105(23), 413–418. https://doi.org/10.3238/arztebl.2008.0413
Mattina, G. F., Van Lieshout, R. J., & Steiner, M. (2019). Inflammation, depression and cardiovascular disease in women: The role of the immune system across critical reproductive events. *Therapeutic Advances in Cardiovascular Disease*, 13, 1753944719851950. https://doi.org/10.1177/1753944719851950

Mayberry, R.M., Mili, F., & Ofili, E. (2000). Racial and ethnic differences in access to medical care. *Medical Care Research and Review, 57,* 108–145.

Mauer, M. (2013). The changing racial dynamics of women's incarceration. https://www.sentencingproject.org/publications/the-changing-racial-dynamics-of-womens-incarceration/

McEwen, B. S. (1998). Stress, adaptation, and disease: Allostasis and allostatic load. *Annals of the New York Academy of Sciences, 840*(1), 33–44. https://doi.org/10.1111/j.1749-6632.1998.tb09546.x

McEwen, B. S. (2005). Stressed or stressed out: What is the difference? *Journal of Psychiatry and Neuroscience, 30*(5), 315–318.

McEwen, B. S., & Gianaros, P. J. (2010). Central role of the brain in stress and adaptation: Links to socioeconomic status, health and disease. *Annals of the New York Academy of Sciences,* 1186, 190–222.

McGlade, A., Ware, R., & Crawford, M. (2009). Child protection outcomes for infants of substance-using mothers: A matched-cohort study. *Pediatrics, 124*(1), 285–293. https://doi.org/10.1542/peds.2008-0576

Meaney, M. J., Diorio, J., Francis, D., Weaver, S., Yau, J., Chapman, K., & Seckl, J. R. (2000). Postnatal handling increases the expression of cAMP-inducible transcription factors in the rat hippocampus: The effects of thyroid hormones and serotonin. *The Journal of Neuroscience, 20*(10), 3926–3935. https://doi.org/10.1523/JNEUROSCI.20-10-03926.2000

Meaney, M. J., & Szyf, M. (2005). Environmental programming of stress responses through DNA methylation: Life at the interface between a dynamic environment and a fixed genome. *Dialogues in Clinical Neuroscience, 7*(2), 103–123.

Méndez-Bértolo, C., Moratti, S., Toledano, R., Lopez-Sosa, F., Martínez-Alvarez, R., Mah, Y. H., Vuilleumier, P., Gil-Nagel, A., & Strange, B. A. (2016). A fast pathway for fear in human amygdala. *Nature Neuroscience, 19*(8), 1041-1049. https://doi.org/10.1038/nn.4324

Merwin, S. M., Barrios, C., Smith, V. C., Lemay, E. P., & Dougherty, L. R. (2018). Outcomes of early parent-child adrenocortical attunement in the high-risk offspring of depressed parents. *Developmental Psychobiology, 60*(4), 468–482. https://doi.org/10.1002/dev.21623

Mesquita, A. R., Pêgo, J. M., Summavielle, T., Maciel, P., Almeida, O. F. X., & Sousa, N. (2007). Neurodevelopment milestone abnormalities in rats exposed to stress in early life. *Neuroscience, 147*(4), 1022–1033. https://doi.org/10.1016/j.neuroscience.2007.04.007

Michael, N. (2020a, September 1). Neurobiology of implicit bias part 1 [Webinar]. NEFESH International. https://therapistexpress.com/workshops/NeurobiologyofImplicitBiasandTransgenerationalTrauma/login

Michael, N. (2020b, September 8). Neurobiology of implicit bias part 2: Implicit biases, racism and transgenerational trauma [Webinar]. NEFESH International. https://therapistexpress.com/workshops/NeurobiologyofImplicitBiasandTransgenerationalTrauma/login

Mickelson, K. D., Kessler, R. C., & Shaver, P. R. (1997). Adult attachment in a nationally representative sample. *Journal of Personality and Social Psychology, 73*(5), 1092–1106.

Mimura, C., & Norman, I. J. (2018). The relationship between healthcare workers' attachment styles and patient outcomes: A systematic review. *International Journal for Quality in Health Care, 30*(5), 332–343. https://doi.org/10.1093/intqhc/mzy034

Morsy, L., & Rothstein, R. (2016). Mass incarceration and children's outcomes. https://www.epi.org/files/pdf/118615.pdf

Muennig P., Fiscella K., Tancredi D. & Franks P. (2010). The relative health burden of selected social and behavioral risk factors in the United States: Implications for policy. *American Journal of Public Health, 100*(9), 1758–1764.

Murphy, G., Peters, K., Wilkes, L., & Jackson, D. (2018). Adult children of parents with mental illness: Parenting journeys. *BMC Psychology, 6*(1), 37. https://doi.org/10.1186/s40359-018-0248-x

Murray, J., Farrington, D. P., & Sekol, I. (2012). Children's antisocial behavior, mental health, drug use, and educational performance after parental incarceration: A systematic review and meta-analysis. *Psychological Bulletin, 138*(2), 175–210. https://doi.org/10.1037/a0026407

National Academy of Medicine. (2020). Resources to support the health and well-being of clinicians during the Covid-19 outbreak. https://nam.edu/initiatives/clinician-resilience-and-well-being/clinician-well-being-resources-during-covid-19/#.XtT8O2KZoFI.email

National Child Traumatic Stress Network. (2021). www.nctsn.org

National Child Traumatic Stress Network, Secondary Traumatic Stress Committee. (2011). Secondary traumatic stress: A fact sheet for child-serving professionals. https://www.nctsn.org/sites/default/files/resources/fact-sheet/secondary_traumatic_stress_child_serving_professionals.pdf

National Child Traumatic Stress Network. (2004). Child traumatic grief educational materials. http://dcfs.nv.gov/uploadedFiles/dcfsnvgov/content/Tips/Child_Safety/ChildhoodTraumaticGriefEducationalMaterials1013.pdf

National Human Genome Research Institute. (n.d.). Human genome project results. https://www.genome.gov/human-genome-project/results

National Institutes of Health. (2018). Intramural research program personnel demographics (end FY 18). https://oir.nih.gov/sourcebook/personnel/irp-demographics/intramural-research-program-personnel-demographics-end-fy18)

Neblett, E. & Roberts, S. O. (2013). Racial identity and autonomic responses to racial discrimination. *Psychophysiology, 50*(10), 943–953. doi: 10.1111/psyp12087

NEJM Catalyst. (2017) Social Determinants of Health (SDOH). https://catalyst.nejm.org/doi/full/10.1056/CAT.17.0312

Nelson, C. A., Zeanah, C. H., & Fox, N. A. (2019). How early experience shapes human development: The case of psychosocial deprivation. *Neural Plasticity,* 2019, 1–12. https://doi.org/10.1155/2019/1676285

Nerd Nite (2017, November 4). The Polyvagal Theory: The new science of safety and trauma, Seth Porges, presenter [Video]. YouTube. https://youtu.be/br8-qebjIgs

Neumann, I. D. (2008). Brain oxytocin: A key regulator of emotional and social behaviours in both females and males. *Journal of Neuroendocrinology, 20*(6), 858–865. https://doi.org/10.1111/j.1365-2826.2008.01726.x

Nosek, M., Stillman, J. A., & Whelan, Z. (2019). Youth experiences of parent incarceration: Doing time from both sides. *Journal of Psychosocial Nursing and Mental Health Services, 57*(6), 22–29. https://doi.org/10.3928/02793695-20181220-03

Nuru-Jeter, A., Dominguez, T. P., Hammond, W. P., Leu, J., Skaff, M., Egerter, S., Jones, C. P., & Braveman, P. (2009). "It's the skin you're in": African-American women talk about their experiences of racism. An exploratory study to develop measures of racism for birth outcome studies. *Maternal and Child Health Journal, 13*(1), 29–39. https://doi.org/10.1007/s10995-008-0357-x

Office of Refugee Resettlement, U.S. Department of Health and Human Services. (2018). Facts and data. https://www.acf.hhs.gov/orr/about/ucs/facts-and-data

Ogden, P., Minton, K., & Pain, C. (2006). *Trauma and the body: A sensorimotor approach to psychotherapy*. Norton Series on Interpersonal Neurobiology. New York: Norton.

Ogden, P. (2018). Polyvagal theory and sensorimotor psychotherapy. In S. W. Porges & D. A. Dana (Eds.), *Clinical applications of the polyvagal theory: The emergence of polyvagal-informed therapies*. Norton Series on Interpersonal Neurobiology. New York: Norton.

Olausson, H., Lamarre, Y., Backlund, H., Morin, C., Wallin, B., Starck, G., Ekholm, S., Strigo, K. W., Vallbo, A. M., & Bushnell, M. C. (2002). Unmyelinated tactile afferents signal touch and project to insular cortex. *Nature Neuroscience, 5*(9), 900–904.

Onaka, T., Takayanagi, Y., & Yoshida, M. (2012). Roles of oxytocin neurones in the control of stress, energy metabolism, and social behaviour. *Journal of Neuroendocrinology, 24*(4), 587–598. https://doi.org/10.1111/j.1365-2826.2012.02300.x

Orme, W., Bowersox, L., Vanwoerden, S., Fonagy, P., & Sharp, C. (2019). The relation between epistemic trust and borderline pathology in an adolescent inpatient sample. *Borderline Personality Disorder and Emotion Dysregulation, 6*, 13–21. https://doi.org/10.1186/s40479-019-0110-7

Panksepp, J., Burgdorf, J., Turner, C., & Gordon, N. (2003). Modeling ADHD-type arousal with unilateral frontal cortex damage in rats and beneficial effects of play therapy. *Brain and Cognition, 52*(1), 97–105. https://doi.org/10.1016/S0278-2626(03)00013-7

Panksepp, J., Normansell, L., Cox, J. F., & Siviy, S. M. (1994). Effects of neonatal decortication on the social play of juvenile rats. *Physiology & Behavior, 56*(3), 429–443. https://doi.org/10.1016/0031-9384(94)90285-2

Panter-Brick, C., & Leckman, J. F. (2013). Editorial commentary: Resilience in child development - Interconnected pathways to wellbeing. *Journal of Child Psychology and Psychiatry, 54*(4), 333–336. https://doi.org/10.1111/jcpp.12057

Paquette, D. (2004). Theorizing the father-child relationship: Mechanisms and developmental outcomes. *Human Development, 47*(4), 193–219.

Parker, K. J., Buckmaster, C. L., Sundlass, K., Schatzberg, A. F., & Lyons, D. M. (2006). Maternal mediation, stress inoculation, and the development of neuroendocrine stress resistance in primates. *PNAS USA, 103*(8), 3000–3005. https://doi.org/10.1073/pnas.0506571103

Parker, Karen J., & Maestripieri, D. (2011). Identifying key features of early stressful experiences that produce stress vulnerability and resilience in primates. *Neuroscience & Biobehavioral Reviews, 35*(7), 1466–1483.

Patrick, S. W., Dudley, J., Martin, P. R., Harrell, F. E., Warren, M. D., Hartmann, K. E., Ely, E. W., Grijalva C. G., & Cooper, W. O. (2015). Prescription opioid epidemic and infant outcomes. *Pediatrics, 135*(5), 842–850.

Paulson, J. F., & Bazemore, S. D. (2010). Prenatal and postpartum depression in fathers and its association with maternal depression: A meta-analysis. *JAMA, 303*(19), 1961–1969.

Pereyra, P. M., Zhang, W., Schmidt, M., & Becker, L. E. (1992). Development of myelinated and unmyelinated fibers of human vagus nerve during the first year of life. *Journal of the Neurological Sciences, 110*(1–2), 107–113. https://doi.org/10.1016/0022-510X(92)90016-E

Perry, B. D., & Dobson, C. L. (2013). Application of the neurosequential model of therapeutics (NMT) in maltreated children. In J. D. Ford and C. A. Courtois (Eds.), *Treat-*

ing *complex traumatic stress disorders in children and adolescents: Scientific foundations and therapeutic models.* Guilford Press.

Pew Research Center. (2015). Parenting in America: Outlook, worries, aspirations are strongly linked to financial situation. https://www.pewresearch.org/wp-content/uploads/sites/3/2015/12/2015-12-17_parenting-in-america_FINAL.pdf

Phillips, R. (2013). The sacred hour: Uninterrupted skin-to-skin contact immediately after birth. *Newborn and Infant Nursing Reviews, 13*(2), 67–72. https://doi.org/10.1053/j.nainr.2013.04.001

Pompa, C. (2019, June 24). Immigrant kids keep dying in CBP detention centers, and DHS won't take accountability. ACLU. https://www.aclu.org/blog/immigrants-rights/immigrants-rights-and-detention/immigrant-kids-keep-dying-cbp-detention

Porges, S. W. (1995). Orienting in a defensive world: Mammalian modifications of our evolutionary heritage. A Polyvagal Theory. *Psychophysiology, 32*(4), 301–318.

Porges, S. W. (1996). Physiological regulation in high-risk infants: A model for assessment and potential intervention. *Development and Psychopathology, 8*, 43–58.

Porges, S. W. (2001). The polyvagal theory: Phylogenetic substrates of a social nervous system. *International Journal of Psychophysiology, 42*(2), 123–146.

Porges, S. W. (2011). *The polyvagal theory: Neurophysiological foundations of emotions, attachment, communication, and self-regulation* (1st ed.). Norton Series on Interpersonal Neurobiology. New York: Norton.

Porges, S. W. (2014). The transformative power of feeling safe. Presented at the Cape Cod Institute. Eastham, Massachusetts.

Porges, S. W. (2015a). Making the world safe for our children: Down-regulating defence and up-regulating social engagement to 'optimise' the human experience. *Children Australia, 40*(2), 114.

Porges, S. W. (2015b). Play as neural exercise: Insights from the polyvagal theory. In D. Pearce-McCall (Ed.), *The power of play for mind brain health.* (pp. 3–7). http://mindgains.org/

Porges, S. W. (2019). Social connectedness as a biological imperative: Implications of Polyvagal Theory in the Classroom. Educational Neuroscience Symposium. Presented September 20, 2019. Butler University. Indianapolis, Indiana.

Porges, S. W., & Dana, D. A. (2018). *Clinical applications of the polyvagal theory: The emergence of polyvagal-informed therapies.* Norton Series on Interpersonal Neurobiology. New York: Norton.

Porges, S. W., Doussard-Roosevelt, J. A., & Maiti, A. K. (1994). Vagal tone and the physiological regulation of emotion. *Monographs of the Society for Research in Child Development, 59*(2/3), 167. https://doi.org/10.2307/1166144

Porges, S. W., & Furman, S. A. (2011). The early development of the autonomic nervous system provides a neural platform for social behaviour: A polyvagal perspective. *Infant and Child Development, 20*(1), 106–118." https://doi.org/10.1002/icd.688

Putterman, A., Fawcett, E. (2020, April 1). Newborn baby among 16 additional COVID-19 deaths in Connecticut, as state opens new mobile hospital. *Hartford Courant.* https://www.courant.com/coronavirus/hc-news-coronavirus-updates-0401-20200401-hdee5iawvncgjdq5qoa7zc6vye-story.html

Pynoos, R. S., Steinberg, A. M., Layne, C. M., Liang, L.-J., Vivrette, R. L., Briggs, E. C., Kisiel, C., Habib, M., Belin, T. R., & Fairbank, J. A. (2014). Modeling constellations of trauma exposure in the National Child Traumatic Stress Network Core Data Set.

Psychological Trauma: Theory, Research, Practice, and Policy, 6(Suppl 1), S9–S17. https://doi.org/10.1037/a0037767

Raby, K.L., Yarger, H.A., Lind, T., Fraley, R.C., Leerkes, E., & Dozier M. (2017). Attachment states of mind among internationally adoptive and foster parents. *Developmental Psychopathology.* 29(2), 365–378. https://doi:10.1017/S0954579417000049

Redford, G. (2019, November 12). Amy Edmondson: Psychological safety is critically important in medicine. *AAMC News & Insights.* https://www.aamc.org/news-insights/amy-edmondson-psychological-safety-critically-important-medicine

Reihl, K. M., Hurley, R. A., & Taber, K. H. (2015). Neurobiology of implicit and explicit bias: Implications for clinicians. *The Journal of Neuropsychiatry and Clinical Neurosciences,* 27(4), 248–253. https://doi.org/10.1176/appi.neuropsych.15080212

Reilly, K. (2013, June 21). Sesame Street reaches out to 2.7 million American children with an incarcerated parent. Pew Research Center, Fact Tank. https://www.pewresearch.org/fact-tank/2013/06/21/

Rifkin-Graboi, A., Bai, J., Chen, H., Hameed, W. B., Sim, L. W., Tint, M. T., Leutscher-Broekman, B., Chong, Y.-S., Gluckman, P. D., Fortier, M. V., Meaney, M. J., & Qiu, A. (2013). Prenatal maternal depression associates with microstructure of right amygdala in neonates at birth. *Biological Psychiatry,* 74(11), 837–844. https://doi.org/10.1016/j.biopsych.2013.06.019

Riley, R. (2020, Jan 9). Mich. kids are going to school traumatized — and teachers lack training, resources to help. *Detroit Free Press.* https://www.freep.com/in-depth/news/columnists/rochelle-riley/2019/12/13/special-education-trauma-kids-michigan-schools/3739003002/

Robinson, B. (2008). A review of NICHD standardized nomenclature for cardiotocography: The importance of speaking a common language when describing electronic fetal monitoring. *Reviews in Obstetrics and Gynecology, 1*(2), 56–60.

Rogers, E. M. (1995). *Diffusion of innovations.* (4th ed.). Free Press.

Rogers, F. D., Rhemtulla, M., Ferrer, E., & Bales K. L. (2018) Longitudinal trajectories and interparental dynamics of prairie vole biparental care. *Frontiers in Ecology and Evolution.* https://doi.org/10.3389/fevo.2018.00073

Rosen, M. A., DiazGranados, D., Dietz, A. S., Benishek, L. E., Thompson, D., Pronovost, P. J., & Weaver, S. J. (2018). Teamwork in healthcare: Key discoveries enabling safer, high-quality care. *American Psychologist,* 73(4), 433–450.

Sambo, C. F., Howard, M., Kopelman, M., Williams, S., & Fotopoulou, A. (2010). Knowing you care: Effects of perceived empathy and attachment style on pain perception. *Pain, 151*(3), 687–693. https://doi.org/10.1016/j.pain.2010.08.035

Sameroff, A. (2010). A unified theory of development: A dialectic integration of nature and nurture. *Child Development, 81*(1), 6–22.

SAMHSA, Center for Behavioral Health Statistics and Quality, National Surveys on Drug Use and Health (NSDUHs), 2009-2014.

Sanders, M. R., & Hall, S. L. (2018). Trauma-informed care in the newborn intensive care unit: Promoting safety, security and connectedness. *Journal of Perinatology, 38*(1), 3–10. https://doi.org/10.1038/jp.2017.124

Sanders, M. R. (2018). Strengthening the safety circuit: Applying polyvagal theory in the newborn intensive care unit. In S. W. Porges and D. Dana (Eds.), *Clinical applications of the polyvagal theory: The emergence of polyvagal-informed therapies.* (pp. 359–377). Norton Series on Interpersonal Neurobiology. New York: Norton.

Sandhu, N., Eppich, W., Mikrogianakis, A., Grant, V., Robinson, T., & Cheng, A., for the Canadian Pediatric Simulation Network (CPSN) Debriefing Consensus Group. (2014). Postresuscitation debriefing in the pediatric emergency department: A national needs assessment. *Canadian Journal of Emergency Medicine, 16*(05), 383–392. https://doi.org/10.2310/8000.2013.131136

Sandman, C. A., Davis, E. P., Buss, C., & Glynn, L. M. (2011). Prenatal programming of human neurological function. *International Journal of Peptides, 2011*, 1–9. https://doi.org/10.1155/2011/837596

Schaal, B., Marlier, L., & Soussignan, R. (1998). Olfactory function in the human fetus: Evidence from selective neonatal responsiveness to the odor of amniotic fluid. *Behavioral Neuroscience, 112*(6), 1438–1449. https://doi.org/10.1037//0735-7044.112.6.1438

Schirmer, S., Nellis, A. & Mauer, M. (2009). Incarcerated parents and their children. 1991–2007. https://www.sentencingproject.org/wp-content/uploads/2016/01/Incarcerated-Parents-and-Their-Children-Trends-1991-2007.pdf

Schmidt, L. A., Burack, J. A., & Van Lieshout, R. J. (2016). Themed issue on developmental origins of adult mental health and illness. *Journal of Developmental Origins of Health and Disease, 7*(6), 564–564. https://doi.org/10.1017/S204017441600060X

Schore, A. N. (1996). The experience-dependent maturation of a regulatory system in the orbital prefrontal cortex and the origin of developmental psychopathology. *Development and Psychopathology, 8*, 59–87. https://doi.org/10.1017/S0954579400006970

Schore, A. N. (2014). Early interpersonal neurobiological assessment of attachment and autistic spectrum disorders. *Frontiers in Psychology, 5*, 1–13. https://doi.org/10.3389/fpsyg.2014.01049

Shatz, C. J. (1992). The developing brain. *Scientific American, 267*(3), 60–67. http://www.jstor.org/stable/24939213

Sherman, M. D., & Hooker, S. A. (2018). Supporting families managing parental mental illness: Challenges and resources. *The International Journal of Psychiatry in Medicine, 53*(5–6), 361–370. https://doi.org/10.1177/0091217418791444

Shin, L. M., Rauch, S. L., & Pitman, R. K. (2006). Amygdala, medial prefrontal cortex, and hippocampal function in PTSD. *Annals of the New York Academy of Sciences, 1071*, 67–79. https://doi.org/10.1196/annals.1364.007

Shonkoff, J. P., & Phillips, D.A. (Eds.). (2000). *From neurons to neighborhoods: The science of early childhood development.* National Academy Press.

Shonkoff, J. P., Garner, A. S., Committee on Psychosocial Aspects of Child and Family Health, Committee on Early Childhood, Adoption, and Dependent Care, and Section on Developmental and Behavioral Pediatrics, Siegel, B. S., Dobbins, M. I., Earls, M. F., Garner, A. S., McGuinn, L., Pascoe, J., & Wood, D. L. (2012). The lifelong effects of early childhood adversity and toxic stress. *Pediatrics, 129*(1), e232–e246. https://doi.org/10.1542/peds.2011-2663

Short, T. D., Stallings, E. B., Isenburg, J., O'Leary, L. A., Yazdy, M. M., Bohm, M. K., Ethen, M., Chen, X., Tran, T., Fox, D. J., Fornoff, J., Forestieri, N., Ferrell, E., Ramirez, G. M., Kim, J., Shi, J., Cho, S. J., Duckett, K., Nelson, N., Zielke, K., . . . Reefhuis, J. (2019). Gastroschisis trends and ecologic link to opioid prescription rates — United States, 2006–2015. *Morbidity and Mortality Weekly Report (MMWR), 68*, 31–36. http://doi.org/10.15585/mmwr.mm6802a2

Siegel, D. J. (2012). *The developing mind: How relationships and the brain interact to shape who we are* (2nd ed.). Guilford Press.

Simmons, R. A. (2009). Developmental origins of adult disease. *Pediatric Clinics of North America, 56*(3), 449–466. https://doi.org/10.1016/j.pcl.2009.03.004

Skogen, J. C., & Øverland, S. (2012). The fetal origins of adult disease: A narrative review of the epidemiological literature. *JRSM Short Reports, 3*(8), 1–7. https://doi.org/10.1258/shorts.2012.012048

Smyke, A. T., Zeanah, C. H., Fox, N. A., Nelson, C. A., & Guthrie, D. (2010). Placement in foster care enhances quality of attachment among young institutionalized children. *Child Development, 81*(1), 212–223. https://doi.org/10.1111/j.1467-8624.2009.01390.x

Sonu, S., Post, S., & Feinglass, J. (2019). Adverse childhood experiences and the onset of chronic disease in young adulthood. *Preventive Medicine, 123*, 163–170. https://doi.org/10.1016/j.ypmed.2019.03.032

Sørensen, H. J., Manzardo, A. M., Knop, J., Penick, E. C., Madarasz, W., Nickel, E. J., Becker, U., & Mortensen, E. L. (2011). The contribution of parental alcohol use disorders and other psychiatric illness to the risk of alcohol use disorders in the offspring. *Alcoholism: Clinical and Experimental Research, 35*(7), 1315–1320. https://doi.org/10.1111/j.1530-0277.2011.01467.x

Southwick, S. M., & Southwick, F. S. (2020). The loss of social connectedness as a major contributor to physician burnout: Applying organizational and teamwork principles for prevention and recovery. *JAMA Psychiatry, 77*(5), 449–450. https://doi.org/10.1001/jamapsychiatry.2019.4800

Specter, M. (2020, April 20). How Anthony Fauci became America's doctor. *The New Yorker.* https://www.newyorker.com/magazine/2020/04/20/how-anthony-fauci-became-americas-doctor

Spinazzola, J., Hodgdon, H., Liang, L.-J., Ford, J. D., Layne, C. M., Pynoos, R., Briggs, E. C., Stolbach, B., & Kisiel, C. (2014). Unseen wounds: The contribution of psychological maltreatment to child and adolescent mental health and risk outcomes. *Psychological Trauma: Theory, Research, Practice, and Policy, 6*(Suppl 1), S18–S28. https://doi.org/10.1037/a0037766

Steinberg, A. M., Pynoos, R. S., Briggs, E. C., Gerrity E. T., Layne, C. M., Vivrette, R. L., Beyerlein, B., & Fairbank J. A. (2014). The National Child Traumatic Stress Network Core Data Set: Emerging findings future directions, and implications for theory, research, practice, and policy. *Psychological Trauma: Theory, Research, Practice and Policy, 6*(S1): S50–S57.

Steinberg, Z., & Kraemer, S. (2010). Cultivating a culture of awareness: Nurturing reflective practices in the NICU. *Zero to Three Journal, 31*(20), 15–21.

Steinberg, Z., & Patterson, C. (2017). Giving voice to the psychological in the NICU: A relational model. *Journal of Infant, Child, and Adolescent Psychotherapy, 16*(1), 25–44. https://doi.org/10.1080/15289168.2016.1267539

Substance Abuse and Mental Health Services Administration. (2017). Children living with parents who have a substance use disorder. https://www.samhsa.gov/data/sites/default/files/report_3223/ShortReport-3223.pdf

Szabo, S., Tache, Y., & Somogyi, A. (2012). The legacy of Hans Selye and the origins of stress research: A retrospective 75 years after his landmark brief "Letter" to the Editor" of Nature. *Stress, 15*(5), 472–478. https://doi.org/10.3109/10253890.2012.710919

Thompson, G. (2018). Brain-empowered collaborators: Polyvagal perspectives on the doctor–patient relationship. In S. W. Porges and D. Dana (Eds.), *Clinical applications of the polyvagal theory: The emergence of polyvagal-informed therapies.* (pp. 127-148). Norton Series on Interpersonal Neurobiology. New York: Norton.

Toepfer, P., Heim, C., Entringer, S., Binder, E., Wadhwa, P., & Buss, C. (2017). Oxytocin pathways in the intergenerational transmission of maternal early life stress. *Neuroscience & Biobehavioral Reviews, 73*, 293–308. https://doi.org/10.1016/j.neubiorev.2016.12.026

Torvik, F. A., Rognmo, K., Ask, H., Røysamb, E., & Tambs, K. (2011). Parental alcohol use and adolescent school adjustment in the general population: Results from the HUNT study. *BMC Public Health, 11*(1). https://doi.org/10.1186/1471-2458-11-706

Trevarthen, C. (1996). Lateral asymmetries in infancy: Implications for the development of the hemispheres. *Neuroscience & Biobehavioral Reviews, 20*(4), 571–586. https://doi.org/10.1016/0149-7634(95)00070-4

Tronick, E. Z. & Cohn, J. F. (1989). Infant-Mother face-to-face interaction: Age and gender differences in coordination and the occurrence of miscoordination. *Child Development, 60*, 85–92.

Tronick, E. Z. (2007). *The neurobehavioral and social-emotional development of infants and children.* Norton Series on Interpersonal Neurobiology. New York: Norton.

Twohey, M. (2020, April 7). New battle for those on coronavirus front lines: Child custody. *The New York Times.* https://www.nytimes.com/2020/04/07/us/coronavirus-child-custody.html

Ulmer-Yaniv, A., Djalovski, A., Priel, A., Zagoory-Sharon, O., & Feldman, R. (2018). Maternal depression alters stress and immune biomarkers in mother and child. *Depression and Anxiety, 35*(12), 1145–1157. https://doi.org/10.1002/da.22818

United Health Foundation. (2017) America's Health Rankings 2016. https://www.americashealthrankings.org/

U.S. Census Bureau. (2019) Quick facts. https://www.census.gov/quickfacts/fact/table/US/PST045219

U.S. Customs and Border Protection. U.S. Border Patrol southwest border apprehensions by sector FY2018. https://www.cbp.gov/newsroom/stats/usbp-sw-border-apprehensions

van Dernoot Lipsky, L. (2009). *Trauma stewardship. An everyday guide to caring for self while caring for others.* Berrett-Koehler Publishers.

Verghese, A. (2009). *Cutting for stone.* Knopf.

Verschueren, K. (2020). Attachment, self-esteem, and socio-emotional adjustment: There is more than just the mother. *Attachment & Human Development, 22*(1), 105–109.

Videlock, E. J., Adeyemo, M., Licudine, A., Hirano, M., Ohning, G., Mayer, M., Mayer, E. A., & Chang, L. (2009). Childhood trauma is associated with hypothalamic-pituitary-adrenal axis responsiveness in irritable bowel syndrome. *Gastroenterology, 137*(6), 1954–1962. https://doi.org/10.1053/j.gastro.2009.08.058

Waller, E., Scheidt, C. E., & Hartmann, A. (2004). Attachment representation and illness behavior in somatoform disorders. *The Journal of Nervous and Mental Disease, 192*(3), 200–209. https://doi.org/10.1097/01.nmd.0000116463.17588.07

Washington, H. A. (2006). *Medical apartheid: The dark history of medical experimentation on Black Americans from colonial times to the present.* Random House.

Weinstein, A. (2016). *Prenatal development and parents' lived experiences: How early events shape our psychophysiology and relationships.* Norton Series on Interpersonal Neurobiology. New York: Norton.

Widström, A. M., Wahlberg, V., Matthiesen, A. S., Eneroth, P., Uvnäs-Moberg, K., Werner, S., & Winberg, J. (1990). Short-term effects of early suckling and touch of the nipple on maternal behaviour. *Early Human Development, 21*(3), 153–163. https://doi.org/10.1016/0378-3782(90)90114-x

Williams, D. R., & Cooper, L. A. (2020). COVID-19 and health equity: A new kind of "herd immunity." *Journal of the American Medical Association, 323*(24), 2478–2480. doi:10.1001/jama.2020.8051

Williams, J. F., Smith, V. C., & the Committee on Substance Abuse (2015). Fetal alcohol spectrum disorder. *Pediatrics, 136*(5) e1395–e1406. https://doi.org/10.1542/peds.2015-3113

Williams, S. K., & Johns, J. M. (2014). Prenatal and gestational cocaine exposure: Effects on the oxytocin system and social behavior with implications for addiction. *Pharmacology Biochemistry and Behavior, 119*, 10–21. https://doi.org/10.1016/j.pbb.2013.07.004

Wilson, C. (2018). *Grounded: Discovering the missing piece in the puzzle of children's behaviour.* CHEW Initiatives.

Winnicott, D. W. (1960). The theory of the parent-infant relationship. *The International Journal of Psychoanalysis, 41*, 585–595.

Wong, B. (2020, April 10) Medical workers wear pics of themselves smiling to comfort COVID-19 patients. *HuffPost.* https://www.huffpost.com/entry/medical-workers-pics-smiling-covid-19-patients_l_5e8f725bc5b6b371812da523

Wordsworth, W. (1802). *My heart leaps up.* Poems in Two Volumes (Published 1807).

World Health Organization. (2008). *Closing the gap in a generation: Health equity through action on the social determinants of health.* https://www.who.int/social_determinants/final_report/csdh_finalreport_2008.pdf

Yamamoto, R., & Keogh, B. (2018). Children's experiences of living with a parent with mental illness: A systematic review of qualitative studies using thematic analysis. *Journal of Psychiatric and Mental Health Nursing, 25*(2), 131–141. https://doi.org/10.1111/jpm.12415

Yule, A. M., Wilens, T. E., Martelon, M., Rosenthal, L., & Biederman, J. (2018). Does exposure to parental substance use disorders increase offspring risk for a substance use disorder? A longitudinal follow-up study into young adulthood. *Drug and Alcohol Dependence, 186*, 154–158. https://doi.org/10.1016/j.drugalcdep.2018.01.021

Zanetti, D., Tikkanen, E., Gustafsson, S., Priest, J. R., Burgess, S., & Ingelsson, E. (2018). Birthweight, type 2 diabetes mellitus, and cardiovascular disease: Addressing the Barker hypothesis with Mendelian randomization. *Circulation: Genomic and Precision Medicine, 11*(6), e002054. https://doi.org/10.1161/CIRCGEN.117.002054

Zeanah, C. H., Egger, H. L., Smyke, A. T., Nelson, C. A., Fox, N. A., Marshall, P. J., & Guthrie, G. (2009). Institutional rearing and psychiatric disorders in Romanian preschool children. *American Journal of Psychiatry, 166*, 777–785.

Zigler, E., Piotrkowski, C. S., & Collins, R. (1994). Health services in Head Start. *Annual Review of Public Health, 15*, 511–534.

Zigmont, J. J., Kappus, L. J., & Sudikoff, S. N. (2011). The 3D model of debriefing: Defusing, discovering, and deepening. *Seminars in Perinatology, 35*(2), 52–58. https://doi.org/10.1053/j.semperi.2011.01.003

INDEX

Note: Page numbers in italics indicate figures and tables.

Abbas, K., 139–40
acute stress disorder, 139–40
adaptive survival responses, respecting, 134, 135–36
Adler, Herbert, 123
adrenaline, 110, 247
adrenocortical attunement, 83–84
adrenocorticotropin releasing hormone (ACTH), 36, 72
Adult Attachment Interview, 27
adults, polyvagal-informed, 247–48, 250–54
adverse childhood experiences (ACEs)
    gastrointestinal disorders and, 111
    health outcomes and, 101–3
    toxic stresses and, 98–101
Adverse Childhood Experiences (ACEs) survey, 98–99
Affordable Care Act (ACA), 78
Ainsworth, Mary, 25–26, 29–30, 38, 59
alcohol, 86–87
Allison, Elizabeth, 164, 226
allostatic load, 75, 105, 239
Als, Heidelise, 17–20, 266–67
American Academy of Pediatrics, 61
American Psychological Association, 61
amygdala, 33, 50, 53–54, 56, 72, 107–8, 132, 247
Anda, R. F., 98–99
adrenocorticotropic hormone (ACTH), 11–12

Andrews, H., 39
anger, 11, 68, 168–73
anti-Black violence, xxvi
anxiety, 7, 39, 55, 68, 72, 80, 99, 100, 103, 106–7, 131, 163, 231
apologies, 250
approach behaviors, *127*, 234
approach expressions, 6
Ardern, Jacinda, 242–43
arousal zones, 38–40, *38*, 41–42
Association of American Medical Colleges (AAMC), 121–22
atrioventricular (AV) node, 34–35
attachment, xxiii, xxv, 36, 249, *249*, 258–59
    attachment histories, 127, *127*, 128–31
    attachment styles, *127*, 128–29, 130
    attachment theory, 124
    co-regulation and, 38–39
    maternal-infant co-regulation and, 38–41
    mid-range balance model of, *31*
    secure, 23–26
    social connectedness and, 25–26
    social engagement and, 25–26
autonomic ladder, *40*, 41–46, 72–73, 134–35, 142, 162
    bystander traumas and, 163
    infants and, 41–46
    language of, 234–35, *234*
    primary caregivers and, 41–46

autonomic nervous system (ANS), xxvi,
    4–7, 35, 39, 42–43, 56, 105, 135, 180,
    246, 248, 250
  attending, 165, 166
  befriending, 165–66
  danger and, 118–19
  examining, 264
  fetal, 10–11
  in fetal and intrauterine life, 8–9
  opiate exposed newborns and, 22
  personal profile map and, 199
  recalibrating, 223–26
  relationship with, 134–38
  respecting, 252
  safety circuits and, 248–51
  shaping, 165, 166
autonomic reactions, 165
autonomic states, 182. *See also* autonomic
    nervous system (ANS); *specific states*
  effect on functioning, 188, 197
  recognizing, 134–35
  regulation of, 188, 197
autonomic wisdom and expertise
  accelerating momentum of, 268
  intergenerational transmission of,
    251–54
avoidance behaviors, *127*
avoidant attachment, 130

Bahrick, L., 39
Bailey, B., 259
Bailey, E., 259
Bales, K. L., 97
Barcelona de Mendoza, V., 106
Barclay, L., 161
Barker, D. J. P., 93–94
Barnett, Elizabeth, 79
Barrows, H. S., 259
Bartholomew, K., 128–29
Baylin, Jon, 44–45, 131, 167, 184, 199
becoming more present, 174–77
Beebe, Beatrice, 30–31, 38, 39
behaviors, evolutionary determined hierarchy of, 4–6, *5*
being there, vs. virtuality, 266
Belin, T. R., 71
belonging, safety and, 211

Bennefield, Z., 104
bereavement
  border separations and, 77–79
  emotional proximity and, 81–85
  parental incarceration and, 79–81
  unaccompanied minors and, 77–79
Berkwitt, A. K., 21–22
birth, 3, 15–16
  disruption of the expected environment, 14–17
  preterm infants, 17
  transition to the expected environment, 13–14
birth weight, health outcomes and, 93–94, 101–2
Bizzarro, M. J., 21–22
Black, T., 71
blocked care, 44–45
"blocked trust," 167
border separations, forced, 77–79
Bostwick, W., 232
Bowlby, John, 23–24, 25, 28, 32–33, 38, 59, 255, 266–67
brain
  developing, 81, 86–91
  embracing, 184–85
  mammalian, 33–34, 247, 248
  nurturing of, 3
  stress allostasis and, 74–75
  substance misuse and, 86–91
brain cells, 9
Braun, K., 27–28
Braveman, P., 69, 101–2
Brazelton et al., 29
breastfeeding, 89
Bremner, J. D., 99
Brenner, M., 259
Bricusse, Leslie, 233
Brierley, J., 139–40
Briggs, E. C., 71
Brindley, P. G., 147–48
Bronfenbrenner, Urie, 47
Bucharest Early Intervention Project, 75–76, 96–97
Buck, K., 39
Buckmaster, C. L., 59
Burford, T. I., 105

Burgess, S., 94
burnout, 138–39
bystander traumas, 162–64

Cage, B. N., 105
Caldji, C., 96
caravans of risk, children and, 73–74
caravans of risk passageways, 89, 103
cardiovascular disease, 93, 94, 100, 109, 111, 128
caregiver-child relationships, 26–29. *See also* mother-infant interactions
caregiver-child dyadic regulation, xxv, 14–15
caregivers. *See also* providers
  arousal zones and, *38*, 41–42
  autonomic ladder and, *40*, 41–46
  awareness of children's neuroceptions and, xxiii–xxiv
  cortisol and, 108–9
  demographics of, 26–27
  essential to young mammals, 124
  hyperaroused or high-tracking, *38*, 39–40
  hypoaroused, *38*, 40–41
  polyvagal-informed, 247–48
  teaching to be polyvagal-informed, 251–54
caregiving
  child development and, 27–28
  epistemic trust and, 227–28
  impaired, 81–86
  mental illness and, 81–85
  substance misuse and, 85–86
Center for the Study of Social Policy (CSSP), 61
  Strengthening Families framework, 252
Center on the Developing Child, 26, 56–57
  parental mental health concerns and, 81
  stress taxonomy, 61–62
Chamberland, C., 71
Champagne, F. A., 27–28, 97
Chen, H., 39
child abuse, 250. *See also* psychological maltreatment
child development, caregiving and, 27–28
childhood, toxic stresses of, 70

children. *See also* infants
  caravans of risk and, 73–74
  mentalizing experiences of, 251–52
  motivating to seek novelty, 50–51
  nurturing of, 116–19
  preparing to live in families and larger world, 47–64
  supporting toward ventral vagal, 201–3
  traumatic loss and, 70–73
Children's Health Insurance Plan (CHIP), 78
child-serving professionals, 115–19. *See also* caregivers; providers
Chokshi, D. A., 77–78
chronic disruptions of connectedness, from a lifespan perspective, 93–111
chronic inflammation, 110–11
Ciesla, J. A., 109
Circle of Security, 253, 255
City of Kindness campaign, 240–41
climate, enhancing, 218
Clinton, Bill, 78
code messages, 214
Cohen, P., 39
collaboration, 216
collateral damage, 162–64
Colville, G., 139–40
Committees of the American Academy of Pediatrics, 59
communication. *See also* language; nonverbal communication
  closing loops in, 148
  limiting at critical moments, 148
  polyvagal-informed, 247–48
  social engagement and, 147–48
  teamwork and, 147–48
community, 242, 265
compassion, 156, 185, 224, 249
compensatory paternal involvement, 97
Connaughton, J. F., Jr., 21
connectedness/connection/connectivity, 13–15, 81, 142, 182–83, 187–88, 209, 211, 216, 219, 238, 241, 249, *249*. *See also* social connectedness
  disruption of, 67–91, 234, 250
  science of, 164–65
  survival and, 265

conservation of resources (COR) theory, 73
conversations, explicit discussions of emotions and emotional states, 230–31
Cooklin, Alan, 84
Cooper, G., 253
Cooper, Lisa, 231, 233
cooperation, neurobiology of, xxvi
coping strategies, 200
　parental mental health concerns and, 84–85
co-regulation, 254
　attachment and, 38–39
　maternal-infant, 38–39
　providers and, 161–62
　self-regulation and, 115–49
corticotropin-releasing hormone (CRH), 11–13, *12*, 36
cortisol, 11–13, *12*, 36–37, 48–49, 72, 82, 96, 108, 111, 247
　caregivers and, 108–9
cortisol awakening response (CAR), 83–84
Costello, P. C., 24
COVID-19, xxvi, 148–49, 245–46, 252
　acknowledging impact on daily routines and relationships, 235–36
　connection and, 233–34
　establishing epistemic trust while social distancing, 226–31
　face-heart connection and, 233–34, 236–37
　polyvagal leadership in time of, 239–43
　provider deaths from, 237–39
　racial disparities in infection and outcomes, 231–33
　repair strategies and, 266
　social connectedness in time of, 223
　social engagement and, 266
　vaccinations for, 265–66
Coyle, D., 215–16
crisis, optimal response to, 143–47
culture, enhancing, 218
"culture of action," 140–41
"culture of awareness," 140
Curley, J. P., 97
cytokines, 110–11

daily routines, COVID-19 and, 235–36
Dalia, C., 139–40
Dana, Deb, 62, 118, 133, 134–37, 156, 164–66, 170, 199, 234, 259, 266–67, 268
danger
　assessment of, 53–54 (*see also* neuroception)
　autonomic nervous system (ANS) and, 118–19
　clues of, 107
　COVID-19 and, 223–24
　neuroception of, xxiii–xxv, 39–40, 53–54, 163, 234–37, 250, 267
　socialization for, 51–53
　sympathetic mobilization and, 7
Davis, F., 259
Davis, Wade, 265
Deans, Dean, W. 95
debriefing sessions, 142
DeFede, J., 90
defensiveness, 185
defensive states, 45, 137, 204, 211, *213*. *See also* fight-or-flight behaviors
Deferred Action for Childhood Arrivals (DACA), 78
Deferred Action for Parents of Americans (DAPA), 78
depression, 99, 106–7, 109–10, 231. *See also* maternal depression; parental depression; parental mental health concerns
developmental systems theory, 62
development origins of health and disease hypothesis (DOHaD), 93–94, 97–98, 102
　fetal programming and, 93–94
Devine, P. G., 133
diabetes, 94, 98, 100, 101, 128
Diagnostic and Procedural Coding (ICD) labelling, Polyvagal Theory and, 46
Diagnostic and Statistical Manual (DSM), Polyvagal Theory and, 46
Diamond, G., 109
Diorio, J., 96
disconnectedness, chronic disruptions of connectedness, 93–111
discrimination, 101–2. *See also* racism

dismissive-avoidant attachment, 129–30, 131
disruptions
  in childhood, 67–91
  chronic, 93–111
  of connectedness, 67–91
  not repaired, 37
  repair of, 36–37
Djalovski, A., 102–3
Dobbing, J., 25
doctor-patient relationships, 123–26. *See also* providers
  attachment styles and, 128–31
  co-regulation and, 161–62
  physiological state and, 162
Dominguez, T. P., 101–2
dorsal motor complex (dorsal motor nerve nucleus, DMNX), 33–34, 36
dorsal vagal collapse, 142, 183
dorsal vagal states, 45–46, 134–35, 177, 182, 183–84
dorsal vagus, 7–8, 11, 13, 16, 40, 108
Doussard-Roosevelt, J. A., 25, 35
Dozier, M., 27
drugs, 86–87. *See also* opiate exposed newborns; substance misuse
Drusto, C. A., 106
Dube, Sh. R., 99
Duhigg, C., 216, 220
Dyadic Developmental Psychotherapy (DDP), 166–67, 168–73, 199
dysregulation, 152, 153, 180, 200, *210*, 214, *215*, 234
  handling, 144–46
  uncertainty and, 228–29
  use of term, 156–57
early adopters, 267, 269
early childhood services, providing accessible polyvagal-informed, 260–65
early childhood social-emotional development, xxv
Early Head Start, 264
early life toxic stresses, 98–101
early majority, 267
Eat, Sleep, Console, 21–22, 88
eco-bio-developmental (EBD) model, 58
Edmondson, Amy, 121–22, 156

education
  parent education and, 251–54
  professional education and training, 254–60
  professional education and training and, 254–60
  safety and, 178–79
Edwards, V., 98–99
Egerter, S., 101–2
Egger, H. L., 75–76
embedded mental health clinicians, 140–41
emergency department staff, 143–44, 157–62
emerging humanity, supporting an, 151–85
Emich, J. P., 21
emotional neglect, 89
emotional proximity, traumatic loss and, 81–85
emotional safety
  creating in service of learning, 179–81
  supporting employees' ventral vagal states, 203–9
emotions
  explicit discussions of, 230–31
  high stakes and, 153–56
empathy, 165, 250
employees, mission and, 218, 220
Engel, George, 124–26
environment, modifying, 218, 219
epigenetics, 58, 72, 101, 108
  fetal environment and, 97–98, 100
  genetic susceptibilities and, 95–97
  neuroception and, 246–47
  poverty and, 108
  stress and, 108
  systemic racism and, 101–2, 106
epinephrine, 110
epistemic mistrust, 228
epistemic trust, 226–31
Esserman, D. A., 21–22
evolutionary biology
  groundwork laid by, 4
  Polyvagal Theory and, xxv
evolutionary determined hierarchy of behaviors, 4–6, *5*
exploration, 47–50

face-heart connection, 5–6, 34, 50, 145, 233–34, 236–37
face-to-face connection, 145, *210*, 234–39
facial expressions, 6, 29, 32, 34, 54, 107, 198, 230, 233, 247
facial reactivity, 107
Fairbank, J. A., 71
Fallon, B., 71
families
  nurturing of, 116–19
  preparing children to live in, 47–64
family separations, immigration policy and, 77–79
Fauci, Anthony, 228–29
Feagin, J., 104
fearful-avoidant attachment, 130, 131
Feinglass, J., 99
Feldman, R., 102–3
Feldstein, S., 39
Felitti, V. J., 99
Fenwick, J., 161
Ferrer, E., 97
fetal central nervous system, bricks and mortar of the, 9
fetal environment, 3–22, 93–94
  epigenetics and, 97–98, 100
  fetal sensory environment, 9–10
  hormonal regulation of, 11–13
  sensory-rich, 9–10
fetal heart, neural regulation of, 10–11
fetal programming, developmental origins of health and disease (DOHAD) and, 93–94
fetal sensory environment, 9–10
fetuses, 13–15. *See also* maternal-fetal dyadic interactions
fight-or-flight behaviors, 7, 110, 134, 135–36, 162, 174, 177, 179, 181, 183, 198, 199–200, 211, *213*
Finnegan, L. P., 21
Finnegan Neonatal Abstinence Scoring System, 21
first responders, 143–44
Fonagy, Peter, 164, 226, 252
Ford, J. D., 71
"four R's," 134–37

Fox, N. A., 75–76, 96–97
Fraley, R. C., 27
Francis, D., 96
Frankel, Elizabeth, 78–79
Freedman, A., 96
freeze-shutdown, 162, 174, 177, 184, 199–200, 228
freezing in place, life threat and, 8–9

Garber, J., 109
gastrointestinal disorders, 111. *See also specific disorders*
gastroschisis, 87
genetics, epigenetics and, 58, 95–97
genetic susceptibilities, epigenetics and, 95–97
genotypes, 95–96, 97–98
Gerretsen, P., 124
gestures, 247
Giles, W. H., 99
Gil-Nagel, A., 54
global community, Polyvagal Theory and, xxvi–xxvii
Gottleib, L., 69
gratitude, 220
Green, S., 105
Gross, Ken, 240
Grossman, M. R., 21–22
group culture, 215–16
Gustafson, S., 94
Guthrie, G., 75–76

Habib, M., 71
Hagiwara, N., 133
Hammond, W. P., 101–2
Harrell, C. J., 105
Hatzenbuehler, M. L., 103
Head Start, 264–66
healing, embodying Polyvagal Theory and, 246
healthcare
  health outcomes and, 68–70
  systemic racism and, 104–5
health outcomes
  adverse childhood experiences (ACEs) and, 101–3
  birth weight and, 93–94, 101–2

development origins of health and disease hypothesis (DOHaD) and, 93–94
discrimination and, 101–2
marginalized groups and, 103
medical care and, 68–70
racism and, 101–2, 104–5
social connectedness and, 123
social determinants of, 68–70
stress and, 102–3
healthy development, paradigm shift in promoting, 58–59
heart rate, fetal, 10–11
heart rate variability (HRV), 6–7, 17
Hebb, D. O., 52
hierarchy of behaviors, 4–6, *5*
high stakes, emotions and, 153–56
hippocampus, 50, 247
HIV/AIDS, 103
Hodgdon, H., 71
Hoffman, K., 253
hormonal influence, behaviors and, 36–37
hormonal regulation, of intrauterine environment, 11–13
Horowitz, L. M., 128–29
Huang, Y., 106
Hughes, Dan, 44–45, 131, 166–68, 184, 199, 266–67
hyperarousal, *38*, 39–40
hypervigilance, 7, 50, 62, 101, 140, 163, 179, 228
hypoarousal, *38*, 40–41
hypothalamic-pituitary-adrenal axis, 7, 11–13, *12*, 37, 83–84, 101, 102, 105, 107, 110, 247

immigration policy, family separations and, 77–79
immune response, 101
parasympathetic nervous system (PNS) and, 110–11
stress and, 102–3
implicit biases, as obstacles to interpersonal safety, 131–33
implicit biases, development of, 53–54
indifference, 250
infants. *See also* newborns
autonomic ladder and, *40*, 41–46

exploring the world, 48–50
opiate exposed newborns, 20–22
preterm, 16–20, 101–2
self-regulation and, 108–9
separation as threat to survival of, 32–33
video analysis of infant behavior, 26
information
discussing sharing of, 231
reducing uncertainty by providing, 236
reevaluate sources and timing of receiving, 229–30
Ingelsson, E., 94
Institute of Medicine, 119, 121
intensive care staff, 143–44
intentional "we," promoting, 265–67
Interleukins, 110–11
intervention, provider-patient relationships as, 123–24
intrauterine environment. *See* fetal environment
irritability, 11, 72, 74, 75, 176, 177, 185
irritable bowel syndrome (IBS), 100, 111
isolation, 231, 239

Jaffe, J., 39
Jinpa, Thupten, 3, 6
Johns Hopkins University & Medicine Coronavirus Resource Center, 245–46
Johnson, Lyndon B., 264
joint attention, 57
Jones, C. P., 101–2

Kennedy, John F., 268
Keogh, B., 84
Khullar, Dhruv, 77–78, 239
KidsTLC Constitution, 219, 271
Kim, S. J., 232
kindness, 240–41
King, Martin Luther, 268
Kisiel, C., 71
Knox, Isabella, 254
Korn, Deborah, 39
Koss, M. P., 98–99
Kron, F. W., 133
Kron, R. E., 21

laggards, 267
language
    of autonomic ladder, 234–35, *234*
    importance of, 156–57
    motherese, 247
    straightforward and direct, 147
late majority, 267
Layne, C. M., 71
leadership, 268
    polyvagal-informed, 216–20, *217*, 239–43
    in time of COVID-19, 239–43
learning, playing and, 55–58
Leerkes, E., 27
Lester, Barry, 95
Leu, J., 101–2
Levine, Peter A., 182–83, 245, 260
Liang, L.-J., 71
life threat, freezing in place and, 8–9
limbic system, 247, 248
Lind, T., 27
Link, B. G., 103
Lipari, R. N., 85
Liu, D., 96
Lopez-Sosa, F., 54
loss, 224
    trauma and, 70–73, 77–85
love hormone, 13. *See also* oxytocin
Lyons, D. M., 59

Maggert, K.A., 95
Mah, Y. H., 54
Main, M., 26
Maiti, A. K., 25, 35
Major Life Discrimination scales, 106
Malins, Peta, 85
mammalian brain, 33–34, 247, 248
mammalian cultures, 216, 219
Margetts, B., 94
marginalized groups, 133
    health outcomes and, 103
    maltreatment of, 103
Markese, S., 39
Marks, J. S., 98–99
Marlier, B., 10
Marshall, P. J., 75–76
Martínez-Alvarez, R., 54

Mashoodh, M., 97
masks, 225, 233–34, 236. *See also* personal protective equipment (PPE)
Masten, A., 62, 63
maternal depression, 81–85, 106–7
maternal-fetal dyadic interactions, 13–15
maternal-infant co-regulation, attachment and, 38–41
maternal tracking, 38–40, *38*
McCauley, E., 109
McEwen, B. S., 74, 75
Meaney, M. J., 96
Medicaid, 78
medical errors, reducing through psychological safety, 121–22
medications, 95–96
Méndez-Bértolo, C., 54
mental illness, stigmatization of, 103
mentalizing, 251–52
mental models, building shared, 147
MERS epidemic, 223
metabolic syndrome, 101
Michael, Nancy, 52, 53–54, 132–33
mid-range balance model of attachment, *31*
mismatch, in mother-infant interactions, 29–32
missions, 216–17, 218
mistrust, epistemic, 228
Moratti, S., 54
motherese, 247
mother-infant interactions
    felt state of mother-infant dyad, 36
    maternal styles of, 30–31
    mismatch and repair in, 29–32
    newborns and, 13–15
    secure attachment and, 23–26
    skin-to-skin contact, 14–15
Myers, J., 124

National Child Traumatic Stress Network (NCTSN), 70–71, 73
National Institutes of Health (NIH), 104
National Perinatal Association, 141
National Traumatic Stress Network, 140
Neblett, E., 105
need to know and be known, 124–26

neglect, 89, 250
Nelson, C. A., 75–76, 96–97
Nelson, T. M., 105
neonatal abstinence syndrome (NAS), 21, 74, 88
neurobiology
 of cooperation, xxvi
 of safety, xxii–xxiii, xxvi
neuroception, xxiii–xxv, xxiv, 4, 38–40, *38*, 132, 172, 182, 246
 of danger, xxiii–xxv, 39–40, 163, 234–37, 250, 267
 epigenetics and, 246–47
 neuroceptive states, *38*
 neuroceptive thumbprint, 249, 268
 of others, 264
 recognizing, 252
 of safety, xxiii–xxv, 39, 219, 234
 of security, 234
 of threat, 250, 267
neurons, 9, 52–53
neurotransmitters, 10, 72
Newborn Individualized Development Care and Assessment Program (NIDCAP), 18–20
newborn intensive care unit (NICU), 17–19, 20
newborn intensive parenting unit (NIPU), 20
newborns, 15–16
 mother-infant interactions and, 13–15
 opiate-exposed, 20–22, 87–88
 parental depression and, 81–85
New England Journal of Medicine Catalyst, 68–69
nonverbal communication, 156, 247
 personal protective equipment (PPE) and, 236–37
 polyvagal-informed, 247–48
 positive, 133
noradrenaline, 110
Nordenberg, D., 98–99
norepinephrine, 110
novelty, motivating young children to seek, 50–51
nucleus, 34
nucleus ambiguus (NA), 33–34

nurturing ourselves, 138–43
Nuru-Jeter, A., 101–2
nutrition, 93–94, 95–96, 97

Obama, Barack, 78
obesity, 99, 101
Ogden, Pat, 164
openness, safety conveyed through, 126–28
opiate-exposed newborns, 20–22, 87–88
optimal human functioning, building a safe environment to nurture, 187–220
ordinary disruptions, mastering, 59–61
organizations, *210*
 actions to support safe environment in, 218–20
 culture and leadership in polyvagal-informed organization, 215–20
 leadership and, 216–20, *217*
 missions of, 216–17, 218, 220
 organizational culture, 215–20
 polyvagal-informed, 146–47, 187–220, 267–68
 ventral vagal teams and, 209–14
orphanages, 75–76
Osborn, R. R., 21–22
Osmond, C., 94
others
 neuroception of, 264
 regard for, 128–29
 regulation of, 134, 136, 155–56, 173–74, 212–13, *215*
oxytocin, 11, 13, 14, 37, 89
oxytocin/vasopressin systems, 11, 13

Panksepp, Jaak, 55
Panter-Brick, C., 62
Paquette, D., 29
parasympathetic nervous system (PNS), 5, 110–11
parental depression, 81–85
 child depression and, 109
parental environment, as second womb, 23
parental incarceration, 79–81
 epidemiology of, 80–81

parental mental health concerns, 106–7, 109
  children's understanding of, 84
  coping strategies and, 84–85
  stigma of, 84–85
  stress reactivity and, 106–9
parent education, Polyvagal Theory and, 251–54
parent-infant system, 13–20
  preterm infants and, 17–20
parents, teaching to be polyvagal-informed, 251–54
Parker, K. J., 59
paternal depression, 106–7
pathogens, 95–96
Pearson, D., 96
peek-a-boo, 55–56
perception, xxiii
Perry, Bruce, 99, 248
persistent structural stigma, 103–4
personal profile map, 199
personal protective equipment (PPE), 225, 234, 236, 237, 239
Pew Research Center, 26–27
phenotypes, 96
Phillips, D. A., 58
Phillips, R., 14
physiological state, doctor-patient relationships and, 162
Pittman, R. K., 107
play, 29, 47–48
  as coping strategy, 84–85
  learning and, 55–58
  as neural exercise, 55
  risk and, 55
  serve and return/back and forth interactions, 55–58
Playful, Accepting, Curious, and Empathic (PACE) attitude, 167–68, 175–77, 199
Plotsky, P. M., 96
polyvagal-informed
  becoming, 250–51
  performance for the, 267–69
polyvagal-informed leadership, 216–20, 217, 239–43, 268
polyvagal-informed organizations, 146–47, 267–68
  action steps for building, 197–220
  culture and leadership in polyvagal-informed organization, 215–20
  educating staff on polyvagal theory, 197–201
  foundations of, 194–96
  scaffolding organization's safety with ventral vagal teams, 209–14
  supporting children toward ventral vagal, 201–3
  supporting employees' ventral vagal states, 203–9
  what is a polyvagal-informed organization, 188–94
polyvagal-informed society, 266–67, 268
polyvagal leadership, in time of COVID-19, 239–43
Polyvagal Theory (PVT), 164
  application to psychotherapy, 134–35
  applying, 268
  attachment histories and, 128–31
  coining of the term, 5
  COVID-19 and, xxvi
  Diagnostic and Procedural Coding (ICD) labelling and, 46
  Diagnostic and Statistical Manual (DSM) and, 46
  early adopters of, 269
  embodying, xxvi–xxvii, 152–56, 246
  epistemic trust, 227
  evolutionary biology and, xxv
  global community and, xxvi–xxvii
  intergenerational transmission of autonomic wisdom and expertise and, 251–54
  introduction to, xxi–xxvii
  larger issues of life and, xxvi
  parent education and, 251–54
  as powerful organizing principle, xxi–xxiii
  professional education and training and, 254–60
  provider-patient relationships and, 128–31
  for providers, 151–85
  self-regulation and, xxv–xxvi
Porges, Stephen, xii–xviii, xxiv, 4–5, 25, 29, 33–36, 35, 67, 126, 134, 216, 266–68

on compassion, 185
on connectedness, 266
on lifting the vagal brake, 144–46
on neuroception, 53
on play, 55
on power of social engagement, 233
on safety, 216
on threats, 218
on trauma, 70
Post, S., 99
postpartum depression, 81–85, 106–7. *See also* maternal depression
post-traumatic stress syndrome (PTSD), 80, 107, 139–40
poverty, stress and, 108
Powell, B., 253
prefrontal cortex, 247
pregnancy, 3–22
  anxiety and depression and, 106–7
  substance misuse in, 86–91
Priel, A., 102–3
Priest, J. R., 94
primary caregivers, autonomic ladder and, 41–46
prior generations, experiences of, 97–98
privacy concerns, 231
problem-based learning, 259
professional education and training, 254–55, 258–59
  attend to and repair disruptions in, 254–60
  Polyvagal Theory and, 254–60
provider-patient relationships
  as intervention, 123–24
  polyvagal theory and, 128–31
providers
  attachment theory and, 124
  burnout and, 138–39
  bystander traumas and, 162–64
  co-regulation and, 161–62
  COVID-19 and, 224–25, 237–39
  critical care, 147–48, 163 (*see also* emergency department staff)
  dying from COVID-19, 237–39
  education of, 258–59
  face-to-face connection and, 234–39
  implicit biases and, 131–33

personal protective equipment (PPE) and, 225
polyvagal-informed, 152
polyvagal theory for, 151–85
role in neuroception of patients and families, xxiv
secondary traumatic stress and, 139–43
social support among, 238–39
proximity-seeking behavior, 23–24, 25–26, 48
psychological first aid (PFA), 141
psychological maltreatment, 71–73, 89, 250
psychological safety, reducing medical errors through, 121–22
purpose, establishing, 216
Pynoos, R. S., 71

quickening, 9

Raby, K. L., 27
racial disparities in infection and outcomes, COVID-19 and, 231–33
racism, xxvi
  epigenetics and, 101–2
  health outcomes and, 101–2, 104–5
  medical abuse and, 104–5
  preterm infants and, 101–2
  systemic, xxv, xxvi, 101–2
  transgenerational transmission of stress and, 108
rage, 12
Rauch, S. L., 107
regard for others, 128–29
regulating others, 134, 136, 155–56, 174, 215
  teams and, 212–13
  through self-regulation, 173–74
"Regulating Resources Map," 136
regulation, 188, 197, 268
relationship building, 259
relationship disruptions, xxv–xxvi
  prevention of, xxv–xxvi
  repair of, xxv–xxvi
relationships. *See also specific relationships*
  beyond the mother-child interaction, 26–29
  COVID-19 and, 235–36

repair
  of disruptions, 36–37
  in mother-infant interactions, 29–32
reptiles, 33
reptilian cultures, 216
resilience, 59, 123, 211
  building platform for, 59–61
  everyday stress and, 62
  key factors, 63
  mastering ordinary disruptions and, 59–61
  science of, 61–64
resource caravan passageways, 75
resources within us all along, 183–84
respiratory sinus arrhythmia (RSA), 6–7, 34–36, 83, 105, 107, 108
re-storying, 134, 136–37
"resuscitate by voice," 147
Reynolds, S. F., 147–48
Rhemtulla, M., 97
righting reflex, 60–61
Riley, Rochelle, 177
risk, 47–48, 55
risk factor caravan passageway, 73–74
Roberts, S. O., 105
Robertson, James, 25, 32–33, 59
Rodriguez, Robertino, 234, 237
Rogers, E. M., 266–67
Rogers, F. D., 97
Rogers, Fred, 187

safety, 14, 47–48, 182–83, 187–88, 216, 268
  assessment of, 53 (*see also* neuroception)
  belonging and, 211
  building, 216
  communication of, 247
  conveyed to patients through openness, 126–28
  as critical, but not the destination, 267–68
  cues of, 247, 254–60
  definition of, 119
  disruptions of sense of, 36–37
  education and, 178–79
  felt sense of, 178–79
  implicit biases as obstacles to, 131–33
  as more than absence of danger or risk of injury, 119–21
  neurobiology of, xxii–xxiii, xxvi
  neuroception of, xxiii–xxv, 39, 219, 234, 247
  psychological, 121–22
  reflected in ventral vagal social engagement system, 6–7
  science of, 164–65
  socialization for, 51–53
  what it is and where to find it, 116–19
safety circuits, 249–50, *249*
  autonomic nervous system (ANS) and, 248–51
  disruptions of, 250
safety deficit disorder, 179
Sanders, Marilyn, background of, xxi
Sanders, Paula, 241–42
SARS epidemic, 223
SBAR strategy (Situation, Background, Assessment, and Recommendations), 148
Scerbo, M. W., 133
Schaal, B., 10
Schatzberg, A. F., 59
Schloredt, K. A., 109
Schmied, V., 161
Schore, Allan, 24–25
secondary traumatic stress, providers and, 139–43
secretory IgA (sIgA), 82, 102–3, 108–9
secure attachment, 23–26, 47–48, 129, 130, *249*
security
  disruptions of sense of, 36–37
  neuroception of, 234
Seidman, Dov, 223
self-compassion, 165, 249
self-concept, 128–29
self-organization, 24–25
self-regulation, 15, 24–25, 39, 119, 123, 134, 136, 155, 174, 188, 197
  child-serving professionals and, 115–19
  co-regulation and, 115–49
  infants and, 108–9
  Polyvagal Theory and, xxv–xxvi
  to regulate others, 173–74
  teams and, 212–13
Selye, Hans, 74–75

Sentencing Project, 79–80
separations
   as threat to infant survival, 32–33
   traumatic, xxv, 16, 67–91, 90
September 11, 2001, terrorist attacks, responses to, 90–91
serve and return/back and forth interactions, 55–58
sexual abuse, 89
sexual orientation, stigmatization of, 103
shame, working with, 168–73
Shapiro, E. D., 21–22
Sharma, S., 96
Shatz, C. J., 52–53
Shearon, S., 105
sheltering in place, xxvi, 224, 226
Shin, L. M., 107
Shonkoff, J. P., 58
Short et al. 2019, 87
Siegel, Dan, 174
Simmonds, S. J., 94
sinoatrial (SA) node, 34–35
Skaff, M., 101–2
slowing down, 133
smart vagus, 34
Smyke, A. T., 75–76
social connectedness, xxvi, 14, 47, 101, 126, 142, 165, 241, 267
   attachment and, 25–26
   biological imperative of, 79
   as coping strategy, 84–85
   COVID-19 and, 223–26
   definition of, xxiii
   disruptions fo, xxv
   health outcomes and, 123
   promoting intentional "we" through, 265–67
   safety and, 249–50
social determinants of health, 68–70
social distancing, xxvi, 224, 226–31, 239–40
social engagement, xxiii, 14, 162, 182, 184–85, 216, 238, 241, 249, *249*, 267
   attachment and, 25–26
   boosting, 143–47
   children fighting before, 174–77
   communication and, 147–48

creating sense of, 242
power of, 90, 233
preparation for, 9
promoting intentional "we" through, 265–67
teamwork and, 147–48
ventral vagal, 39–40, *211*, 212
social engagement system, 6, 143–44, 174–77, 183–84, *210*, 211, *211*, 212, 219, 245–69
socialization, for safety and danger, 51–53
social vulnerability, 232
Solomon, J., 26
Somogyi, A., 74–75
Sonu, S., 99
soul, embracing, 184–85
Soussignan, R., 10
Southwick. F. S., 139, 238–39
Southwick. S. M., 139, 238–39
Spinazolla, J., 71
Spitz, A. M., 98–99
the state, as signal, 181–83
"state begets state," 174, 200, 209, 266
Steinberg, A. M., 71
stigmatization, 103
Still Face intervention, 29–30
Stolbach, B., 71
stories, importance of, 156–57
Strange, B. A., 54
Strange Situation paradigm, 26, 29–30
stress, 96. *See also* hypothalamic-pituitary-adrenal axis
   acute stress disorder, 139–40
   adverse childhood experiences (ACEs) and, 98–101
   amygdala and, 107–8
   chronic, 107–8
   epigenetics and, 108
   health outcomes and, 102–3
   immune response and, 102–3
   positive, 61, 62
   poverty and, 108
   racial, 105 (*see also* racism)
   stress inoculation, 59–60, 63
   teamwork and, *215*
   tolerable, 61

stress (*continued*)
   toxic, 61–62, 70, 90
   transgenerational transmission of, 108
     (*see also* epigenetics)
stress allostasis, 74–77
stress reactivity, 111
   downstream effects of impaired, 109–11
   impact of parental mental health concerns on, 106–9
stress responses, 68
   disrupted by autonomic reactions, 105
   taxonomy of, 61–62
structural stigma, 103–4
substance misuse, 82, 85–86, *86*, 100
   developing brain and, 86–91
   impaired caregiving and, 85–86
   opiate exposed newborns and, 20–22
   perinatal, 87–91
   in pregnancy, 86–91
substance use disorder (SUD), 85–91, *86*. *See also* substance misuse
Sun, Y. V., 106
Sundlass, K., 59
surfactant, 13
survival. *See also* fight-or-flight behaviors; freeze-shutdown
   adaptive survival responses, 134, 135–36
   community and, 265
   connectivity and, 265
   survival strategies, 224
sympathetic activation, 42–43, 48–49, 68, 142, 163, 247
sympathetic mobilization, 7
sympathetic nervous system (SNS), 5, 7, 9, 10, 110, 144, 183
sympathetic states, 134–35, 182
synactive theory, 17–20
systemic racism
   epigenetics and, 106
   healthcare and, 104–5
   health outcomes and, 104–5
Szabo, S., 74–75

Tache, Y., 74–75
Tait, Tom, 240–41
Tamblyn, R. M., 259
Tannenbaum, B., 96

Target, M., 252
Taylor, J. V., 106
teachers, polyvagal-informed, 177–83
teamwork, 147–48, 209–10, *210*, 211, *212*, *213*, *215*
telehealth, 239
"tender age" facilities, 78
teratogens, 96
therapists, polyvagal-informed, 164–68
Thompson, A., 105
Thompson, George, background of, xxi
threat, 218. *See also* danger
   neuroception of, 250, 267
   sympathetic mobilization and, 7
thrifty phenotype hypothesis, 94
Tikkanen, E., 94
Toledano, R., 54
toxic stresses, 90
   adverse childhood experiences (ACEs) and, 98–101
   of childhood, 70
   early life, 98–101
   traumatic, 70
toxins, 97
transgenerational transmission of stress, racism and, 108
trauma, xxv, xxvi–xxvii, 67. *See also* traumatic loss; traumatic separations
   of being there, 162–64
   bystander traumas, 162–64
   developmental, 250
   epidemiology of, 70–71
   loss and, 70–73, 77–85
   toxic stresses and, 70
   trauma-informed services and, 260
   triumph over, 245
   types of, 71
   of working with and through others' traumas, 138–43
"trauma exposure response," 139
trauma-informed services, 260
traumatic loss
   border separations and, 77–79
   children and, 70–73
   emotional proximity and, 81–85
   parental incarceration and, 79–81
   unaccompanied minors and, 77–79

traumatic separations, 67–91
Trocmé, N., 71
Tronick, E. Z., 29–30, 38
Trump, Donald, 78
trust, 37, 167–68
  "blocked trust," 167
  epistemic, 226–31
  gaining, 234
  social distancing and, 226–31

Ulmer-Yaniv, A., 102–3
unaccompanied minors, 77–79
uncertainty, 131, 228–29
unseen wounds, 71

vagal brakes, 35, 41, 48, 56, 105, 143–47, 215
vagal tone, 6–7, 34–36, 48, 108, 110, 123, 144
vagus, 5–8, 144
van Dernoot Lipsky, Laura, 139, 141
Van Horn, S. L., 85
vegetative vagus, 34
ventral vagal anchor, 142
ventral vagal social engagement system, 6–7, 39–40, *211*, 212
ventral vagal states, 41, 115–16, 119, 123, 134–36, 162, 164–65, 174, 177, 183, 199–200, 209, 211–12, *211–12*, 220, 237, 247, 260, 268
ventral vagal teams, 209–14, *212*
ventral vagus complex (nucleus ambiguus, NA), 33–34, 36
Verghese, Abraham, 151

Verschueren, K., 28, 29
video technology, study of infant behavior and, 26
virtuality, vs. being there, 266
Vivrette, R. I., 71
voices, intonation of, 247
Vuilleumier, P., 54
vulnerability, 216, 232, 234, 236

Waddington in Deans and Maggert, 95
Walker, J. D., 99
wandering nerve, 5–6. *See also* vagus
War on Poverty, 264
Watson, G. S., 133
"white-framed language," 104
Whitfield, Ch., 99
Williams, David, 231, 233
Williamson, D. F., 98–99
Wilson, Clare, 115, 116
"window of tolerance," 174
Winnicott, D. W., 42
Winter, P. D., 94
Wong, B., 234
World Health Organization, 68, 109–10, 224

Xu, Y., 21–22

Yamamoto, R., 84
Yarger, H. A., 27

Zagoory-Sharon, O., 102–3
Zanetti, D., 94
Zeanah, C. H., 75–76, 96–97

ABOUT THE AUTHORS

MARILYN R. SANDERS, M.D., is a pediatrician/neonatologist at Connecticut Children's Medical Center in Hartford, Connecticut and Professor of Pediatrics at the University of Connecticut School of Medicine. She incorporates the principles of the Polyvagal Theory into the intensive care of critically ill babies and their families. Dr. Sanders also provides developmental follow-up for babies who were hospitalized in an intensive care unit. She serves on the advisory board of the Polyvagal Institute. Dr. Sanders lectures to health, mental healthcare, and other professionals throughout the United States and internationally.

GEORGE S. THOMPSON, M.D., is a psychiatrist devoted to assisting families and healthcare organizations to build emotionally safe, curious, and collaborative cultures that transform trauma into wisdom. He serves on the Polyvagal Institute advisory board and the board of directors of the Dyadic Developmental Psychotherapy Institute. Dr. Thompson teaches widely about his observation that trust happens when we demonstrate an understanding of another's experience. He lives with his family in Lawrence, Kansas and, with his team, is creating a model youth psychiatric residential program, the Thompson Centers for Heroic Change.